THE WARDEN

Thomas Chippendale

Oxford Junior Encyclopedia – Home Volume

Cream Coloured Earthenware

Japanese Crafts

Into Japan

Into China

Corsica

Edward James – A Surrealist Life

A Guide to the Kyoto Museum of Archaeology

Glimpses of Kyoto Life

THE WARDEN
A Portrait of John Sparrow

JOHN LOWE

HarperCollins*Publishers*

In affectionate memory of my friends,
Trenchard and Maisie Cox

HarperCollins*Publishers*
77–85 Fulham Palace Road, Hammersmith,
London W6 8JB

1 3 5 7 9 8 6 4 2

First published in Great Britain by
HarperCollins*Publishers* 1998

ISBN 0 00 215392 0

Designed by Humphrey Stone

Set by Rowland Phototypesetting Ltd,
Bury St Edmunds, Suffolk

Printed in Great Britain by
Caledonian International Book Manufacturing Ltd,
Glasgow

CONTENTS

LIST OF ILLUSTRATIONS

Reynolds and Humphrey Stone
John Betjeman
John with Edward Hussey
The last visit to Venice in 1985
John's last days at Beechwood House

ACKNOWLEDGEMENTS

IN MARCH 1951 two New College friends, Adrian House and
Richard Ward, introduced me to John Sparrow. In March 1988
Adrian House suggested to me that I should write some kind of
life of John Sparrow and, to my surprise, John seized on the idea
and appointed me his official biographer in April 1988. Since then,
Richard Ward has read and corrected the typescript, chapter by chapter. I am grateful to both of them.

In the last years of John's life I stayed often at Beechwood House.
This was only possible through the kindness of Inge Gerstl, who
looked after him then. At the same time John's friend Sally Owen
gave me a great deal of help in starting my researches.

I owe special thanks to Peter Lewis, Librarian of All Souls College,
who has been quick to supply me with information, and patient over
the return of John's papers which I had on loan while writing the
book.

Since 1988 I have talked or corresponded with dozens of people
about John's life, and I would like to express my sincere thanks to
all of them; friends, Oxford colleagues, and colleagues at the Chancery Bar. John died at the age of eighty-five, but it is surprising how
many near-contemporaries he left behind with excellent memories,
notably his brother Tim and his sister Daphne.

I am particularly grateful to Peter Levi, who contributed an
appraisal of John's Latin verse, and to Sir Michael Fox for evoking
3 New Square and its practice when John returned to those Chambers
in 1946.

I have received most valuable help from Sir Michael Howard, and
from two other former Fellows of All Souls and close friends of John
Sparrow, the late Sir Isaiah Berlin and Sir Stuart Hampshire.

I have also had a great deal of help and encouragement from Henry
Hardy, Isaiah Berlin's editor and archivist at Wolfson College.

I have also received help through conversation and correspondence with Mark Amory, Lord Annan, Nicolas Barker, Richard Brain, Mrs Beatrice Brocklebank, D. J. R. Bruckner, Professor William M. Calder III, Sir Raymond Carr, the late Robert Charleston, Colette Clark, Dr John Clarke, Honor Clerk, David Crane, Roger Custance, John Davies, Fram Dinshaw, Durham University Library, Charles Egleston, Kenneth Garlick, the late John Gere, John Gurney, Lady Harrod, Sir Rupert Hart-Davis, the late Colin Haycraft, the late Sir William Hayter, Edmund Heward, Derek Hill, Jonathan Hill, Philip Howard, Edward Hussey, Susanna Johnston, Milo Keynes, Sir John Lawrence, Jeremy Lewis, Bryan Magee, Giles Mandelbrot, James McConica, Harvey McGregor, the late Jock Murray, Sir Patrick Neill, the late Anthony Newnham, Nigel Nicolson, Norma Aubertin-Potter, Malcolm Radcliffe, Rodney Radcliffe, Simon Rendall, Sir Denis Rickett, the late A. L. Rowse, George Rylands, James Sabben-Clare, St Andrews University, the late Edward Shils, John Simmons, Francis Sitwell, Thomas Snow, the late Brian Spiller, Lord Stockton, Humphrey Stone, the late Janet Stone, Dr Anthony Storr, Mrs John Sutro, the Tate Gallery, Mark Tennant, the University of Texas, the Library of Victoria, British Columbia, the late Charles Wenden, Robert J. Wickenheiser, Lord Wilberforce, Bryan Wilson, Winchester Cathedral archives and Wolverhampton Public Library.

I am grateful to my friend and former editor, Carol O'Brien, who first took on this book, and to Amanda Starkey, Arabella Pike and Georgina Laycock who saw it through the press.

Shortly after John Sparrow's death I was asked by the editor of the *American Scholar* to write an obituary essay, which was published under the title 'John Sparrow: The Warden of All Souls' in the autumn issue of 1992. Although I have seldom quoted directly from the article, and several of my opinions have changed since then, its composition has remained an important moment in my researches.

I have made every effort to trace the owners of the copyright of the photographs I have used in the book. In several cases they were casual 'snapshots', and it was impossible to identify the photographer. (Although numbers 23, 25, 30, 31 and 32 were taken by Janet Stone.) I shall be glad to receive any information about the photographs, so that acknowledgements can be made in any future edition.

FOREWORD

I FIRST met John Sparrow in March 1951. Thirty-seven years later, on 19 April 1988, he appointed me his official biographer, giving me permission to see all his letters, papers and any other relevant material. He kept most of this archive at Beechwood House in Iffley, where he had been living in retirement since he gave up the wardenship of All Souls in 1977. Beechwood House belonged to All Souls College. I had already been visiting John regularly throughout the 1980s, or as often as living most of the year in Japan and France allowed. From 1988 until his death in January 1992 I spent several weeks at Beechwood House each year, partly to start sorting and reading his large collection of papers, but also to enjoy the pleasure of his company.

It was a strange experience to be working on the biography of a man – one of my oldest friends – who was usually sitting just across the room, while I was reading some of his most personal letters. The reader may well wonder what influence he may have tried to exercise on my researches. The answer is very little. He was keen to be remembered in a biography, but his lack of interference during those years was remarkable. Often, he asked what particular letter or paper I was reading, and if the subject stirred his curiosity he would read it, but without comment. From the beginning he betrayed his impatience to be in print through the frequent exhortation, 'I hope you are getting on with it.' The assumed sharpness of tone was softened by the inimitable Sparrow grin.

There were two occasions when he did express opinions of considerable interest, the only times he questioned my intent. The first time, when I thought he was dozing, he spoke suddenly with a sense of purpose unusually firm in his old age:

'How do you intend to treat my homosexuality?'

'How do you want it treated?' I replied.

'No, you tell me.'

'Well, I'm going to deal with it as naturally as I have always done.'

'Good. That is how I wanted it treated.'

He never mentioned the subject again in relation to the biography. I think he knew that I understood exactly what he wanted to say. He wanted this side of his nature dealt with 'naturally' but, more important, he wanted it dealt with.

His second intervention was just as sudden:

'While you are doing all this research, you will find out many bad sides to my character. But just supposing you were also to discover a few good things about me, which would you put at the top of your list?'

I replied, without hesitation, 'Your gift for friendship.'

'Will you really write that?'

'Certainly.'

'Good.'

John could express enormous satisfaction with that short word. In both cases it had the force of an imprimatur. I hope that I have delivered what I promised him.

Unconsciously, John did make one other contribution to the book. He had a large collection of photographs of himself illustrating his whole life. In old age he never tired of looking through these, often with me.

'I like that one very much,' he would say, pointing to himself in mid-wardenship and a red shirt.

'I'm not very keen on it,' I observed.

'Oh, why not?' Slightly nettled.

'I think it makes you look rather raffish.'

'That's why I like it,' replied John, and we moved on to another snapshot. And in this way we went through the collection many times, until I knew exactly which were John's favourite photographs. I have included most of them in the book, including the raffish one.

Although he never mentioned it to me, his friend Sally Owen told me that he read the typescript of the first two chapters, describing his childhood and schooldays. She observed him in his armchair, turning the pages and occasionally saying to himself, 'Fascinating.' I do not think he was commenting on the quality of the book, but rather enjoying having his memory jogged about incidents in his early life which he had forgotten. In those last years I spent a lot of time reminding him of favourite stories that had long slipped his memory.

I must explain why I have called this life of John Sparrow 'a portrait'. He and I agreed from the start that a shorter, more selective book, rather than a full dress biography, best suited his life and character. Beyond that, while I had every intention of telling the truth about him, I wanted to be free to select certain episodes or friendships to illustrate the man, omitting a few others which I thought would be hurtful to those John had left behind. I can assure the reader that this selectivity in no way distorts the portrait.

Finally, I must apologize to those readers who prefer the modern biographical practice of referring to people by their surname, and I was urged by some to call my subject 'Sparrow' throughout this book. But I knew John Sparrow for over forty years, and almost from the day we met I called him 'John'. To write about him using his surname would have seemed completely artificial, to the extent of causing a small snag in my mind each time I wrote it. Whether I write of him as 'John' or as 'Sparrow' my objectivity is in no way affected. When, from time to time, we disagreed in life, we did not suddenly revert to our surnames. It has not always been easy to put aside forty years of friendship, and no doubt a biographer who had never known John would have written a different book. I have simply tried to tell the truth about him as I, aided by many others, see it, because that was what he wanted. He wished to be remembered as he was, faults and all.

My dear Warden,

(I shall always write to you under this title on the same principle by which the Rev. Septimus Harding after he had resigned from the post of Warden of Hiram's Hospital was always known by his old title)

I repeat, My dear Warden, . . .

Yours ever,

H.M.

*Harold Macmillan to John Sparrow on his
retirement, 3 November 1977*

I

THE CHILD

1906–19

═══

When he was a pink and white bundle of six weeks, his future
nurse looked at him in his cradle with the eye of a connoisseur,
and declared that her new charge was different from any baby
she had ever seen. 'He seems to look right through you,' she said,
referring to an extraordinary penetrating way he had of looking
at a stranger, which had even earlier caused the good woman
to say, 'You must make a judge of this child.'

From a memoir written by John Sparrow's mother

JOHN HANBURY ANGUS SPARROW was born on 13 November
1906 at New Oxley, Bushbury, near Wolverhampton. The above
quotation comes from an account of his childhood which his
mother wrote when he was about nine. Her nursery observations
contain prophetic glimpses of his future character; and taken with
other events of his early years, they suggest that John came into the
world fully armed. The stories of his childhood show an unusual
precocity in which one can recognize several traits of his mature
character. This child was certainly father to the man.

John's father was Isaac Saredon Sparrow. He was born in 1871,
the son and grandson of rich and renowned ironmasters of the Black
Country. D. H. Wood, in his *History of Ironfounding in the Mid-
lands*, wrote: 'The Sparrow family brought fame to the Stow Heath
Furnaces and Bilston Mill. At the former, Wm. Hanbury Sparrow
made a huge fortune, amounting to between £1,300,000 and
£1,500,000. The specialities of the Bilston Mill were rods, bars and
hoops. The work was carried on for many years under the name of
W. and J. S. Sparrow.' The first of these was John's great-grand-uncle,
William Hanbury Sparrow. William's father had married Mary Hanbury, the origin of John's second name. John Sly Sparrow, the other

[1]

partner, was his great-grandfather. His grandfather, John William Sparrow, continued to run the business, but by the late nineteenth century the foundries had become obsolete and were sold.

Although the rods, bars and hoops of the Bilston Mill were a world away from John's career and interests, there is a certain aptness in his descent from Midland ironmasters, and his character owed something to the provincial world which was his home until he graduated from Oxford. In those days Wolverhampton was a solid, old-fashioned place, which must have contributed to John's conservatism, a certain provincial narrowness, and his love for the Victorian period. And mostly, John was 'plain in his manner', an epithet originally applied by his contemporaries to William Hanbury Sparrow, but equally apt for John.

In the late 1850s, having purchased the land from the Duke of Sutherland in 1849, John's grandfather built a large house called Beckminster on the outskirts of Wolverhampton. He died in 1891, but John's grandmother continued to live in the house until her death in 1916. Isaac Sparrow inherited the house, and the family went to live there. But Wolverhampton was expanding, and in 1923 the corporation, needing land for development, bought the property. The Sparrows moved to a house called The Orchards in Tettenhall Woods, which remained their home until John's parents moved to the edge of Oxford in 1939.

It is difficult to draw an accurate picture of John's father Isaac. He was a disagreeable man, and all his children disliked him and were afraid of him. Daphne, John's younger sister, says that John was the first of the children to stand up to him. John's own dislike was always obvious, but it was hard to discover the reasons for his strong antipathy. He seldom said much about his father, except for such brief and dismissive remarks as 'He was usually at his club' – the Conservative Club in Wolverhampton – the implication being that he neglected his family. Little correspondence between John and his father survives; these letters deal mainly with money – with fees due to New College or the Middle Temple. John dismissed his father, but their negative relationship must have had a deeper influence on him than he allowed. Even in old age John refused to talk about him.

Two surviving letters from Isaac to his mother show that he was sent to school at Lancing in 1884. The letters assured her that he was happy. In 1889 he went up to Corpus Christi College, Oxford, where he read modern history. He took his BA in 1893, but did not receive his MA until 1928.* After Oxford he joined Lincoln's Inn, was called to the Bar, and practised without distinction on the Midland circuit. He was an unambitious man, comfortable with his inherited wealth and the undemanding routine of provincial life in and around Wolverhampton.

Isaac met Margaret Macgregor at a charity bazaar in Edgbaston, Birmingham, where he was living at the time. A number of love letters from Isaac, and a few from Margaret, date from the spring of 1905 and tell of the progress of their courtship. Isaac's letters express his feelings in a naïve and sometimes mawkish style. 'Let us never part again in a misunderstanding when any one of the little hitches happen – for after all we are but mortal and misunderstandings will sometimes come – let us take one another's hands for if we love each other, as we do, nothing can matter.' Margaret, in a typical letter written just after their marriage, writes with more astringency and a shrewish humour: 'I really love you very much, more than any husband I have ever had before, and I don't think I want to have another – just yet at any rate – I am sure I can put up with you for a year at any rate – perhaps two and in the meantime, I am your adorable (!) wife.'

Comparison between the letters of Isaac and Margaret suggests that he was no match for this handsome, intelligent and lively girl. However, one must be cautious since in most cases only one side of the correspondence has survived, and one's impressions are often contradicted by the memories of their children, Tim and Daphne. And though the letters do suggest an imbalance in their relationship, they remained together from 1905 until Isaac's death in 1964.

Isaac and Margaret had five children. John was born in 1906. Then came the twins, Tim and Mollie, in 1908. They were followed by two more daughters, Daphne in 1909, and Penn in 1911. Following the fashion of that time, each child was baptized with a string of names. Those used here are the ones by which they were known from their nursery days, within and outside the family.

* The Oxford MA is a formality and not a mark of academic achievement.

At the outbreak of the First World War, Isaac, aged forty-three, enlisted as a private in the Royal Fusiliers. Margaret disapproved of his refusal to take a commission, as she did in 1939, when John also joined up as a private soldier. Isaac was later commissioned in the Cheshire regiment, in which he served for the rest of the war; in 1916 he joined the staff of a prisoner-of-war camp at Shrewsbury.

After the war he returned to quasi-legal work, serving on a tribunal adjudicating claims for unemployment benefit. To John, his father's career must have seemed provincial and humdrum, entirely alien to his own interests. They shared only one passion – football. Both, throughout their lives, were ardent soccer fans, and supported the then great Wolverhampton Wanderers. Isaac was a director of the club, and the only place where John met his father with enthusiasm was in the directors' box at the Molyneux ground. In his rare letters to his father the fortunes of the 'Wolves' were often mentioned. John's love of soccer, both as a player and as a spectator, was never, as one of his obituaries suggested, any kind of affectation. Quite the contrary: it was an affair of the heart, and at the end of his life there were few occupations he enjoyed more than watching a match on television, or one of his videos of former championship games.

Margaret, John's mother, was the eldest of the six daughters of Angus and Jean (née Chisholm) Macgregor. The Macgregor family came originally from the Scottish Highlands, but had migrated to Birmingham at some unrecorded date in search of employment. Angus Macgregor was in commerce, not particularly prosperous, and no doubt anxious at the thought of marrying off six daughters. Margaret was born in Birmingham in 1871; she was only six months younger than Isaac. Her wedding photograph shows that she was tall, with striking and intelligent looks. Her father must have felt that she had made a good match. She had been educated at Edgbaston High School, and she graduated from St Andrews University in 1900 with an ordinary degree in mathematics – an unusual achievement for a girl in the late nineteenth century. Women's studies were not included in the university curriculum in those days, but if they had been, the subject might well have been chosen by Margaret. Her surviving notebooks include a number of feminist essays deploring the suppression of women in Japan and other countries. She was never a suffragette, but her sympathies must have leaned in that direction. Other essays, and some of her letters, show that she held

[4]

strong views about the responsibilities of a wife in running her home and bringing up her children; territory where a husband should never trespass. Margaret was loyal to Isaac, but there were to be clashes on such points.

John was baptized at Bushbury on 9 January 1907. The names John and Hanbury were chosen to honour the Sparrow family. Margaret seems to have been unhappy with this one-sided choice and, at the last moment, sent a note to R. H. Sargent, the vicar of Bushbury. His reply reads: 'Compliments. Definitely *ANGUS. RHS.*' So John was christened John Hanbury Angus, and both sides of the family were duly commemorated. In later years John Betjeman, who loved unusual names, was to have a lot of fun with 'Hanbury'.

The service of baptism was conducted by a relation, Frederick Weaver, vicar of Milton Clevedon in Somerset. John's grandfather had been married twice: first to Charlotte Eyre and, after her death, to Mary Weaver, John's grandmother. Frederick Weaver was his great-uncle. Another Weaver relation, Reginald, became Master of Trinity College, Oxford, the only other academic in the family. The two marriages of his grandfather, together with the numerous brothers and sisters of his mother and father, produced a family tree of intricate cousinage.

Two of John's relations are, in very different ways, worthy of note. Isaac's notorious younger brother Hugh went off to Argentina in search of adventure and wealth. A fragment of his diary, and a snapshot showing him on horseback in the company of three gauchos, suggest that his first years were rough. Eventually he married an Argentinian girl, but the marriage ended in a double tragedy: he murdered his wife and committed suicide. The affair was hushed up, and it is now impossible to find out what really happened. It is the only flash of melodrama in an otherwise respectable family history, but perhaps John inherited something of his uncle Hugh's wildness, along with a love of riding.

One member of the Macgregor family, the youngest daughter, Augustine, shared John's early love of art. She was a painter and illustrator of professional skill, and with a style of considerable charm. She may have encouraged the young artist of six when he struggled with local landscapes and views of Beckminster – a few of which survive – but at Winchester he abandoned painting on the advice of his friend Kenneth Clark.

[5]

The Sparrows were frequently separated as Isaac's work in the Birmingham courts often involved absences from the family home near Wolverhampton. Arguments and conversations continued through letters. Their marriage, in both its harmonies and its discords, centred on their children. A number of letters, all from Margaret to Isaac, survive from the early years. Although Margaret frequently refers to Isaac's answers, none have survived. Her letters describe the children's lives: seaside holidays, childish ailments and the progress of their education. Many of the letters are undated, and in all of them Margaret's strong opinions on domestic matters may give a distorted view of her husband's character. They suggest that she found Isaac insensitive to the needs of both her and the children, until at one point – perhaps only in momentary exasperation – she claims that they have little in common. Isaac seems to have infuriated her with his stubborn silence, by means of which he usually got his own way. They were at odds about various matters, but most frequently over the upbringing and education of the children.

Many of the letters are bland accounts of daily life. From Westgate-on-Sea in May 1912, Margaret reports that the girls have gland trouble although the boys have recovered. 'They are able to paddle. John caught 12 shrimps yesterday, but I think I have told you of that excitement.' But in 1914 Margaret begins to complain, first about Isaac's enlistment in the ranks and, in the following year, about the children's education. John had already briefly attended the junior house of Wolverhampton Grammar School, but had soon been moved to Brockhurst, at Church Stretton in Shropshire, as a boarder. Now Isaac proposed to send Tim and Mollie, aged only seven, to join John at Brockhurst. The suggestion incensed their mother:

I think it would be *sheer cruelty* to take them away from this country home . . . with the hot weather coming on to send them to a cooped up place like that. It is not as if their education has been neglected, I have given them a good start and they would do well at school if they had a little longer at home.

Now I have just seen a most excellent governess, the sort of person that I never expected to come across in Wolverhampton . . . She has learnt French abroad and can teach music and is not in the least a common person – in fact she looks a born governess of the old fashioned type . . . There is no prejudice or love of opposition on my part but they are only seven and I have given a great deal of time and thought to their education and I feel very strongly about it.

A compromise was reached, and only Tim joined John at Brockhurst.

Not long after this, with Margaret's strong disapproval, John was sent to a preparatory school called The Old Hall, at Wellington in Shropshire. He was nearly ten, the normal age to start prep school then. His mother took him there at the beginning of his first term in September 1916, and the next day wrote a disparaging report to Isaac about his choice of school:

I had lunch at The Old Hall – and two things rather disgusted me – we, Mr H. [Hickman, the headmaster] and I were helped first and given a most delicious rice pudding and apples and I thought well anyway the boys get good milk puddings but to my horror there was no milk pudding for the boys only a piece of pastry and some stewed apples – pastry! A thing we practically never give them at home – and we pay these enormous fees to have them as I have said before worse fed – and at the present time worse taught for the teachers were a queer lot – the men looked as if they had no pretensions to be gentlemen and the rest were women who compared unfavourably except one – with Miss Boulton [the favoured governess]. The second thing I criticize was Mr H.'s whiskey, I should have thought at lunch with the boys he could have done without it . . . I can't say why there is something about Mr Hickman that does not satisfy me, and really I think the way you have rushed these boys off to school is simply wicked. If I were an incompetent fool but I have taken so much trouble about their education, it is to me of such infinite importance and I should have spared no time or pains to see schools till I felt I had found not only the right school but the right man.

I think I have said all that is necessary, it is a pity I have to be disagreeable but I only wish there were no cause – After all children mean much more to their mother than their father – necessarily from the fact that they are their mother's chief work in life – men are fond of saying this – they might therefore not so ignore it in action.

After his mother's death in 1916 Isaac decided to move from New Oxley into Beckminster. His decision caused further 'disagreeable' correspondence from Margaret. She liked their house at New Oxley and thought Beckminster old-fashioned, gloomy and ill-equipped for raising a young family. Isaac was parsimonious, but Margaret refused to move until the house had been redecorated and modernized: a downstairs cloakroom was, in her view, essential for the children. It is not recorded how far she had her way, but the family moved in the spring of 1917.

Isaac's enlistment in the ranks, the children's schooling, the plumbing at Beckminster – all seem to have been symptoms of a basic incompatibility between Isaac and Margaret. This was revealed more openly in a letter that she wrote to him in November 1916, just after she had visited him in London:

> I am writing this after my arrival home . . . I heard some soldiers say the 2.30 was much more crowded, so I was thankful I hadn't gone by it, though I didn't do so because I could not bear to part from you like that, I had no idea I was not agreeable and I am very sorry you thought I was not. You were very kind to me in London, and as long as we were happy together I enjoyed it very much. You often accuse me of being horrid when I have no intention or idea of being so – and it simply makes me feel utterly helpless. Every time I go to meet you I make up my mind it shall be all happiness and it always ends the same way, till now I really begin to think we may as well reconcile ourselves to the fact that we shall never get on – it may be neither of our faults but simply our temperaments . . . It is very sad and if you ever thought anyone else could and would make you happy I wouldn't stand in your way for a moment. Peace gives me happiness but you don't value peace, you sacrifice it constantly for trifles and make a tragedy of life when it might be a joy.

Such personal letters, written in the heat of emotional moments, must be interpreted with caution, particularly without Isaac's replies. The family deny any obvious conflict, and say that although their mother had strong views on the upbringing and education of her children, in other matters she was a compliant wife, usually patient with Isaac's stubborn and disagreeable nature. In these letters Margaret lays all the blame on Isaac, but her strong views and outspokenness would probably only have strengthened his conventional, male attitudes, making him more determined to have his own way.

At an early stage Isaac may have felt that his wife was exerting too much womanly influence on the children, particularly on John and Tim. He almost certainly shared the view of many fathers that boarding school would 'make men' of them. Whether or not the children sensed an antagonism between their parents, their mother was the centre of their lives. There is no doubt where John's love and loyalty lay.

From John's earliest childhood his mother sensed that he was exceptionally talented, and did everything she could to foster his gifts and to encourage his interests. In doing this, she may appear to have made John her favourite. That is a false impression. According to Tim and Daphne, the other children felt no jealousy towards John, because they were never deprived of their mother's love on his account. She was an equally good mother to all her children, though her favourite was Penn, her youngest child. John adored his mother, an adoration that lasted throughout his life. He often wrote to her, sometimes at length, once or twice each week, until her death at the age of ninety-two in 1963. She wrote as often to John. Many of their letters survive, and they give an intimate account of John's life from his days at Winchester to well into his wardenship of All Souls. They also show that his relationship with his mother, while deep, was never sentimental; she never hesitated to disagree with him when she thought him in the wrong. Her love of John was always guided by her considerable intelligence.

Margaret wrote a fascinating memoir of John's childhood, which she must have finished during his time at The Old Hall, though the essay gives no exact dates. Her judgement of his character and promise may have been coloured by her love and her ambitions for him, but the sketch is wonderfully true to life. Each story she tells suggests a familiar trait in his adult character. His precocity was legendary in their nursery: talking at six months, an early reader, and always clever beyond his years:

Nor from the first could you cajole him with any of those time honoured fictions on which nursery diplomacy exists. I remember as a baby of two his nurse coaxing him to lie down with the threat that if he did not, he 'wouldn't grow big'. 'I *shall* grow big if I lie down or not, Nannie,' he said and it was not defiance, it was refusal to be humbugged, for having uttered this protest he lay down submissively. But even at the early age of three he realised the need for expediency. 'You mustn't say what you think, but what people like,' he observed on being reproved for the expression of some unpopular or heterodox opinion; yet I fear his want of expediency will always militate against his popularity.

John continued to hold 'unpopular' opinions and lacked 'expediency' throughout his life. It endeared him to some, but not to others – particularly some of his colleagues – and it certainly militated against his worldly success.

John, wrote his mother, 'had been given no religious instruction', but when, at the age of four, he asked how the world had come about, he was told that God was its creator. He asked immediately, 'Who made God?' He was born with a questioning mind and, perhaps, a tendency to intellectual arrogance. As he was driven through the back streets of an ugly Black Country town, he said in a tone of contempt, 'I could have made a better world than this.'

His mother's essay continues:

John is not an only child, left to speculate to himself, but the eldest of a close running family of boys and girls from the next of whom he is only separated by a year – though it seems a century. He was a difficult member of the nursery community owing to a peculiar and tiresome trait that was very subversive of discipline, and that yet had a curious element of chivalry in it. He could not bear his brother or sisters to be punished or even reproved for anything, and as a protest he at once proceeded to do whatever the forbidden thing may have been, and when some misdemeanour had been discovered he has even been known to assume responsibility for it though entirely guiltless! He is extraordinarily sympathetic with suffering of any kind, merited or not, and he pours his philosophy like balm even on nursery troubles. When his little sister of three was crying for something as unobtainable as the moon, I overheard him, then a year older, say comfortingly, 'Never mind, Mary [Mollie], we can't have everything we want, we learn that.' 'Have you learned it?' I asked in surprise. 'We learn without knowing,' he answered sententiously.

At an early age John developed an ambition to be an artist. He pored over a book given him when he was six, *The Hundred Best Pictures*, and his greatest treat was to visit the Birmingham Art Gallery. A few of his childhood paintings have survived, but they show no real talent. His mother noted that he only revealed his artistic ambitions to her, except on one occasion: 'I had taken him to a neighbouring house for tea, and he sat absolutely silent the whole afternoon till as we were coming away, a young lady who was helping him with his coat said, in a kindly, patronizing way, "He is getting quite a little man." "A great artist and a poet," came from the depths of the overcoat.'

At the age of six the poet was already at work. John's first recorded poem was called 'Dead Leaves and Fairies':

> Dead leaves when Summer's drifted by
> Upon the ground they withered lie,
> And fairies on them trip about
> Each singing a gay song.
> And skipping on by lake and pond,
> They care of nothing but of joy,
> They look up laughing to the Sun.

Later, according to his mother, though she gives no dates, his verse had matured considerably, and he produced some lines imitative of Browning, showing that his gift for poetic pastiche made an early start:

> And this the worst?
> No, Worst, Best and Past are gone
> And I arrived at my stage.
> And this the tone of a parting
> When all is ended? Done?
> I have read the last page,
> I have been of the stage
> Of life. That is done –

John also started writing plays, which were performed by him and the other children. His mother recalled two: *The Way of Happiness* was inspired, she wrote, by Oscar Wilde, while *Life and Money*

Matters showed the influence of Ibsen: 'It was the style that held him in both, but he was too young for the matter to hurt him.' She then quotes two lines from his 'Wilde' play which, with hindsight, make one wonder if John might not have been taking in rather more of the matter than his mother supposed. Mabel, the heroine, says enthusiastically to Jack, '"Don't you think life is made happier for people by marrying?" Jack (*gloomily*), "Possibly."'

Margaret was aware of Isaac's concern about all the artistic interests which she was so obviously encouraging in John:

> Any orthodox Englishman would wonder what he had done to deserve such a son as John, but a sympathetic mother hid John's artistic eccentricities from his orthodox father, and John himself, instinctively hiding them as far as possible, revealed fortunately a promise in cricket and football that helped to relieve any possible parental anxiety.
>
> Nevertheless when John was barely eight the orthodox Englishman made up his mind to cut short his son's precocious career and packed him off to boarding school ... The rigidity of school life naturally came hard to him and his first letters were pathetic reading. 'I am crying nearly all the time that there is no one to hear me, and to myself nearly all the time – I will give you my five shillings to take me home with you at half term.' ...
>
> His masters declare that he never showed any signs of homesickness. He apparently relieved his feelings in his letters, and outwardly preserved his usual stoicism.

His mother then turns to his relations with the other boys, exemplifying the extrovert and introverted sides of his nature which were to mark his character throughout his life:

> Among the boys he quickly earned a reputation as a teller of wonderful stories and on account of his promise at games. 'He shows great promise both in and out of school, and the boys are extraordinarily nice to him,' wrote the headmaster. The last sentence does not convey the idea of popularity. John was not popular, his curiously cussed opinions which he will no doubt learn to compromise or keep to himself, made him an eccentric, who was forgiven and tolerated for certain virtues in cricket and

football that no schoolboy ignores. Besides, he was a character. 'It's only Saredon,'* the boys used to say, 'and he is so clever.' His art and his poetry were his secret garden, hidden from the world, and to which he returned with all his old passion in the holidays. A curious dual existence for a child of nine!

John's mother could be extremely shrewd, and prophetic. Much of that passage, omitting the cricket and football, might describe his wardenship of All Souls since, contrary to her hopes, he never learned to compromise his 'cussed opinions', nor did he ever court popularity. And if he led a dual existence at the age of nine, the duality in his life multiplied into various forms as he grew older.

After mentioning again John's sympathy for others in trouble, Margaret reaches her conclusion:

Curious child! How little power one feels one has of moulding such a character; it seems as if with all its twists and knots it was unmalleable! It has been moulded perhaps by the ages, by hereditary forces that are beyond our control. Yet one does not fear for him, he has the inner vision; with his childish spiritual eyes he sees into the heart of things ... He has, nevertheless, the sin of angels, inwardly and secretly he is consumed with ambition. When the Home Rule agitation was going on he said one day, 'Isn't it funny to think that these men who are in things like Sir Edward Carson, were once quite unknown to me, and they got on and made themselves known.' I suggested that some men had very few chances of getting on. 'You mean the "mute inglorious Miltons?"' he asked at once. 'I mean that some men are helped by circumstances,' I answered. 'I should hate that, I should like to get on by my own brains,' he said vigorously.

One wonders what he will do, or whether he will do anything.

These often rather solemn observations must not obscure the fact that for the most part John enjoyed a happy childhood with his brother and sisters, cared for by an intelligent mother who took great pains to provide for the needs of all her children. John appears in early photographs as a lively, robust and attractive little boy. His sense of humour is already present in a somewhat impish look, to develop later into the characteristic mischievous grin. His life was by

* Schoolboy teasing by using an unusual family name.

no means all confined to a 'secret garden'. Other snapshots show him with the family, playing cricket, picnicking, enacting nursery rhyme charades, going out in the pony cart, or simply climbing trees and walls. No doubt his mother was the organizer behind every activity. It is noticeable that Isaac does not appear in a single snapshot of these childhood days.

John was the cleverest member of the family and soon became the leader of their activities. But his siblings lacked neither intelligence nor interests. Tim later joined John at Winchester with an exhibition. He went on to be a successful professional soldier in the Royal Engineers, rising to the rank of brigadier. When he retired from the army he worked for many years as Peter Scott's administrator at the Slimbridge Wildfowl Trust.

Tim's twin sister Mollie was in some ways the most remarkable member of the family, her character as distinctive as John's and almost the exact opposite. After qualifying as a doctor, she made an unsuccessful marriage to George Corbyn Barrow, a Birmingham solicitor who later became Lord Mayor of the city. After the collapse of her marriage her independence asserted itself. She became a member of the Communist Party, and devoted herself to practising medicine and charity work in Sparkbrooke, a wretchedly poor district near the centre of Birmingham. In 1956, following the Russian invasion of Hungary, she left the party, but continued to devote her life to helping the poor. To further her aims she founded the Sparkbrooke Association, and her work and selflessness became widely admired in Birmingham. She died in 1970. She saw little of the family during the Birmingham years, except for Penn, who once went to live with her after suffering a breakdown. Her relationship with John is recorded in only one letter, in which, with considerable stringency, she told her brother to pull himself together.

John's two younger sisters, Daphne and Penn, after a brief period when they were both stagestruck, pursued interesting and responsible careers. In later life they devoted themselves to the care of their ageing parents, both of whom lived to over ninety. Penn was John's favourite. She was a frequent guest at the Warden's lodgings, be-friended some of John's closest friends, and sometimes joined him on foreign holidays. She died in 1986.

John started at The Old Hall in 1916, and stayed there until the end of the summer term, 1919. Most of his school reports have survived, and it is interesting to compare the impressions they give of John's school career with those recorded by his mother. Like so many prep school reports of that time, they are perfunctory and are more concerned with how John 'played up' at football than with his academic progress. He was frequently criticized for his work in classics, maths and French, those subjects marred by untidiness, inaccuracy and lack of attention to detail, and in his later reports he is accused of being smug.

He always had good reports for English. 'Takes interest in Analysis,' commented the English teacher – a perceptive appraisal. The headmaster thought John popular, and a good all-rounder, including a talent for boxing. However, the reports do not suggest that John would end his academic career at The Old Hall by winning a scholarship to Winchester. If his mother was surprised, she was also delighted. She added a footnote to her essay: 'He is a scholar of the finest school in England with every opportunity for fulfilling the promise he showed so early.'

John's childhood is exceptionally well-documented. A few photographs taken at The Old Hall – team groups and the like – show a self-assured small boy, with a slightly questioning and inward-looking grin, giving an air of self-confidence and independence. John never complained about his time at the school, though he probably shared his mother's opinion of Mr Hickman. His main memories were of soccer and cricket, but he gave the impression that his days there were happy enough.

Let John have the last word. He had a favourite story about his final interview with the headmaster. Like a number of John's stories, it is almost certainly apocryphal. And like so many of his stories, it is humorous, with the joke against himself.

I was very innocent in those days. I don't think I knew anything about sex. On my last day at The Old Hall, the headmaster sent for me. That was R. H. Hickman, you know. [John always remembered the initials of everyone he had ever known.]

Mr Hickman stood in front of the fireplace. I stood behind the sofa, which occupied the centre of his study.

'Well, Sparrow, off to Winchester, eh? Thought I'd wish you luck ... well, just say a word of ... um ... a word about your future. You'll find Winchester a bit different ... a ... well, a bigger sort of pond ... older boys and ... well, that sort of thing.'

Mr Hickman drew a deep breath and looked at the carpet. 'The point is, Sparrow ... I mean, I'm sure you know all about the *birds and the b*—'

Mr Hickman looked up. I had vanished.

I had fainted behind the sofa. Even the thought of the 'birds' was too much for me. I was *very* innocent, you see.

II

THE WYKEHAMIST

1919–25

I hope that he will not use his abilities too selfishly and will
work for the good of others as well as himself.
Final report of R. M. Wright, Second Master, 1925

JOHN SPARROW went to Winchester College in September 1919,
two months before his thirteenth birthday. His school career was
to create, or to emphasize, a conflict of interests which he never
resolved. Winchester is well known for leaving an indelible mark
on the character of its pupils. In John's day it demanded of its scholars
an undivided attention to their classical studies, in preparation for
the classical school at Oxford. Even the format of the junior school
reports of those days left minimal space for subjects regarded as
peripheral, such as English and French – subjects at which, in his
first few years, John did best. His knowledge and love of English
literature developed prodigiously at Winchester, but it was not his
schoolmasters who encouraged him. They frowned on his enthusiasm
for such a marginal subject.

Winchester, like Eton, separates its scholars in their own house,
known as 'College', still occupying the chambers around Chamber
Court which the founder, William of Wykeham, built for his original
'poor scholars to the number of sixty and ten' in 1382. There can
be few institutions in England in which one is so aware of a living
tradition, a tradition that is strong yet flexible enough to foster a
modern and liberal schoolboy life. It was a less tolerant place when
John arrived, like other public schools at that time, with its roots
still in a brutal past. In his autobiography Kenneth Clark recalled
his first journey to Winchester on the school train. Unaware of Winchester *mores*, during the journey he chatted to the other boys. On
arrival he was immediately beaten for uppishness.

John, as a scholar, was a College man, and his housemaster – the head of College was then called the Second Master* – was A. T. P. Williams. He became headmaster in 1924, succeeding M. J. 'Monty' Rendall, and subsequently Dean of Christ Church and Bishop of Durham. During his last two years John's housemaster was R. M. Wright. Both Williams and Wright liked John, and defended him when he was criticized by other masters in his termly reports. He was commended as a good member of College, active in all school affairs, not least football.

It is often said that Winchester tends to produce men with left-wing views. Richard Crossman was a contemporary of John's, Hugh Gaitskell another. It might be more accurate to say that the Winchester ethos encourages a social conscience, often revealed in individual Wykehamists by a sense of public service. It is another indication of the school's lasting tradition. Wykeham's purpose, through the school and its sister foundation, New College, Oxford, was to produce well-educated public servants. Both foundations have fulfilled his ambition to a remarkable degree for over 600 years.

John was an exception to the general rule, growing up with a strongly conservative nature, and with little sense of public duty or corporate loyalty. But John was not a rebel at school; he enjoyed his years at Winchester, though as far as possible he went his own way, pursuing his own interests. Winchester was only to experience the more intransigent side of his character during his many years as a Fellow of the governing body.

A few of John's contemporaries have survived him and retain clear memories of him at Winchester. William Hayter† recalled that throughout their time together in College, nobody ever took it for granted that John would win a scholarship to Oxford. Lord Wilberforce,‡ another College contemporary, gave a more detailed account in his memorial address:

---

* Since 1990 the two posts have been separated: the scholars' housemaster is the Master in College, and a senior ex-housemaster is Second Master.
† Sir William Hayter, KCMG (1906–95). Contemporary of JS at Winchester and New College. Diplomat, British ambassador USSR 1953–57. Warden of New College 1958–76.
‡ Richard (Lord) Wilberforce, CMG. Contemporary of JS at Winchester and New College. Prize Fellow, All Souls 1932, Chancery Bar, QC 1954, Lord of Appeal 1964–82.

I first met Sparrow in 1920 when he was fourteen and a scholar at Winchester College. He was a quite ordinary schoolboy, reasonably lazy, a bit of a bully in a kindly way, but we could see very soon that he and one other, Richard Crossman, stood out as marked for national distinction.

He was good at games. I have a vivid mental picture of his prowess at football. He was acrobatic and ingenious but he was also a good scorer/striker.

He did well enough in the school subjects, but we noticed that he was already 'into' English literature, not, or hardly, in the curriculum and considered a 'soft' subject.

Lord Wilberforce is not the only one to remember John as something of a bully, though a 'kindly' bully seems something of a contradiction. James Sabben-Clare, the present headmaster, told me that he had seen a report book kept by the senior boy in John's chamber which also referred to him as something of a bully. Unfortunately, the building where these books were kept was being restored and now they cannot be found.

John's mother kept all his school reports, which reveal the official attitude to his career and progress. His classics teachers, and the headmaster in his termly summary, frequently complained about his inaccuracy and his lack of effort to do himself justice. At the end of his first term Rendall wrote: 'Clearly he lacks the staying power and must develop it.' In a sense Rendall was right. John never developed the staying power for the long sustained effort. But when it suited him he did not lack application. He simply saved himself for those things which interested him most.

John's first English report said, 'His English work shows special promise of originality.' His interest in English literature, particularly that of the seventeenth century, was evident even at the age of thirteen, informed by his precocious tastes in book-collecting. It was his mother who first stimulated his love of literature, although not his book-collecting, for she was not a collector of anything. During the school holidays she encouraged all the children to devote a part of their time to art and literature. John needed little encouragement and soon became the leader of these activities, some of which must have been a little above the heads of his siblings, though Daphne insists that he never bored them.

It was John who, at the start of the Easter holidays in April 1920, encouraged his family to form an Antiquarian Society, which produced a handwritten magazine at the end of each holiday. Brother and sisters were recruited to act as treasurer, museum keeper, and as the audience for John's discourses. Several issues of the magazine survive, including the first.

The opening pages sum up what had been achieved by the society during the holidays. Rules, enforced with severe fines and other penalties, had been agreed, officers appointed, subscriptions levied, and 'the place for the museum was decided and the museum itself was furnished and supplied with coins, books, manuscripts etc. Meetings had been held [Rule 7. Every four days] fairly often since then, and hardly one had passed without more generous subscriptions, and without the addition of old books.' John, of course, was the editor, as the solemn, thirteen-year-old prose suggests. His learned dissertation on antiquarian book-collecting occupies almost half of this first issue, following an explanation of the agreed administration of the society. After so much formality, it is a relief to find a juvenile touch in the final regulation: 'Rule 11. The society *must* be kept secret.'

It is obvious from the start that John's main purpose in founding the society was to collect books – books he was unable to buy from his own resources. The society's library was modest in size, but John's aims were ambitious: 'When the society had started it had only one book, and for this reason it has specialised in books during the past holidays. I am writing, therefore, on the books which are now in its possession.' One can see here the early development of those Machiavellian skills which were later to manipulate the committees of All Souls; in plain language, getting one's own way.

The first book described by John – together with his drawing of the title page – was Ludwig Elzevir's 1652 edition of Plautus' 'twenty remaining comedies', printed in Amsterdam. 'It has the characteristics of all Elzevirs,' he explained. 'It is very well printed and bound, and in excellent condition.' These comments are followed by a description, and a second drawing, of Elzevir's 1665 edition of Terence's comedies. John continued: 'These are the Elzevirs that the society has, but it might have, any day, if it were lucky, the two rarest Elzevirs, one of 1624, the other of 1635. This is a very rare book and would fetch almost any price. A French collector picked up a copy at an old second-hand book stall for six sous! So you never know what may happen!' John was thirteen and all the skills and instincts of a discerning book-collector were in place. His knowledge, his enthusiasm and a canny sense of a bargain may not have meant much to the family audience, but years later the same qualities were to enthral many young Oxford bibliophiles.

All this at an age when most boys were devoting their holidays to Henty and French cricket. John did very much like both cricket and football, and although he developed serious interests at an unusually early age, he was never accused of being a 'swot'. But his literary interests were never mentioned directly in his school reports. There, the demand was always for closer attention to Latin and Greek.

There was in Winchester one person who encouraged John's interest in English literature, and who was convinced that his schoolmasters failed to appreciate his special gifts in this field. This was William Hutton, then Dean of Winchester, whom John met by chance during the summer holidays just before he went to the school. John and his sister Daphne were visiting an aunt in Ingoldisthorpe in Norfolk, where the Dean happened to be staying with a Mrs Tilden, the lady of the manor. She had heard from John's aunt about his scholarship, and he was invited to tea to meet the Dean. It was the beginning of an important friendship and Hutton became the first major influence in John's life outside his family.

William Hutton had been a fellow of St John's College, Oxford, and by repute the most popular lecturer on history in the university. He left Oxford to become Archdeacon of Northampton, and from there he went to be Dean of Winchester in 1919, where he remained until his death in 1930. When John came to Winchester he was regularly asked to tea at the Deanery. He always said that these visits were frowned on by the school authorities since the Dean had the reputation of being over-fond of young boys. But John always insisted that the visits were entirely innocent. It could be that the college authorities were suspicious of the Dean on account of a different kind of influence: his encouragement of John's literary interests.

Later letters from Hutton, written to John while he was at Oxford, do suggest that the Dean had been openly critical about what he regarded as Winchester's foolishness in failing to recognize John's true gifts. He could be outspoken to the point of extreme rudeness. In one letter he wrote 'with reasoned contempt of the things your schoolmasters said about you', and delighted in each of John's academic successes at Oxford. The letters, particularly those written during his last illness, also show a deep affection for John, though of a wholly proper kind. Undoubtedly he showed John great kindness, which kindled a lasting affection in his protégé. To his death, John kept a photograph of Dean Hutton on his desk; it showed a long, sensitive face, a reticent smile on the lips. This cultivated and kindly man was a vital ally to John during his time at Winchester, particularly in the realization of his first major achievement.

If there are 'turning points' in people's lives, then the letter that John wrote to the distinguished bibliographer, Geoffrey Keynes,* on 11 August 1922 was certainly an important one in John's life. The assurance of the letter, masked by an assumed modesty, is impressive and amusing. It was written when John was fifteen.

Dear Sir,

I have just bought your splendid bibliography of Donne, and I wonder if you would be at all interested in a copy of the 'Devotions' which I have.

I am afraid that it is horribly imperfect, since it lacks 2 pages, one of which is the title page, so I cannot tell which of the first two issues it belongs to, though your book makes me certain that it is either the first or the 2nd, owing to the large type (which was made smaller I believe in the second issue) I think that it is of the very first issue . . .

I got the book for 3/- about 2 years ago, when I was 13, so I consider it rather a bargain (tho' the missing title page etc, I suppose make it of not much value). I had never heard of John Donne then, but I was so impressed by the extraordinary nature of the book, and so admired it, that I remedied my ignorance very soon by reading everything about him and by him that I could find. Quite lately I won at Winchester College (where I still am) a prize for Literature, and I spent it on the Poems and Life and Selected Sermons, and your book.

I am so enthusiastic about the Devotions that I am trying to

---

* Sir Geoffrey Keynes (1887–1982). Surgeon, bibliographer and literary scholar: younger brother of John Maynard Keynes. Educated at Rugby and Pembroke College, Cambridge, he combined the life of a distinguished surgeon with bibliographical and editorial work of the highest quality.

'edit' them by transcribing them, writing notes, and an introduction. I don't know if you think that my youth is a fatal handicap to my success. I don't think I lack the little intelligence, the familiarity with Donne or the enthusiasm for him which seems to be needed.

Do you think (supposing that I don't do it too badly), that such a book would have any chance of success? It is a great ambition with me.

I also want if I can to collate the various editions and record the various readings – could you tell me in which the text varies, and about how much? I suppose that it would be difficult though, to find copies of the other editions to compare with mine.

If you would like to see my copy of the Devotions, and think that its self or its binding are of any interest, I should be very pleased to send it to you immediately.

I hope that you will forgive my writing in this way, with so very little claim to your interest.

Yours truly,
John Sparrow

It was an irresistible letter, and Geoffrey Keynes did not resist. As enthusiastic about John Donne as his young correspondent, he answered immediately, suggesting that they meet in London. They met on the steps of St Paul's, and Keynes recalled in his memoirs the small but solid figure advancing up the steps towards him, a broad grin just evident beneath the brim of a large schoolboy bowler hat. It was the beginning of a long friendship, and the consolidation of an interest in seventeenth-century English literature which was to absorb John for the rest of his life. Fifty years later he said in a lecture, 'Geoffrey Keynes turned me from a book-lover into a book-collector.'

Only sixteen months later, in December 1923, when John had just turned seventeen, the Cambridge University Press published *Devotions Upon Emergent Occasions, by John Donne, edited by John Sparrow, Scholar of Winchester College, with a Bibliographic Note by Geoffrey Keynes, Fellow of the Royal College of Surgeons.*

From letters to his mother and to Kenneth Clark we know that John stayed with the Keyneses, and must have received considerable help from Geoffrey Keynes. It is also clear that his mother feared that this task was distracting him from his school work and his

[23]

chances of gaining a scholarship to Oxford, a view undoubtedly shared by his schoolmasters. His mother must have been torn, for while she appreciated the immediate need of the scholarship, in the longer term she favoured a literary career for John. She did not foresee that Oxford might lead him in a different and, to her, less sympathetic direction – the law.

Whatever help John may have received, his edition of the *Devotions* was a triumph. The book was warmly praised by Edmund Gosse in *The Times* of 24 January 1924:

> . . . The 'Devotions', issued by the Dean himself in 1624, is a different matter. I am told that Mr John Sparrow, who edits the new Cambridge reprint, is a schoolboy still at Winchester. If I am indiscreet in revealing this, I beg to be pardoned. I should not mention the rumour were I not astonished at the ripeness and elegance of the work so early accomplished. I recall what was said of the juvenile writings of George Stepney – that 'they made grey authors blush'. The 'Devotions', which have never been adequately edited before, is one of Donne's most personal compositions. He wrote it during his recovery from a severe attack of gastritis, when for some weeks his life was despaired of. It is a very entertaining production, as theological entertainment counted in the reign of Charles I; and Mr Sparrow's account of it will be read with interest.

There were other admiring reviews, opinions summed up by George Saintsbury who, having emphasized the beauty and importance of the *Devotions*, wrote: '. . . Of the material production . . . too much good can hardly be said; and as for the editing, the most unabashed beggar could only ask for a "Contents" of the Devotions.'

Had John been a mature scholar and a recognized authority on Donne, the book could not have been more favourably received. In a letter to Kenneth Clark of 29 January 1924 John gives his only surviving reaction to his reviewers. Like so many of his letters it is difficult to separate his mordant asides from his genuine feelings: 'I've only seen two reviews – i. Gosse in the Sunday Times, very flattering, *but fatuous*. ii. The leader of the Lit. Supp. of Dec. 20th, which is good. But it talks of Christianity at Christmas (and too little of me).'

Although John did most of the work on the book during the

holidays, his schoolmasters cannot have been unaware of it, before and after publication. In a letter to his mother he wrote that there had been some kind of fuss surrounding the publication of the *Devotions*. However, there is not one mention of his achievement in his school reports. John Donne was neither Latin nor Greek, and comments in his reports like 'he must be careful not to stray into paths of dilettantism,' or 'I hope that he will realise at Oxford the danger that his efforts may be dispersed over *too* wide a field,' reflected a dislike of his extra-mural activities, with a total disregard for the talent he displayed in that particular field. At that date, at Winchester and elsewhere, the educational system was narrow and inflexible, with little conception of encouraging a boy's particular gifts and interests.

The effects of this regime, reinforced by Greats at Oxford, were, for John, long-lasting and divisive. For the rest of his life his passion for literature distracted him from serious classical scholarship, while his Oxford training in logical thinking blunted his creative imagination and his gifts for literary criticism. Winchester and Oxford left him with an intellectual split personality which, in general terms, left him restless at the Bar, and unproductive at All Souls. One wonders if his life would have been markedly different if, instead of Winchester, he had gone to Eton – even then a more liberal school where Harold Acton and Brian Howard flourished and the publication of the aesthetic *Eton Candle* was allowed. At Eton the 'ripeness and elegance' of his literary gifts might have been recognized and encouraged early enough to set him on a course where his talents could find greater fulfilment.

A footnote to John's introduction to the *Devotions* shows that he had at least one ally in Winchester: 'I cannot say how grateful I am to both him [Geoffrey Keynes] and to the Dean of Winchester, who has read through the proofs and has made many helpful suggestions. J.S.' William Hutton was a versatile man. Before he became a distinguished cleric he had been Oxford University reader in Indian history and, more relevant in helping with Donne, had published books on *The English Church* during the seventeenth century, together with a life of Laud. John could not have wished for a better adviser. And beyond that, he was not afraid to champion John's literary interests and to support him with his friendship.

John's edition of the *Devotions* – whatever help he may have received from Keynes and the Dean – shows his own extraordinary understanding of Donne and his work. He edited the text with scholarly notes and wrote an illuminating introduction to this long-neglected and difficult prose work. The quality of his writing and the perception of his critical analysis proved that his youth was no handicap. Over the years he frequently pencilled corrections into his own copies of his earlier books. There are few suggested changes in his copy of the *Devotions*. It was an assured and accomplished piece of work.

Donne wrote down this miscellany of 'Meditations', 'Expostulations' and 'Prayers' during a grave illness in 1623. It is a spiritual, almost mystical autobiography. It reveals how Donne, the young and passionate philanderer, had turned into an ascetic and passionate believer. According to John's mother, he 'had been given no religious instruction' and, by temperament and the cast of his mind, was never drawn to religious speculation. Yet here, he was completely at home with the difficult turns of thought, and the religious experience of this strange seventeenth-century divine. He may have had guidance from the Dean, but the introduction was his own work. One quotation must suffice to show John's clarity of thought and style, and his deep understanding of Donne:

> This book is not a model of Donne's prose style, though it does contain glorious examples of his work; its value is not its philosophy, its theology, or any reasoning or argument that it contains; but it is extraordinarily interesting as a unique revelation of a unique mind. It shows us the intensity and the complexity of Donne's feelings; it shows us his personal philosophy – not his studied opinions on intellectual or theological problems, but his secret thoughts on what concerned him most. It does not explain, it reveals; it makes clear that 'natural, unnatural' perversity in Donne's nature which made him at once the most human and the most incomprehensible of beings.

John's introduction is not only remarkable for its lucid prose and its perception. It also reveals – at the age of sixteen – a self-assurance that was so characteristic of his more adult life; the critic, the occasional scholar and the man.

If John's publication was not appreciated by his schoolmasters, it was recognized in the wider world. On 17 May 1924 he wrote to his mother from Winchester, telling her of another proposed literary commission. Typically, his feet firmly on the ground, he begins with cricket:

Dearest Mummy,

(a) When will Tim be coming back? [He had been ill.]

(b) When he does, will he see if there is a cricket bat of mine in the cricket bag, and if so, to bring it with him?

(c) May I press for the order of photographs which I lately sent you?

(d) *Strictly Confidential*. This will be a great surprise (provisionally at any rate). Last holidays, when with the Keynes, I collated a ms. of Henry King's poems. There was no idea of 'editing' the poems, as of course I have renounced 'Literature' till after the scholarship exam – Mr K. fully concurred with that, in deference to what you wish, (though his creed is that 'there is time for everything if you waste none'). However he asked the Nonesuch Press whether they are thinking of an ed. of King in the future, and they seemed favourable, though in no hurry. (N.B. Be patient, don't jump to conclusions.)

Then, about a week ago, they wrote asking if I would undertake an edition of Herbert (a glorious poet) for next year. But how could I? It would have meant a large job, and I have only one holidays (and not all that) for it. I told Mr K. that it wouldn't be possible to accept that unconditionally tho' it was a great opportunity, and I should have loved to do it. Then he found out that Herbert had already been done in America, very thoroughly and well, and all that would be needed would be an adaptation of that – simply three days solid work, I should say – no more and no less. My conscience couldn't make me refuse that. But now comes the thunderbolt.

There comes to me this morning a letter from the Nonesuch, saying that they would like me to do King for next year – terms: 50 guineas and 7½% of the profits of subsequent editions. You may well be surprised – but no more than I was.

Now listen: 'doing King' means 'collating' one more MS (in the Bodleian – no doubt Uncle [Reginald Weaver] would do it for me this term – about 12 hours work), comparing that ms with the one I did last holidays in the weekend in London, and with the one printed edition; selecting the notes from a modern

[27]

edition of King, and writing a short introduction. No copying out, as in Donne, no looking up, or comparing three editions word for word, and the whole thing about one-quarter of the bulk of the Devotions – no sets of proofs to correct.

I think, *honestly*, that if I worked a full day every day for a week, I could get the whole thing finished, when the Bodleian MS is collated . . .

Then you ask, why is the editorial fee so large? Well, the Nonesuch limit all their editions, and must make £500 on every book they publish – unlike the C.U.P., who are very poor – and they can well afford it . . .

If you say 'yes' *I undertake solemnly*, to spend under ten days, or if you like under sixty hours, on the job, during next holidays, and not to look at King this term or next: also to do what work you or Daddy think fit next holidays (so far, I may say, I am getting on *very* well with this term's work, and if I fail for a scholarship, to devote all the profits of the book to my education! 50 guineas is nearly as good as a scholarship for one year).

Now 50 guineas is a lot to me: a scholarship at Oxford is far far more.

The pleasure of doing this is great: a university education is incomparably greater . . .

N.B. I am keeping this quiet, and telling no one – as I don't want it noised abroad like Donne. If you really trust me – if you doubt my estimate of the work, write to ask Mr Keynes – you can answer without telling Daddy, for I know it would worry him unspeakably, and he would exaggerate the whole business – so say nothing! You must answer *by return*, as I must answer the publisher *this week*.

Best love
John

This long and carefully argued letter – the embryonic Chancery lawyer putting his case before a difficult judge – offers several insights apart from the matter of editing the poems of Henry King. It suggests something of his collaboration with Geoffrey Keynes; of the high opinion he must have earned of Francis Meynell, who had founded the Nonesuch Press in 1923; and of some kind of fuss at Winchester surrounding the editing of the *Devotions*. And of John himself, the strength of his literary ambitions; his rather over-businesslike concern with fees and percentages; his obvious closeness with his mother at this time, and the deliberate way in which his father was to be kept out of such important deliberations.

His mother's reply has not survived, but she must have been persuaded since *The Poems of Bishop Henry King*, edited and with an introduction by John, were published by the Nonesuch Press in 1925. He must have been allowed to work on the book during the summer holidays of 1924. Ultimately, the limited edition ran to 900 copies, making a larger profit for the editor than he had predicted.

John began his last year at Winchester in September 1924. The letter to his mother, and his school reports, show that he was not allowing his literary interests to interfere with his school work. That autumn he was awarded the second closed scholarship in classics to New College, Oxford. The top scholarship was awarded to William Hayter who, after a distinguished diplomatic career, became Warden of New College in 1958.

At the end of that term John's housemaster, R. M. Wright, wrote:

> I am very glad that he has secured his New College scholarship. He is evidently a boy of real intellectual gifts and originality, though I gather from his reports that he has something to learn in mental discipline and accuracy of thought; he must be careful not to stray into paths of dilettantism and superficiality.
>
> I have liked very much what I have seen of him in his life in College. He is pleasant in his manner, full of intellectual vigour and goes hard and straight in all departments. He is filling his position as a senior prefect with authority and trustworthiness.

It is puzzling that a boy who had shown such meticulous care in editing the *Devotions* should have been accused so often of inaccuracy and failure to take trouble in his school work.

There exists another letter to his mother in which John writes of his own attitude to his school work, and tries to explain the difficulties he had during his earlier years at Winchester. The letter is not dated, but the contents suggest that it was written in the winter term of 1920, at the start of his second year. He begins, typically enough, by apologizing to his mother for failing to send her the results of the inter-house football matches. These he now lists, with brief comments which reflect his own enthusiasm for the game. There follows the hope that his home team, Wolverhampton Wanderers, will maintain the good form they had shown recently. He then turns to college affairs:

Today I went to tea with the Second Master [also his house-master], he was very kind, and so was Mrs Williams. I find carpets and pleasant teacups and wallpapers have a nice effect upon me after so much of the opposite! . . .

I am pleased . . . because I feel I did a very good Latin Prose last night. I *do* enjoy work when I do it well – but I find that when there is no opportunity of doing well, and where just *doing* it counts, I cannot work – I do not say so *hard* – but, with such success. That sums up, with a great deal of truth, a lot of more or less similar things that have been told me on the same subject. However, since nobody believes I try at this kind of work (because they judge by *results* which don't tell a bit whether I have tried or not) I used to be discouraged. However, I *do* try now, because I see that success is worth while being deserved, if not won. All this may seem amazingly untrue and absurd and conceited, but it is really not so in the least. I have quite against my will, and in the slightest accordance with my mood, been talking seriously!

This youthful analysis by John of his attitude to his school work remained valid long after he had left Winchester. He needed to do well: he was a perfectionist, he was vain and he had an accurate opinion of his own abilities. Throughout his life he tried to accept only those pieces of work at which he could excel. He made occasional mistakes which left him floundering and miserable. But when he had done well, his vanity required more than personal satis-faction. He thrived on the good opinion of others. The encourage-ment he received from Keynes and Hutton resulted in work of the highest standard, lacking the faults he displayed in the classroom.

His reports for the spring and summer terms of 1925 did at last recognize his literary talents, and an effort to improve in all his studies. The headmaster remained worried by his 'versatility', but his housemaster was more sympathetic:

I congratulate him on his excellent performance in English Lit. Exam. He has evidently literary abilities of a high order.

He has showed himself prominently in all departments of College life and thought, and has done well to distinguish himself athletically by getting into 2nd XI. I hope he will not use his abilities too selfishly and will work for the good of others as well as himself.

The same Wykehamical aspiration is echoed in the headmaster's final report: 'He ought not to be content with any less than a really worthy ambition, for he has the capacity to do much service.'

These may just have been typical schoolmasterly exhortations, or they may have been shrewder observations about John's innate selfishness. His personal interests and extra-curricular activities must have been regarded as self-centred. Until recently, public schools had discouraged such non-team games as tennis and golf. The editing of John Donne and Henry King doubtless aroused similar suspicions. John was already a master at getting his own way, but at Winchester at that time this would have been seen not as a strength, but as a flaw in his character. It is easy to laugh at schoolmasters, but in their assessment of John they were to be proved correct.

Although John's adolescence is better documented than that of most boys, the letters and reports do not give a vivid idea of what he was like between the ages of thirteen and eighteen. Existing photographs show a slightly solemn boy, but neither in those nor in the letters is there much sign of that sense of humour so potent in his adult life. Lord Wilberforce recalled him as a 'quite ordinary schoolboy'. At one level he may have been, but ordinary fifteen-year-old schoolboys do not set about editing Donne's *Devotions*. He did well at school 'in all departments', as his housemaster was fond of saying, and enjoyed his schooldays. The friendship and sympathy of Dean Hutton were also gifts from Winchester which he always valued. And his time at Winchester was underpinned by a happy home life and his close relationship with his mother. There, his personal interests were respected and he enjoyed the 'carpets and pleasant teacups' noticeably absent from the austere life in College chambers.

John made a few close friendships at Winchester; that with Kenneth Clark was lifelong and well documented. K, as he was known even as a schoolboy, was three years older than John. They first met in Gilbert's bookshop in Winchester during John's first year. K later recalled a learned lecture on the finer points of certain rare books, and that often noted lock of hair falling over John's forehead. There and then a friendship was formed which continued until K's death in 1983. Friendships between boys of different ages, and in different houses – K was not a College man – were discouraged, but John and K met regularly in the art school. Both had ambitions to paint and both were on the verge of realizing that they lacked the necessary talent. K, influenced by the lectures on Italian art given by Monty Rendall, turned to art history; John to literature.

K left Winchester for Trinity College, Oxford, in 1922, but the friends continued to correspond, and K kept a number of letters from John, written between 1923 and his last term in 1925, when he left Winchester for Oxford. The letters are revealing in several respects. They are the first surviving ones written to a friend, rather than to his family, and show a new style. For the first time one sees John's maturing sense of humour, with its self-mockery and deprecation, and an artful modesty, all wrapped up in a spirit of teasing. So, also for the first time, it becomes necessary to distinguish between John's humorous effects and his real feelings.

The letters are moderately reticent, but there are several hints of John's romantic friendships – wished for, achieved or abandoned. His admiration for K is obvious, but the absence of K's replies makes it difficult to judge the exact nature of their friendship. The letters are a mixture of school gossip, arrangements to meet, the exchange of gifts of books, and more private matters like John's poetry and friendships. The first letter, dated 16 June 1923, starts with an apology that cricket and work have prevented John from answering K's previous letter:

> I was so delighted and so surprised when I got your letter; and I must try to answer it.
>
> I feel very diffident about my 'poems', and I am afraid that I honestly have not time to copy them out, at any rate before you come down; but when you do (in just a week), I will give you the book which contains them all, so that you may be disillusioned to the full! I hope you don't mind waiting till then. And I hope that I shall see you and be able to talk to you – (if you can spare a minute).
>
> There isn't, of course, any 'news' here; everything goes on as

it always does; there are (is?) a certain number of 'nice' people and things, a few interesting, a great many *nasty*, and very few any more than *nice*.

But I think I must appeal to you to help me in a very serious affair, in which I think you would have great influence! I don't know if your principle at school was to have very few and very important friendships – with me it isn't so much a principle which I practice, as the way in which things seem to happen to me without my control; though it does seem the best way. I think it is the result of practically everyone being on the whole hateful, and very few people quite perfectly nice – but you must preach to me about all that.

Anyhow my friendship which is such a sad problem at the moment is with WG, and you know him and like him – so perhaps you have some influence with him! If you have, you must convince him that I am a very nice and (more important) a very *sensible* person, and that he is only rather lazy and rather selfish when he refuses to tolerate me on the ground that I am sentimental and foolish! This looks silly when it is so badly expressed in a letter, but I'd like to explain the situation to you when you come down. Therefore avoid me, (and miss getting my poems) when you do!

They did meet and K did see the poems, as John's next letter confirms:

... But I must also thank you for being so very long suffering and letting me plague you as I did when you were down here – the only excuse is that I enjoyed it. And thank you for taking the trouble to read and criticise my poems, I hope you will always be as frank! (I don't mean that your frankness was hard to bear but good for me – it didn't even seem a bit unkind!)

These first two letters do not start with any form of address. The third begins, 'My dear K (– There!)'

In this letter, and in the seven others John wrote to K while he was at Winchester, occasional paragraphs help to bring him to life:

17 July 1923
I enjoyed the Eton match very much, and the weekend which Mr Keynes spent here. Since then each day has been so hot and heavy that it has seemed two, and I have been trying to work –

All of which makes me rather tired and longing for the tension of term to be loosed – though Camp has to come before that. I wonder whether I shall survive it, or die as you so nearly did!

2 November 1923
But everything has convinced me (as every visit to Oxford does convince me) that I *must* satisfy a stern parent and get a scholarship next year – to do which I must work this term and get into Senior Div. The possibility of not getting a scholarship is a sort of cloud over my existence ... I'd rather like to write a long letter, because enjoying anything very much makes me reflective, and I often like imparting my reflections to people who understand the enjoyment. (That sentence will probably convey a wrong impression: it is very badly expressed.)

[n.d. but 1923]
But here is a confession I must make, and one which honestly rather troubles me. I promised S. that I would stay with him for a few days on my way home; and I feel perplexed because it is so difficult to know whether he will be (a) like what he was three years ago (b) like what I now imagine he was like then, (c) whether he is really the same and I shall change my mind about him. I only know that *then* I really did think him nice.

16 June 1924
My dear K,
    This is a letter. I think it is rather an indignant letter, too. I must answer your accusations in order – your gibes I cannot answer ...
    [He begins with a visit to Oxford and some discussion about Saintsbury's collection of Caroline poets. Suddenly, he changes the subject.]
    Moreover I *know* that £50 is simply fabulous for any literary work; for *me* whatever work I were doing, and for *me* doing as little work as I shall have to, still more ridiculous. But don't be scornful. As a matter of fact it would not have been so much, only Francis Meynell was told that I was going in for a scholar-

ship this year which I *had* to get (really this was said to explain that I should not have much time to devote to King), and he took it to imply (nor was he very wrong) extreme *indigence*, and so encouraged youth and poverty in the way he has.

Thirdly It is quite untrue to say that I am going to New College. I don't know what scholarship I am going up for – and still less which I'll get. It depends (as far as I can see) on parents and preceptors, who haven't decided yet.

If I do go to Cambridge (which you almost suggest) it would be a sort of exile for me, and you mustn't *blame* me for it . . .

Fifthly I have never seen David Garnett or heard from him. And *please* please name my other hypothetical 'clever friends' that I may repudiate them all – for I don't think they exist.

But as for *stupid* friends!

19 May 1925
My dear K,

I was glad to get your letter after so many years (that I think strikes the right note).

I am very grateful for your defence of me, and I shiver to think of the attacks. You are of course quite right to give away the point if my Humility is contested, but I do stick out for Chastity, though I am sure that the possession of such a quality (I do not say virtue, you observe) is not altogether in my favour! . . .

Yes, I am pleased, I think, that I did not go to Palestine. The reason, however, for my not going (and for my relief at not *going*) was that it wd. have meant missing this term here, which is in many ways very enjoyable. And the Dean's proper setting is in his Deanery; perhaps you wouldn't like him, but I always enjoy his books, his house, his garden, his conversation, his kindness, and his dinners! And what more enjoyment can one get from anyone?

These fragments give glimpses of John's growing maturity and confidence, his early attitude to friendship, a slight overconcern about money, an appreciation of the good things of life and, behind it all, his teasing humour, often aimed at himself. He was close to Kenneth Clark, valuing his opinion on everything, including his relationships.

Though their friendship was to last for sixty years, it was closest in these early days.

There were one or two other older boys for whom he had romantic feelings – at that stage, that is probably the correct description of these friendships. John, in his first year, was 'writer' – the Winchester word for the fag to a senior College prefect – to Anthony Asquith, later a distinguished film director, and always known as 'Puffin'. He was the youngest son of Lord Oxford, four years older than John, and left Winchester for Balliol College, Oxford. Their friendship continued after their schooldays and John said that Puffin introduced him to the ballet. A letter from Margot Asquith to John's mother shows that he was staying with them at Sutton Courtenay in August 1921, when he was still only fourteen: 'Dear Mrs Sparrow, How sweet of you to write to me. Your little John is a charming boy; clever, modest, gay and kind, and my Anthony loves him. We all enjoyed ourselves together.'

When John went up to Oxford he was a frequent guest of the Asquiths. He always kept a copy of *The Oxford Book of English Verse* inscribed 'With love A.A.'. Romantic friendships, often involving the pains of first love, are commonplace at British public schools. Although there is no proof, it is likely that John was aware of his homosexuality during his time at Winchester; possibly earlier than that. More open discussion of these matters has shown that some homosexuals become aware of their orientation even before their teens.

Acting as 'writer' inspired John's first published work, a short poem entitled 'Penitential Ode on a Roker', which appeared in the *Wykehamist* of June 1921. A 'roker' is the Winchester word, or 'notion', for a poker, and the ode is a brief musing on the duty of a 'writer' to stoke his senior's fire:

> Alas and alack! for *il faut que*
> I be an unfortunate stoker,
> Whose duty it is for to poke a
> Large fire (it's an obstinate smoker)
> A thing I must do with a roker.
> I missed this one day, and there spoke a

Rude prefect, who said, 'You young thoker,
The work of combustion is slow, cur!
Get another.' His face is pale ochre,
And the man's an inveterate croaker,
But I had to obey, and thus broke a
Strict rule, and by Brooks εαλωκα.

John's last day at Winchester is recorded most charmingly in a letter written by his sister Daphne, describing the 'Domum Day', as the end of year celebrations are called. John's parents and Daphne stayed for the occasion with Dean Hutton, and Daphne was much impressed by the charm of both the Dean and the Deanery:

5 August 1925
... I went home on Saturday, the 25th and on Sunday motored down to Winchester with Mummy and Daddy. Mummy stayed the first night with Mrs Gooden, the mother of one of the boys at Winchester who is a friend of John's – she is very, very, very nice.

John, Tim and her boy all came to dinner that night.

The next morning the boys spent their time packing and I saw the College and the Cathedral. We went to the Deanery for tea and spent the night there. The medal speaking was at 5 o'clock – it was very thrilling – John said his speech wonderfully – it was a speech of Disraeli's about Gladstone.

He got four prizes (King's Silver Medal for English Speech; Hawkins Prize for English Literature; the Headmaster's Prize for French; the Leslie Hunter prize) and each time a boy went up to get his prize, the warden or the headmaster made a short complimentary speech.

The domum dinner was from 6–8, it consisted only of men – all the boys who were leaving and the masters and also some distinguished people specially down for the occasion eg. Lord Jellicoe, and Sir Henry Newbolt. Mummy, Tim and I had dinner at the Deanery.

'Domum' took place at 8. It is simply this – All the boys and everyone, walk about 'meads' (their huge and lovely playing fields) and talk and say goodbyes while a band plays in the middle.

This lasted until about 10, then they all rushed into a courtyard place and sang Dulce domum and Auld lang syne and gave different cheers – it was almost dark by that time and it seemed terribly sad that John was leaving.

After this there was chapel and then we returned to the Deanery.

John came up at some early hour in the morning and said goodbye to us as he was going up to town by an early train. He flew over to Holland with his friends the next day.

Mummy, Daddy, Tim and I started back soon after breakfast, picking up Penn at Oxford. The Dean was very amusing and perfectly delightful.

I have never had a more interesting, exciting or nicer time in my life.

And what did John feel on leaving Winchester? His immediate thoughts are recorded in another letter seeking advice from K. The expedition to Holland – or rather, one of his companions – had caused more heart-searching. Would K approve of his Anglo-Catholic companion, and 'Please assure me (a) that I shall enjoy my week in Holland . . . (b) that (the critical point) I do not suffer in your estimation.'

Of his years at Winchester as a whole, a few days after going up to Oxford he wrote to his Aunt Margaret: 'I did *hate* saying goodbye to Winchester; I never thought I should hate it so much. And I went down there for a day or two before coming up here, and found it as lovely as ever.' Although he was to love Oxford more deeply, he retained a deep affection for Winchester throughout his life.

III

THE UNDERGRADUATE

1925–9

But Oxford must begin some time, and of course it is *lovely*
now it has begun. I am settling down splendidly, and do far
more work, see far more people, see far more things, and
spend far more money than I ever thought possible.

John, in a letter to his aunt, 17 October 1925

JOHN SPARROW went up to New College, Oxford, at the beginning of October 1925. He matriculated on 10 October, becoming
a junior member of Oxford University, which from then on was
to be the centre of his life. He must have felt less of a stranger
than many other freshmen, having made a number of visits while
at Winchester. And New College, sister-foundation of Winchester
College, was built on the same basic plan as Wykeham's school.
New College was on a grander scale, and the front quad had been
considerably altered in the eighteenth century, but enough remained
of the original buildings to make any Wykehamist feel at home.

More important, John came up with some of his Winchester contemporaries – College men such as Richard Crossman and William
Hayter, who had also won closed scholarships to New College. And
soon he caught up with, or got to know, some older Wykehamists,
among them Puffin Asquith and Sylvester Gates.*

A reputation for cleverness, and as a prodigious literary editor,
had preceded John and brought him to the notice of various senior
members of the university. C. S. Lewis referred to him as 'Sparrow

---

* Sylvester Gates, CBE (1901–72). Educated at Winchester and New College. From
1925–7 he held a law scholarship at Harvard, and returned to England in 1928 to
practise law. During the last war he worked in the Ministry of Information, and in
1964 turned to a distinguished career in banking. He was a man noted for his
wisdom, and a friend of JS.

of the Nonesuch Press', having met him at a party given by John Betjeman. And he was soon drawn into Maurice Bowra's circle,* possibly first introduced by K Clark.

John maintained a reasonable balance between work and play: he worked hard enough to achieve notable success; he made a great many friends; and he played soccer. He also continued to collect books. Undergraduate life is a desultory affair. Long nights of work alternate with longer nights of convivial conversation, work and play always in competition. It is less confusing, and hardly less realistic, to examine those two elements of John's undergraduate life separately.

John read Greats, that formidable course of classical and philosophical studies that still dominated Oxford learning at that time. It is a four-year course. The first two years are devoted to Mods (Honour Moderations). These carry the schoolboy's linguistic ability in Latin and Greek, and his appreciation of classical texts, to a more advanced level. Well-grounded at Winchester, John had no difficulty with Mods and in 1927 gained a first, to the delight, but not to the surprise, of his tutors and friends. He now faced the real test with two years of Greats, the study of classical and later philosophy, together with ancient history.

H. W. B. Joseph was his senior philosophy tutor, a leading figure in Oxford at that time. Horace Joseph had been an undergraduate at New College, and became a fellow in 1891; he was senior tutor in philosophy from 1895 to 1932. A few undergraduates, among them Maurice Bowra, were cowed by his rigorous course of dialectic. In his *Memories* Bowra recalled Joseph's tutorials:

> I had made up my mind to do Literae Humaniores, but I havered with extreme indecision how to do it – should I do the full course of Mods and Greats, or should I go straight for Greats? Mods was rather looked down upon, since it consisted only of Greek and Latin language and literature, while Greats offered the alluring prestige of philosophy. I began by going straight for

---

* Sir Maurice Bowra, CH (1898–1971). Educated Cheltenham College and New College, having served in the First World War. Elected Tutorial Fellow, Wadham College 1922, becoming Warden of Wadham 1938–70. Bowra, if a controversial figure in Oxford, was a successful Vice-Chancellor of the university 1951–54 and, surrounding himself with many of the most interesting undergraduates and others in Oxford, established himself as one of the great twentieth-century figures of the university. He had a long, homosexual friendship with JS.

Greats, and was sent for tuition to H. W. B. Joseph, a most formidable and unusual man. He was short and stocky, had a large head, and a pronounced jaw. He was totally devoted to the college and gave to his teaching an energy and care which would have destroyed most other men. His aim was to make his pupils think correctly, and this aim he pursued with no care for their vanity or self-respect. He insisted that words must be used with absolute precision, and before you had read two sentences of an essay he began to point out the contradictions in them. He himself had an astonishing gift for formulating fully shaped sentences which contained no such contradictions, and he expected us to do the same. We could not, partly because we had not drilled our minds to do so, partly because his use of words gave them meanings different from ours. He treated me as he treated everyone else, and I was paralysed . . . I was unable to answer his questions, and this, which was really a total lack of self-confidence, he mistook for conceit, and became even more merciless.

John had no difficulty with Joseph. He thrived on his teaching and became known as Joseph's favourite pupil. They became friends and continued to correspond until Joseph's death in 1943. John had a powerful analytical mind, together with a fascination for words, which made him an ideal pupil for Joseph's stringent logic. Years later – the paper is undated – John made brief notes on the five people who had most influenced his life, and their particular contributions. Of Joseph he wrote: 'From my teacher Joseph: to reverence words and in dialectic to treat my interlocutor as a child, guarding against imagined chances of misunderstanding.'

There were others besides John who thrived on Joseph's teaching and discovered the charming man that lay behind the stern logician. Like all Oxford characters, Joseph attracted legends, many quite untrue. Sir John Lawrence, later to become a distinguished historian of Russia, recalled in a letter to me a very different Joseph to the one described by Bowra:

I knew Horace Joseph well, and my father, also a New College man, knew him before me. He was a bachelor for many years, but then married a most delightful daughter of Robert Bridges, the Poet Laureate. I was not at all good at philosophy, but I am

eternally grateful for having studied it under Joseph and Alec
Smith, the future Warden of New College, because it taught me
the limits of my own understanding. Joseph was a very nice
man, but for some reason he was unpopular. No doubt you
have heard the story that he was crucified with croquet hoops
in New College gardens. The story was afterwards transferred
to Lightfoot, who was also quite undeserving of his unpopularity
– it was untrue in both cases. This I know because at a gaudy
I once sat next to H. D. Henderson, who was a contemporary
of both Joseph and Lightfoot and he told me that the story was
an invention.

There is another Oxford story that Joseph wrote a brief pamphlet –
not more than ten pages – in which he refuted most of Einstein's
theories; to his own satisfaction and, in his view, to everyone else's.
Such stories are directly contradicted by the extreme modesty he
displayed in later correspondence with John, when asked to express
opinions on subjects outside his own field of study.

John enjoyed Joseph's tutorials and derived great benefit from
them. Several of his friends, led by Bowra, thought that Joseph
encouraged the more pedantic side of John's mind, and failed to
encourage his gift for a more creative style of scholarship and literary
criticism. Bowra, who was closer to John than anyone else at this
time, considered this in his *Memories*:

John had a sharp, analytical mind, which could make observations and distinctions beyond the reach of most people. When
he applied it to literature, it was in the field of careful scholarship.
His intelligence found a new and more demanding claim when
he began to study philosophy with Joseph. He took readily, even
eagerly to it, suffered no frustration or humiliation, and liked
Joseph for his own sake, detecting a childlike simplicity behind
the merciless logic, and recognising in this a likeness to himself.
Joseph enjoyed at this time an Indian summer when he was
almost taken up by his pupils, but what John admired was the
uncommon resourcefulness and dexterity of his mind, which
seemed to flinch from no formulation, however complex. At the
time I felt that Joseph's influence on John was deleterious. He
seemed likely to crush the poet by turning him into a logician,
and that of a not very sympathetic kind. But underneath the

new manner the old love was still at work, and John needed something like Joseph's discipline to satisfy his eager intelligence which sought for a foolproof foundation for his thoughts. The drill in logic certainly took away some of his ready responsiveness. His intellectual conscience told him that he must not tolerate slipshod thinking, and at times he would puncture it in not too courteous a spirit. Yet this too was part of growing up and might have come without Joseph, though the manner and the method would have been different. But the gap between the lover of poetry and the young logician widened, and it became more difficult for John to bring the two together. What saved him was his zest for life and enjoyment.

John himself saw Joseph as a major contributor to his intellectual development, and a beneficial one. His direct influence is most obvious during the years immediately after John left Oxford. His demanding standards in dialectic must have been helpful to John at the Chancery Bar, but the accusation that Joseph had 'crushed the poet', or at least the sensitive critic of poetry, is borne out in John's *Sense and Poetry*, published in 1934, and the subject of some interesting correspondence between him and his old tutor (see pp. 73–79).

However, it is fairer to judge Joseph's influence in a longer perspective. Great minds, like great artists, benefit from powerful influences, but they may take a long time to absorb them and to transmute them into their own talents. In later years John was admired for the powerful logic of his arguments, and for his accuracy in choosing the words with which he expressed his ideas. By that time no one was complaining of the 'deleterious' influence of Joseph, though John recognized that these developed powers were rooted in Joseph's teaching.

John had considerable respect and affection for his other philosophy tutor, Alec Smith, who became a Fellow of New College in 1919 and, later, Warden. He was a cultivated and kind man who developed a passion for the college – particularly its architecture, which he wished to restore to its original medieval design. John always liked him, but to most undergraduates of Smith's wardenship he appeared a rather remote character.

Everyone, including Joseph, took it for granted that John would take a first in Greats. But a letter to his mother, written on 24 July 1929, explained that not everything had gone according to plan:

[43]

My dear Mummy,

I write to tell you of my viva.

It lasted three quarters of an hour this morning – 11.15–12.0. Then they told me to wait outside in case they wanted to ask me a few more questions, and after I had waited a few more minutes they told me I was needed no more.

So I must be quite on the border-line, and that must be the border-line between a first and a second; for I couldn't help seeing three αβs in the mark book of the examiner. If, on the viva, I managed to make them into αs it should be all right.

It was all philosophy. I think the question was whether my philosophy was good enough to make up for a bad Greek history paper.

That John should be on the border-line, and his first in doubt, sur-prised many people, not least Joseph. But a letter from his tutor, written two days later, explained everything:

My dear Sparrow,

I gather you rather puzzled the philosophers in your viva, but not so badly but that they took the right decision. I was a little disturbed when I heard that you were to have a serious interview. Your marks on Logic, R. Hist., Phil. Bks and Anc. Hist. were all on the line; but queries about the first two indicate difficulty in judging: Rm. Phil. B+ and Gk. Hist. B (these are all conflated marks: examiners don't reveal the process by which they reach their verdicts). You were helped below the line, where everything but Lat. Unseen (B+?) ranged from A– to A: Lat. prose better than Gk., and Transl. in the order Rom. Hist., Phil., Gk. Hist.

I'm sorry I didn't see you when you were up. I'd have been much sorrier if you had missed your first.

Yours ever,
H. W. B. Joseph

It was a close-run thing, but John was essentially a Latinist, and he skimped his Greek because he had little taste for it.

A further paragraph in his letter to his mother suggests that a second might not have been a disaster: 'I lunched in All Souls with an old Wykehamist Fellow of the college – Dr Jacob.* He encouraged me to go in in October even if the results of today's is only a second.

'I stay at the Deanery till Monday, and then go to the Keyneses at Cogden Farm *for a fortnight*.' John was keeping up with old friends besides making new ones.

Before considering the prize-fellowship exam at All Souls – another turning point in John's life – one should remember that his first in Greats had been preceded by two other academic honours. In 1928 he was awarded the Charles Oldham scholarship.† Dean Hutton, in his letter of congratulation, once again reminded John of the perverse blindness of his schoolmasters as opposed to his own faith in John's academic abilities.

In May 1929, shortly before he took his finals, John won the Chancellor's Prize for Latin Verse. He recited his poem, *Vallum Hadriani, Ecloga*, in the Sheldonian Theatre on 6 July. Joseph sent him a brief note of congratulation: 'I'm very glad that great work secured the prize it deserved. Best congratulations. H.J.'

Being no Latinist, I asked Peter Levi what he thought of the poem, and he sent the following observations, together with his translation of a few lines:

John was a man with many hidden streaks of kindness and of sensitivity, but by no means a simple case of anything. Latin verse is typical. It is just what you'd expect him to be good at, but he is better than that. Nor is his verse at all obviously Wykehamical. I would have diagnosed early to mid 18th century Etonian, which is no doubt the masque he proposes to us. Has he Stukely in mind? I can't tell. But some early visitor to Hadrian's Wall, maybe some friend of Gray. That in itself is quite a clever idea.

But to your questions. His poem won because it was correct as verse and as a pastiche, witty and elegant. The closing passages have a certain hollow and war memorial resonance that would appeal in 1929, and there is one passage of conventional lyric

---

* Ernest Jacob (1894–1971). Educated at Winchester and New College. Fellow of All Souls. Medieval historian and Chichele Professor of Modern History 1950.

† The Charles Oldham Prize, founded by bequest in 1907 in Oxford University by Charles James Oldham, and awarded annually for an essay on a subject connected with Greek or Latin literature.

beauty (the moonlight) which would draw attention. As prize verse this is brilliant, and has very few words one would wish away.

The bit I like and think quotable is on page 3:

nam mihi saepe alta surgentia sidera nocte –
cum sine nube polus, latitantque in vallibus umbrae,
vallibus et silvis, et inundat lumine campus –
illustrant acies fulgentiaque arma per agros
et tacito instructas in muris ordine turmas.

For often in the deep night stars have risen to me
when all the heavens lay cloudless and shadows hid in vales,
in woods and vales, and all the field was flooded with light:
that shone on battle lines and gleams of arms
and squadrons on the walls in silent ranks.

The examination for prize fellowships at All Souls College – written exams and an interview – takes place some three months after the publication of the results of finals. Having obtained his first, John received letters from H. A. L. Fisher, Warden of New College, and other dons, encouraging him to enter the competition. A prize fellowship was the crowning academic achievement at Oxford. The historian and Fellow of All Souls, Ernest Jacob, wrote to advise him how the exam would differ from Greats:

I was thinking over last night, and in doing so remembered that I had made one rather important omission in what I said about All Souls. In Greats you have been accustomed to take your political theory in a purely philosophical way, that is, I suppose, as a kind of aftermath (if I may put it so) of moral philosophy. I do think that you will need to *place* it in relation to its historical setting.

He goes on to recommend a formidable list of books for someone just recovering from his finals, and with only a few weeks to go before the prize exam.

John, confident as ever in his abilities, was enjoying himself with the Dean – 'staying with him was a joy' – and equally with the Keyneses. In a letter to his mother from Cogden Farm he writes of an invitation to go sailing:

That would mean coming home on 19th and 20th (August). Then working at home (unless any *very* tempting invitations received!) till October, early in which month I should have to take the All Souls exam in Oxford – and see about lodgings – in case I am to spend the year there (reading law) *not* at All Souls.

Also, I have just heard that I am needed for an interview *at the Middle Temple* for the Harmsworth Scholarship* on *Oct. 14th* (this doesn't mean I'm getting it – all entrants have an interview).

The '*very* tempting invitations' were received, and mentioned in his next letter to his mother, besides some interesting comments on his attitude to the prize fellowship.

Dearest Mummy,

Very many thanks for your letter and the parcel. The first, with its absurd insinuation about Mrs Nicolson [Vita Sackville-West], I am bound to say, infuriated me at first, but I decided not to take it seriously.

As it turns out [Mrs Nicolson had asked John to tutor her two sons] a letter from her in answer to mine, saying that Harold Nicolson was (unknown to her) making arrangements to get someone else as tutor . . . fits in well with another from Maurice Bowra urging me to come to Munich for a fortnight or a little less on 25th. He generously offers to pay some of my expenses if I can't afford it. This however I shan't allow him to do. Mrs N. suggests I should stay for a day or two at Long Barn and then join Maurice B. at his home (which is only a few miles from Weald where the Nicolsons live) so that we can start off together.

This, you see, interferes with nothing I may do Sept–Oct. Really I should best like then not to be at the Châlet,† nor in Scotland, but at home, with Tim if possible, working undisturbed for a month. Then Oxford at the beginning of October.

* The Harmsworth Scholarship, awarded to members of the Middle Temple.
† The Chalet was a primitive wooden building built on the slopes of the French Alps by the father of Francis 'Sligger' Urquhart, Dean of Balliol and overt homosexual, who organized summer reading parties at the Chalet, which was also open to New College undergraduates. JS attended one summer.

Work would not really be pressing and grinding as for Greats, and would allow for slight diversions. But there is a good deal to get through.

And, as a matter of fact, I am NOT greatly anxious to get the All Souls' thing this year: I would just as soon spend another year in lodgings in Oxford and then get it D.V., in Law in Oct. 1930. I should then have the benefit of a senior scholarship (*if* I do get one) *and* the fellowship consecutively, instead of having to resign the latter for the former. But of course I shouldn't *mind* getting A.S. this year! I only mean to show that there are compensations if I don't. (I don't honestly think there's much chance that I will –)

The results of the All Souls examinations were announced at the beginning of November and the Prize Fellows for 1929 were John Sparrow and Denis Rickett, who was to rise to the highest ranks of the Civil Service. Once again, letters of congratulation poured in, including one from John's father, dated 'Guy Fawkes Day 1929':

My dear John,

Your fireworks display is a good example to those resolved to make this night resplendent with their pyrotechnic efforts.

I told your Mother, who remained in bed with a slight chill, that your own and Rickett's features adorned the pages of the Daily Sketch. Perhaps it was too bad to disappoint her with this figment of my imagination, as she seemed so pleased at hearing it. At any rate we should be hard to please if she were not very proud indeed at your success.

The first thing you must do is to resign your Rowden Scholarship.*

I don't know the actual amount and duration of the All Souls Fellowships. You will at least be comfortable for 3 years. But don't forget that at the end of that time there will be the uncertainties of the Bar and I think you ought to put by a fund of at least £50 per annum for three years. If you do so and I am alive at the end I will make over a like sum of £50 – for each annual £50 saved which will be useful to pay the fees of your call and a year or 2 in a barrister's chambers.

---

* The Jessie Theresa Rowden Scholarship, Oxford University.

When shall you take up residence at All Souls? We hope to come to Oxford before the end of term.

ever your affectionate father
Isaac S. Sparrow

There is little real affection in this letter, though it does suggest that John inherited his own concern with money from his father. Though Isaac must have been comfortably off, he was not generous to John, who always seemed short of money at Oxford, and not because of any undue extravagance. Isaac was an unsuccessful barrister and could not see, or did not wish to see, the glittering future which probably awaited his son at the Chancery Bar.

Among the many letters congratulating John on his prize fellowship, the most important came from the man who was to do more than anyone to advance John's legal career, Cyril Radcliffe (later Lord Radcliffe),* himself a Fellow of All Souls:

My dear Sparrow,

I wouldn't be writing but congratulating you in person if I saw any likelihood of being in Oxford soon, but as I don't, I must just write a line to say how very delighted indeed I am at your election which I hope will be only one, but a very pleasant one of the many things that you will both want and get.

You may – I don't know – find the College somewhat irksome, especially at first, but all the same I don't think that there is anything that you could have done that will suit you better for the next few years and it makes me happy to think that you may come to be as fond of it and as irritated by it as I am myself! Which is only one of the purely selfish reasons why I am so very glad that you have been elected.

Yrs. ever
Cyril Radcliffe

---

* Cyril (Lord) Radcliffe, KBE, (1899-1977). Distinguished lawyer and public servant. Educated Haileybury School and New College, Prize Fellow, All Souls 1922. Called to the Bar 1924, KC 1935. Outstanding Chancery lawyer, invited JS into his Chambers. Director-General of Ministry of Information 1941–45. Appointed Lord of Appeal 1949. Thereafter, chairman of many important public enquiries, and responsible for the boundary partition of India and Pakistan. First Chancellor of Warwick University 1966. One of the most brilliant men of his generation, and a close friend of JS.

Cyril Radcliffe, a brilliant lawyer, and later to be at the centre of public affairs, was also a very private man. A part of him always found All Souls and Oxford 'irksome'. John never shared those feelings, but that did not prevent them from becoming close friends, and Radcliffe a major influence in his life.

So John, through his exceptional cleverness but without undue effort, had, by the age of twenty-three, gained many of the most coveted prizes offered by Winchester and Oxford. And at the same comparatively young age, in being elected a Fellow of All Souls, he became a member of a most select and prestigious club: the one – and he was to join many – that remained his favourite to the end of his life. He could have used his prize fellowship to launch himself on an academic career, but that did not appeal to him. For a year he used the college for the necessary study of the law, and thereafter, having gone to the Chancery Bar, All Souls was a stimulating and agreeable weekend club, and remained so until he became Warden.

All Souls College, Oxford, was planned, built and endowed by Henry Chichele, Archbishop of Canterbury (1414–43). The foundation charter was granted by Henry VI in 1438, the king allowing himself to be called co-founder. The college was originally founded both as a chantry chapel to pray for the souls of the royal family and those who fell at the battle of Agincourt, and as an educational foundation to train administrators and lawyers for public service. Chichele was influenced by William of Wykeham's New College. Until the last war the college was still largely devoted to the study of history and the law. All Souls is unique in Oxford in being the only college without undergraduate or graduate students, and the fellows have no teaching duties within the college, though some have external professorial duties, while a few Fellows volunteer to teach in various departments. Fellows are recruited through the annual prize-fellowship examination, the blue riband of Oxford academic achievement, usually appointing two new Fellows each year. The Prize Fellows form the élite of the college, but there are also professorial and research Fellows and, today, visiting Fellows. The character of the Fellows changed in the second half of the nineteenth century, with the common room dominated by the 'London Fellows' – mostly Prize Fellows who did not wish to follow an academic career but, while keeping their fellowships, left Oxford to pursue distinguished careers in the law, politics and public life. The distinction and influence of these men in college affairs is illustrated by the fact that the Fellows of All Souls have include three viceroys of India: Curzon, Chelmsford and Halifax. These non-academic Fellows were later to be criticized for exercising undue influence in the college. John was always popular with them, and without doubt their votes played an important part in his election as Warden.

Academic success at Oxford was of great importance to John's future career at the Bar, but his friends and his social life were of equal value to him. Of all his friends at Oxford none was so important as Maurice Bowra. He exercised a great influence over John, and also introduced him to many people who became his close companions. Their own relationship is difficult to analyse. They were both homosexual and they were extremely close, but to call them 'lovers' might put a modern gloss on a more old-fashioned kind of relationship. Bowra made a practice of destroying all private letters – he is said to have been haunted by a fear of blackmail – so all John's letters to him are lost. John kept a great many of Bowra's letters which, among other things, make it clear that John wrote frequently to his friend. Bowra's letters tend to be boisterous and discreet, and give few glimpses into the heart of the relationship between the two men.

Needless to say, Maurice Bowra was included in John's list of the five people who had most influenced him: 'From Bowra: zest and a catholic appreciation of the arts; how to enjoy life with freedom of mind, and in society not to play the prude or the hypocrite more than is necessary.' It is a tribute that one should keep in mind while trying to piece together the intricacies of their long friendship. John became waspish about his old friend in later years, but without question their relationship was based on a deep warmth of feeling. If the word 'love' was not used so freely in those days, it does not mean that it did not exist in some form or other.

Bowra's earliest surviving letter to John dates from 12 August 1926, John's first summer vacation. It is a mixture of Oxford gossip, Bowra's home life with his family in Kent, and musings on classical and modern poetry, with a literary 'examination' of the sort that Bowra enjoyed inflicting on his friends:

My dear John,

Yeats, who appeared to me in a dream on Tuesday night, said that his best poem was 'The Wild Swans at Coole'. As he quoted it, the words seemed unfamiliar, but I failed to record them, and now they are gone.

I have broken my type-writer, or perhaps it has rather broken itself. Fortunately Budge got one for her birthday and the house still sounds to the typers typing in tune, but for me it means that I have to read the classics instead of playing at my dull mechanic exercise. So I have read some men like Theocritus, whom I found unlike Platnauer, but poor stuff, too romantic for the real Yeatsian.

Otherwise my life is dull enough. My shares, after their artificial improvement due to the superior qualities of my friends, have slumped. My tennis has disimproved and I tend to lark at meals and to feel ill disposed for conversation.

I have however written a peroration of great beauty to my Pindar preface, nearly all quotations and V. von W.M.

I wrote to K reminding him ever so gently of the bliss anticipated by us all next spring. He has not answered, but has persuaded Ashton* to go with him to Germany instead of with me to Italy. This gives me joy, as I could find no means of getting rid of Ashton, and the thought of him has become irksome.

Maud† and I talked somewhat about money, women, Boase's 'tendencies'.‡ Of the last I had no inklings. I must address myself to the subject next term and extort a confession from him.

There are some good comparative questions for a W. B. [Yeats]–A. E. [Housman] paper.

1. Compare the treatment of death.

2. Compare the influence of male love in Housman with that of female love in Yeats.

---

* Sir Leigh Ashton. Educated Winchester and Balliol. Joined Victoria & Albert Museum, Asst Keeper 2nd class 1922. Director of the museum 1945.

† John (Lord Radcliffe-Maud) Maud, GCB (1906–1982). Educated Eton and New College. Academic and later, senior civil servant. Master of University College, Oxford, 1963–76.

‡ Tom Boase (1898–1974). Educated at Rugby and Magdalen College, Oxford. After a varied academic career, became President of Magdalen College, Oxford 1947–68.

3. Compare the use made of dreams by the two writers.

You were a great success here. The Mandarin [Bowra's father] thinks you will do well at the bar with your appearance, brains and literary gifts.

Yours
CMB

This first letter is typical of all those that followed during John's undergraduate days. The only clue to their deeper relationship was Bowra's frequent and usually malicious reference to homosexual figures in Oxford. Otherwise, there is endless gossip and jibes about their mutual friends, arrangements for journeys abroad, and exhortations to John to do this and that. All these letters were written during the vacations, which explains, for example, why Bowra never mentions J's academic achievements: they were always both in Oxford when results were announced. They saw a good deal of each other during the vacations. In the summer vacation of 1926 John stayed with Bowra and his family in Kent, and in future summers they travelled together to Ireland, Italy and Germany.

John remained deeply fond of Bowra, and was grateful to him throughout his life, though in the later years of their friendship he enjoyed mocking Bowra behind his back. At a dinner party in John's rooms in All Souls in the early fifties Bowra sat at one end of the table telling stories that showed signs of rusting, and booming down the table, 'More wine, John. Do look after your guests.' John took no notice. Bowra had always enjoyed treating him as an incompetent schoolboy, likely to lose his way or, worse, his railway ticket.

In addition to the considerable personal influence that Bowra exercised over John, equally important were the many people he introduced to John who in turn became his close friends, and further influences on his life. They were by no means all academics. Bowra had a most catholic taste in people. The list is long, but the major influences were Cyril Radcliffe, Roy Harrod,* L. P. Hartley,† George

---

* Sir Roy Harrod (1900–78). Educated at St Paul's and New College. Important economist with academic career at Christ Church and Nuffield College.
† Leslie Hartley, CBE (1895–1972). Educated at Harrow and Balliol. Novelist and critic. Friend of JS, who did much to introduce him to the pleasures of Venice.

Rylands,* Bob Boothby,† Sylvester Gates, Harold Nicolson‡ and John Betjeman. Each became a close friend to John, bridging his London and Oxford lives.

Undergraduate lives are not well-documented. They are an irregular patchwork of conversation, parties, club meetings, games and spurts of hard work, often late into the night, to produce an essay for a tutorial the following morning. John's life at New College followed this pattern. He did continue his literary efforts: he edited Abraham Cowley's *The Mistress, with Other Select Poems* for the Nonesuch Press in 1926, and wrote several essays and reviews for various literary journals between 1926 and 1929. In 1926 his sonnet won a competition in the *Saturday Review*. John always found time for the things he enjoyed.

But apart from letters of congratulation on his various successes – all of which he kept – the surviving correspondence with his family and friends throws more light on his life in the vacations. A letter from Richard Wilberforce provided a glimpse of four friends at New College and their deliberations about their futures. These were Herbert Hart,¶ Duff Dunbar, John Sparrow and himself – all exceptionally gifted – who spent hours discussing their work and their careers. By 1927 John had decided to become a barrister, a decision more influenced by his New College friends than by the example of his father.

John did a number of tutoring jobs during his summer vacations. He was glad of the extra money, partly to pay for foreign travel, partly, no doubt, to indulge his continuing taste for book-collecting. When he wrote to his mother on 15 August 1926 he was at Shanklin,

* George Rylands, CBE. Educated at Eton and King's College, Cambridge. As a Fellow of King's he was a scholar of Shakespeare and an influential man in the theatre.
† Robert (Lord) Boothby, KBE, (1900–86). Educated at Eton and Magdalen College, Oxford. MP and well-known character in political life.
‡ Sir Harold Nicolson, KCVO (1886–1968). Educated at Wellington College and Balliol College. Joined Diplomatic Service 1909. Married Vita Sackville-West 1913. Resigned from Diplomatic Service to follow a career of politics and journalism. A close friend of JS, and from 1951 they shared a flat in Albany.
¶ Herbert Hart. Educated Cheltenham College, Bradford Grammar School and New College. Practised at the Chancery Bar 1932–40, but after the war returned to academic life at New College, where he became Professor of Jurisprudence 1952–68. He is generally considered the most brilliant of his contemporaries at New College studying for the law. He disapproved of JS.

on the Isle of Wight, tutoring Peter Pares in Latin. John's coaching was effective since shortly afterwards his pupil won a scholarship to Cambridge. Describing the members of the family he mentions 'The eldest Pares – the Winchester one – is brilliant – All Souls etc.' Little did he know then that this was a man who could have altered the whole course of his own life. For twenty-five years later, Richard Pares* might have defeated John in the election for the wardenship of All Souls, had he not been forced to give up on account of serious illness. John ends his letter, 'everyone is extremely nice and I think I am a "success"'.

Of all the friends introduced by Bowra, no one was more important than John Betjeman† who, one could say, became the friend that John enjoyed most. Together they edited a magazine called *Oxford Outlook*, but their surviving Oxford correspondence is scrappy and unrevealing. They are all letters from John to Betjeman: at that time John did not keep those from Betjeman. Several of John's are humorous or facetious, leaving one to guess how far they are based on fact. The first is dated 13 February 1927:

Dear Mr Betjeman,

You have now kept two books from my Library for thirteen days, and consequently owe me the statutory sum of 13/7½.

However it is not the money I want but the Books and not so much the illegality of your act that I complain of as its damned inconsiderateness. Others (as you seem to forget) have just as much right to them as you have. Come round and see me about it during the next day or two – preferably on FRIDAY EVENING – sincerely yours

John Sparrow

Another undated note, but perhaps written before or just after the above letter, suggests that Betjeman was not only an unreliable borrower of books, but a procrastinating co-editor: 'Tea Friday here to

---

* Richard Pares. Educated at Winchester and Balliol. Prize Fellow, All Souls 192?. A brilliant historian, it is possible that he might have been elected Warden of All Souls instead of JS, but in the early 1950s he developed a creeping paralysis which prevented his candidature.
† Sir John Betjeman, CBE (1906–1984). Educated at Marlborough and Magdalen College, Oxford, where though slightly senior, he became a close friend of JS. Poet and writer on architecture, with a crusading zeal for good nineteenth-century buildings, he was made poet laureate in 1972.

meet Stauffer – if he can come . . . *And bring the two books I lent you*! I hope that the Outlook will be finished by then. J.S.' They were still enjoying this favourite charade, with John as the stern headmaster and Betjeman as the incorrigible schoolboy, fifty years later. And behind their mutual affection Betjeman developed a complete trust in John's gifts as a critic and editor of his poetry. But although Betjeman was already writing poetry, their collaboration lay in the future.

In April John went with Bowra to Florence. Bowra gives him instructions on how to reach the boat at Dover as if he were a small boy, ending, 'Don't lose your ticket or miss the train.' There is an affectionate and slightly envious letter from the Dean, congratulating him on his first in Hon. Mods and continuing: 'I hope you are enjoying Greece, or is it Italy? Where? I wish I were with you. But then how aged I am and how infirm: how Doddering: how like Mr [Sir Edmund] Gosse . . . I wish you'd come abroad with me some time. I would NOT expect you to carry my bag.'

In a long letter of 10 July Bowra says that he is going to Europe with Hugh Gaitskell – 'he can of course never be an "ersatz" for you, who prefer to go with Sligger . . .' John had gone on one of the undergraduate reading parties held by Urquhart at his chalet in the French Alps. But John and Bowra were to meet later in the summer, after he had stayed with the Yorke family at Tewkesbury, from where he wrote to his mother on 9 September:

Everything and everyone here is delightful.
   Mrs Yorke v. nice, Mr Yorke an M.F.H. but not as terrifying as I feared! Don't send the rest of the clothes till I get to Ireland – and Maurice Bowra hasn't yet heard from Pierce Synnott that he can have us and is so mystified by this that he is wiring to him today. But I think we shall go on the 12th to Furness, Naas, County Kildare.

It was his hostess, Mrs Yorke, mother of Henry Green,* who is credited with calling down the corridor, in search of her young guest, 'Where is that clever Mr Partridge?'

John and Bowra did go to stay with Piers Synott at Furness, and

* Henry Yorke (1905–73). Educated at Eton and Magdalen College, Oxford. Wrote novels under the name of Henry Green. A friend of JS at Oxford.

the occasion was recorded in a memorable photograph of Bowra with John seated on the back of a stone lion. 'Jolly lucky lion,' Betjeman is reported as saying, when shown the picture. John appears to be in serious mood, arms folded, the lock of hair falling almost to his left eyebrow, and a forbidding scowl on his face; all in all, still looking like a senior prefect. It was during this visit to Ireland that John first met W. B. Yeats, he and Bowra having been given an introduction to 'A. E.' Russell* in Dublin by Pierce Synnott.

And so 1927 drifted to a close. There were frequent, rather meandering letters from Bowra about people in Oxford and parties in London where Brian Howard† was 'rapturously amusing', and Connolly‡ 'was a great success with all the women and helped them to throw oranges and break balloons'. There were nostalgic letters from Piers Synott, who had done badly in his Oxford exams and consoled himself with the beauties of nature which he thought John too much of a humanist to appreciate. And John Betjeman failed to keep appointments, to return books and to deal with his share of the *Outlook* work. However, such waywardness was never to threaten their friendship.

Despite working hard for Greats in 1928 and 1929, John pursued a busy social life, as is shown in letters from Bowra and other friends. The letters are thicker with gossip than with facts, but they do tell that John was tutoring again during the Easter vacation, this time Angus Stormont Darling, at Fulmer in Buckinghamshire. A letter of thanks from the boy's father confirmed that once again John had been a 'success'. Clearly, his potent charm was already casting its spell.

The nine letters from Bowra written during 1928 tell one nothing about John; little directly about Bowra. But a note written from Ightham, yet on Rousham writing paper – Bowra liked one to know of the exalted company he kept – revealed that they were just about to leave for Germany together. John was also just about to meet a

* George Russell (1867–1935), Irish poet and essayist who wrote under the initials AE. His family went to Dublin when he was young, and he became a friend of W.B. Yeats.
† Brian Howard (1905–58). Well-known aesthete of Eton and Oxford, where he was a contemporary of Harold Acton and Evelyn Waugh.
‡ Cyril Connolly, CBE (1903–74). Educated at Eton and Balliol. Author, literary editor (co-founder of *Horizon*) and journalist.

man who was to become one of his closest friends. Harold Nicolson was Counsellor at the British Embassy in Berlin and, in the absence of his ambassador at that moment, in charge, and busy with diverse official duties. Despite this, he took Maurice and John out to Potsdam, and almost immediately recognized John's cleverness, his charm and his humour. He wrote to Vita Sackville-West, describing John as 'always absolutely correct': 'When I say "correct" I don't mean in a tiresome sense. What I mean is that in every situation he seems to have absolute poise; due, I think, to a perfect sense of values. It is like a singer whose voice has been beautifully trained. There is a sense of security of conduct. A really charming man ... John is very much of a someone.'

Harold Nicolson, in his own way, enjoyed gossip as much as Maurice Bowra, but a wider knowledge of the world made him a shrewder judge of character, as this first assessment of John showed. John was equally drawn to Nicolson, a man of sharply different interests – and, before long, to Vita Sackville-West and their two children, Ben and Nigel. His long friendship with Harold was to be marked by one special quality. In Harold he had found someone as good at teasing him as he was at teasing others.

The correspondence with his mother continued throughout his Oxford years:

I played football and chess for New College ...
   I lunched with David Cecil* and met Anthony Asquith again ... at the New College Essay Society dinner, I proposed the guests in a short and not particularly appropriate speech.
   I am full of plans for work and wish that the weather were worse, to encourage me to carry them out.
   Has Daddy paid my entrance money for Lincoln's Inn?

John's conflicting interests in Latin scholarship, and English literature and life, were perfectly personified in Joseph and Bowra. The division existed at Winchester, but it was considerably widened at Oxford, his pleasure in Joseph's methods of dialectic, temporarily at least, stifling his gift for creative literary criticism. Bowra has more

---

* Lord David Cecil, CH. Educated Eton and Christ Church. Goldsmiths' Professor of English Literature 1948–70 and Fellow of New College 1939–69.

revealing comments to make about John in his *Memories* than anything he ever wrote in his letters:

> He looked very young and had the appearance of a very bright
> schoolboy who also played games, and this was what he was.
> From the first moment he was charmingly at his ease and
> responded with remarkable readiness to a wide range of open-
> ings. In one way he was unusually mature, not merely in his
> knowledge but in his control of it, but he also had the gaiety and
> the humour of youth, the zest for new topics and the freshness of
> outlook to enjoy them.

These were qualities which survived and made him such good company, at least into his early middle age.

> He was already possessed by a love of scholarship, but he was
> more than a mere scholar. For a young man of his age he had
> not only a close and well-founded knowledge of English and
> Latin poetry, but a very keen perception of it and a discriminat-
> ing judgement on its merits. His scholarship was his response to
> his love of poetry, his way of adjusting himself to an experience
> which played a leading part in his life. Having decided in his
> modesty that he could not be a poet himself, he set out to know
> about poetry, and this was his driving passion. Yet this striking
> gift was accompanied by others which might sometimes fortify
> it, but at other times were less easy to combine with it.

This last observation becomes clearer when John starts to write as a
critic. While his clear style and acute judgements owe much to a
mind sharpened by his classical training, at the same time his critical
faculties were sometimes blunted by the rules of logic; they were no
longer able to operate effectively in the imaginative and emotional
world of poetry.

There was a more immediate and more practical choice confronting
John at Oxford: the profession he should follow. Untroubled by any
of the doubts which were to disturb him later, he chose the law.
Bowra comments on this decision and its relation to John's time at
Oxford:

> John combined sensibility and intelligence, with a taste for
> action. He not only played football but liked footballers. It was
> his reaction against the over-cultivated scholasticism of Win-

chester, with its aridity and restraint, but it was also his nature. He liked to mix among strange people, to discover engaging qualities in them to which others were impervious, to savour many sides of the mixed microcosm of Oxford. He was a friend both of John Betjeman and of Hugh Gaitskell, and his taste for enjoyment was not unlike theirs. On one occasion he climbed out of New College after midnight, which was a grave offence, and was roundly dressed down by H. A. L. Fisher, on the principle that 'a college is a fortified place' and that he had 'pointed a pistol at the heart of the University'. Joseph liked him as a good pupil, but also felt at times a need to chide him for his lapses. John took it all in his stride. Without seeming to work, he did quite enough, not always on the sly, and he was able to master any subject in a short time. He got first classes, and though for a time he had to abate his English studies, he never lost his hold on them or his love of them.

John knew that he wanted a life of action, of engagement in affairs. He could have been a don in classics, philosophy, English, or law, but preferred to become a Prize Fellow of All Souls and to go to the bar. As a Chancery lawyer he could apply his sharp subtle mind to sorting out complex problems into their essential components. He settled happily in London, where he hoped to keep up his literary interests and enjoy, with no regard for social distinctions [John has underlined this sentence in his copy, also placing a large exclamation mark in this margin], a wider range of acquaintances than in Oxford.

Bowra disapproved of Joseph. He disapproved of the Bar. Perhaps he also distrusted London, where he himself failed to sustain the reputation he had achieved in Oxford. John showed no hesitation in choosing a career at the Chancery Bar. He was drawn to the law, and drawn to London. And his prize fellowship gave him his weekends in Oxford and a continuing place in Oxford life. He had no wish to teach, and he could indulge in limited scholarship, both classical and literary, in London. There can be little doubt that his homosexual nature was now formed and that he had accepted it. Clearly he felt that this important side of his life could be more easily accommodated in London, both socially and sexually. This must have been what Bowra was hinting at in the last passage.

John's life at Oxford centred on the opposing influences of Joseph and Bowra, but they should not be accused of tearing him apart. John was already divided in his mind before he came to Oxford, and he was drawn to these two men because the two different sides of his nature responded to what each had to offer. In the long term he benefited from both of them. Joseph's tutorials have acquired a reputation as a process of inquisition, but one should also remember that he was a kindly man, a devout Anglican, and that John continued to seek his advice after he had left Oxford.

It is easy to poke fun at Bowra, but those who knew him best, including his colleagues at Wadham, were fiercely loyal to him, even when victims of his sometimes savage humour. His letters misrepresent him. Delivered in person, his scourging gossip was funny and full of vitality. In the letters it takes on a tiresome old-maidish quality, which was not Bowra at all. His brand of malice, redeemed by its energy and wit, and the basic loyalty of the man to his friends, fails to work on paper. He and John remained very close, and on a number of future occasions the Warden of Wadham was to prove a wiser man than the Warden of All Souls.

IV

THE CHANCERY LAWYER

1930–39

———

He [Cyril Radcliffe] is *very* helpful – and I learn a great deal
this way and find it very interesting. I ask him very silly
questions and answer wrongly those that he asks me – so that he
can't think much of me. But it is certainly the work for me, and I
like this particular sort. I do not want ever to go near a jury!

John, in a letter to his mother, 18 October 1931

THIS WAS the only period in John's career when he felt certain
that he had chosen the right profession. He was stimulated by
the exacting work of the Chancery Bar, and soon established a
good reputation under the leadership of Cyril Radcliffe. He also
enjoyed the company of his Chancery colleagues, among them friends
from Winchester and New College.

During the 1930s his legal work left time for him to pursue his
literary and bibliographical interests, and to lead an enjoyable social
life among a growing variety of London friends. As a Fellow of All
Souls, with rooms in college, he could retire there at weekends or
during vacations to keep in touch with Oxford life and his Oxford
friends. It was an ideal life. He was not forced to make a choice,
being able to enjoy the best of these different worlds.

Although John kept many of the letters he received at this time,
they do not give a revealing account of his life during the thirties.
About 250 letters survive. Two of the twenty-eight written to his
mother tell more of his inner feelings than all the rest put together.

In 1934, following the publication of his *Sense and Poetry*, an
ill-considered attack on modern poetry, Edith Sitwell started a regular
correspondence with him. It was largely an obsessive account of
contemporary literary controversies – and of herself. There are seventy-two letters from Edith Sitwell, carefully preserved by John. She

did not keep one of his replies. Ironically, from the moment John was elected Warden of All Souls she kept all his letters, while he ceased to keep hers. Such are the snobberies of literary correspondence.

Two other prolific correspondents were elderly Oxford friends: Edwyn Bevan, classicist and Hellenistic historian; and A. S. L. Farquharson, a Fellow of University College and an Oxford 'wag', always known as 'Farquie'. These letters might be of interest to someone researching the minutiae of Oxford life in the thirties and forties but mean little to a modern reader. John clearly valued them, to the extent of pasting all 'Farquie's' letters in two leather-bound volumes. He also inherited part of Bevan's library.

Of the rest, there are a few letters to John Betjeman, a very few from Bowra, a miscellany from Horace Joseph, Richard Jennings* – the most fastidious of book-collectors – Dean Hutton, and younger colleagues at All Souls, such as Isaiah Berlin† and Goronwy Rees.‡ Occasionally, interesting facts emerge from a welter of social and academic gossip, with much discussion of classical and modern literature. The files bulge with promise, but in fact reveal surprisingly little about John's development during these years; of his deeper feelings, almost nothing. However, they do make it clear that he was enjoying himself.

At the beginning of 1930 John embarked on two years of legal studies necessary to pass the Bar exams and to be called to the Bar. With the Eldon scholarship,¶ a small allowance from his father and

---

* Richard Jennings. Journalist, for many years literary editor of the *Daily Mirror*. Best known for his discriminating book-collecting, in which he would only accept books for his library in almost perfect condition, regardless of age. Hence, in the secondhand book trade, 'a Jennings' came to mean a book in exceptional condition.
† Sir Isaiah Berlin, OM (1909–98). Educated at St Paul's School and Corpus Christi College, Oxford. Prize Fellow, All Souls 1932. Served in Washington DC during the last war. He returned to a distinguished academic life in Oxford, becoming the founding president of Wolfson College 1966–75. A close colleague and friend of JS.
‡ Goronwy Rees (1909–79). Educated Cardiff High School for Boys and New College. Prize Fellow, All Souls 1931. Writer, man of affairs and university administrator. Principal of University College of Wales, Aberystwyth 1953, but forced to resign in 1957 after publishing newspaper articles about his friendship with Guy Burgess, the spy. A close friend of JS.
¶ The Eldon Law Scholarship, Oxford University. Founded as a testimonial to the first Earl of Eldon, Lord High Chancellor of England, and High Steward of Oxford University. Candidates must be Protestants of the Church of England and members of the university who had gained a First, or one of the Chancellor's prizes.

his All Souls fellowship, he was able to support himself. During 1930 he worked in Oxford and spent part of his vacations at home. His affection for his family – except for his father – never wavered.

On 8 May he received a letter from Cyril Radcliffe which was of great importance to his future at the Bar:

Dear John,

I hope that when I am an important barrister advising young men to go to the Bar, as a matter of fact I shan't – I shan't slip in that bit about a solicitor's office and six months in it. I wish that I knew who started it, and why. And what an intending barrister is supposed to gain from watching solicitors' managing clerks who are notoriously the most stupid men in the world mismanaging their clients' affairs by rule of thumb.

Still you do all go, like XVIIIth century young men starting on the Grand Tour: so it would be invidious to try to persuade you against it. So I won't.

Of course I am very glad that you would want to come into my Chambers and I will be very glad indeed to take you any time in 1931. So that is settled.

I must come down to Oxford some weekend before Whitsun. But I have been very busy for a long time and I love London and having only Saturday nights at my command I confess to a certain reluctance actually to take a journey in order to have a glass of port with Reggie Harris,* or to hear Dannreuther [D. S. Dannreuther, PF, 1927]† being amusing. That is very unlike the College spirit, which is more loyal to its mistakes than to its intelligence.

Still I want to see you, and the Warden.

Cyril Radcliffe could never resist a tilt at All Souls, but he and John remained happy to differ on this subject. John had the deepest admiration for Radcliffe's exceptional intellect and his ability to apply it to the law and to the highest affairs of state. Radcliffe was quick to appreciate the power of John's analytical mind, so well suited to work at the Chancery Bar. Beyond that, he had a deep affection for John, which lasted to the end of his life. John found his company

* Reggie Harris, a Fellow of All Souls in the 1920s and 30s, well-known for his sense of fun and linguistic ability.
† D.S. Dannreuther, at Balliol. Prize Fellow, All Souls 1927.

stimulating and, until Radcliffe's marriage in 1939, often spent weekends or went abroad with him. Although he never counted Radcliffe among his closest friends, he never forgot how much he owed to him, and listed him as one of the five great influences on his life. Radcliffe had taught him 'Attention to the matter in hand, and to put a just value on myself and others; in intellectual matters to pay tribute only to reason itself; and generally to scorn and disregard all that is worldly or material, except money.' The last two words may be some kind of Sparrow joke, though John often said that he made more money as Radcliffe's junior in the thirties than at any other time in his life.

Cyril Radcliffe's letter made John two offers: first, in 1931, he would join the Chambers at 3 New Square, Lincoln's Inn, as Radcliffe's pupil; second, when called to the Bar later that year, he would be offered a permanent place in the Chambers. At that time 3 New Square was one of the most highly regarded of the small but élite chambers at the Chancery Bar. It was headed in the early thirties by Wilfrid (later Lord) Greene,* a lawyer of singular brilliance, who in one step became a Lord Justice of Appeal in 1935, leaving Cyril Radcliffe head of the Chambers. Other members were Peter Foster, Raymond Wilton and John's New College contemporary Duff Dunbar. It was a formidable gathering of clever men.

Lord Wilberforce, who had joined another chambers, summarizes the status of 3 New Square at the time, together with some interesting observations on John's particular legal skills:

> The work done by these general chambers consisted of (a) construction summonses (i.e. construction of wills, settlements and other documents) which came before the courts in great numbers three to four days a week; some quite trivial, others of vast importance; (b) motions for injunctions, of which the Chancery Division had a near monopoly; (c) litigation of a non-jury type, involving every sort of dispute as to which the parties preferred the Chancery Division.
>
> No. 3 New Square did all of them, in the upper end of the

* Wilfrid (Lord) Greene, KC (1883–1952). A brilliant Chancery lawyer and head of the Chambers at 3 New Court when JS joined them. Educated at Westminster School and Christ Church. Prize Fellow, All Souls 1907. Lord Justice of Appeal 1935. Master of the Rolls 1937–49. Always a supporter of JS.

market. Greene, and Radcliffe, then a leading junior, attracted
the big money cases likely to go to the Court of Appeal or the
House of Lords. They also attracted the bigger cases in the Privy
Council. There would also be a lot of advisory work – indeed,
except for silks, the majority of the work would be of this kind
– attracting large fees (as arranged by Thresher, their clerk, who
was said to own a Rolls Royce and a house in the South of
France) and drafting work (conveyancing) though much of this
would go to specialist conveyancers.

Sparrow was the brilliant analyst, dialectician, ideally suited
for construction cases – the subtler, the better – and a beautiful
draftsman and stylist . . . [By 1939] Sparrow was making money
but, I should judge, mainly as junior in big cases, led by Greene,
or Radcliffe. I do not think that he was a force in the run of the
mill cases, nor in fighting litigation. He spoke well and wittily
in court – but, surprisingly, rather timidly: he could write a first
class opinion but had not that experience of minor and crude
cases to be really effective against more hardened practitioners;
I doubt if he ever went to a county court.

After World War II he found himself running the chambers
– a task for which he was not well adapted – he did not like
organising or directing people. By 1952 he was certainly building
up a good practice and would have been eligible for silk in a
year or two – and in my view would have got it and made a
success. It was an ungenerous decision by Simmonds* not to
give him silk when he became Warden. He would surely have
been made a judge (though vacancies in the small Chancery
Division were rare) – not Master of the Rolls because that job
was blocked by Denning for a generation – whether the Court
of Appeal or the House of Lords one cannot say – so much
depends on the lack of vacancies. I wonder if he would have
made a good judge of first instance – too much brain and critical
ability can be a handicap: a wise Lord Chancellor would have
seen that he was better fitted for a higher court and then he
might (I cannot say *would*) have been a great success. His ultimate problem was always preferring the *process* (of discussion,

* Gavin (Lord) Simonds (1881–1971). Educated Winchester and New College. Lord
Chancellor 1951–54.

argumentation) to the *result*, but he was a shrewd judge of character – with a firm dislike of some inperfections. All this is one of the big 'Ifs' of the law.

This is an informed appraisal of what John might have achieved, had he stayed at the Bar. But in the thirties his sights were set not on the bench, or taking silk, but in keeping abreast of the difficult work that came his way as a junior. The Chancery Bar is an esoteric world, dry to the outsider but enthralling to its practitioners. Lord Wilberforce outlines the complexities of the work in the Chancery Division, and they are echoed in the complexity of the documents drafted by Chancery lawyers. One can imagine how John's analytical mind was challenged. According to his Chancery contemporaries, his written opinions were circulated among Chancery lawyers, admired as models of their kind. Little of this material is left among his papers. Nicolas Barker, in an obituary in the *Independent*, wrote that he once found John throwing away copies of his opinions; strange, since during the second half of his life he destroyed very few of his papers.

The start of John's legal career is recorded in a letter to his mother of 17 November 1931: 'I have just been called to the Bar, a very ordinary and uninspiring function – but an expensive one: it has cost me about £125 in fees and robes.' The letter is written from 3 Middle Temple Lane. One might have supposed that John was renting these rooms for his own use when he was in London studying under Cyril Radcliffe; they were only a short walk from 3 New Square. No doubt he did use them at times during 1931, but a letter to John Betjeman from All Souls, dated 25 March 1931, shows that in the first instance John took the rooms for Betjeman. It also confirms – which their fragmentary correspondence only suggests – that they had remained close friends after Oxford:

About No. 3 MT Lane.

I have written to the MT [Middle Temple, of which John was a member] for the keys which I will send you. You'd better not communicate directly with them, as they will realize that you are a sub-tenant, which is not strictly allowed.

You had better get beds and bed clothes and saucepans as soon as you can and *at my expense*. Let them be of excellent quality and very cheap.

I have a tea-set. Would you like that to be sent?

[67]

And I have several pictures (e.g. the beautiful mezzotint you gave me for my birthday) which might be hung on the walls.

I am *against the telephone* unless you very much want it. If it is under your name the MT might enquire and complain – if it is under mine, people will always be ringing you up under the impression that I am living in London.

According to Bevis Hillier, Betjeman's biographer, Betjeman's friend John Bowle shared these rooms with him. Despite John's fondness for Betjeman, it is a little surprising that he should risk his reputation with the Middle Temple by putting himself into the hands of this mischievous sub-tenant, who might well have found it hard to resist some prank at the expense of such solemn landlords. But John was not embarrassed, and though he made some use of these rooms, in 1932 he moved to 3 Pump Court, even nearer to 3 New Square.

The letter to his mother of 17 November reports a tempting offer. Despite John's decision to go to the Chancery Bar, there were those in Oxford who did not give up hope of persuading him to return and devote his career to some academic pursuit. The offer he received is interesting for its future implications, and for John's consideration of it:

But the event of the weekend [at All Souls] was one which has rather overshadowed me between Sunday and today – it was this. (Please call Daddy's attention to what follows, if not to the whole of this letter.)

Dr Craster has recently been promoted from being one of the two sub-librarians of the Bodleian (in which capacity he held a £300 fellowship at All Souls to which a sub-librarian may be elected) to being head of the library – Bodley's Librarian. In his new capacity, he has appointed Gibson, one of the assistant librarians, with 40 years service in the library, to succeed him as sub-librarian. The other sub-librarian is Lobel, a well known Greek scholar.

I have always liked Craster, and thought him shrewd and delightful.

On Saturday he summoned me to his new room in the Bodleian, and told me that he proposed, if I was willing, to create a third sub-librarianship, which I should fill. If I said 'No', the number of sub-librarians would remain two. I should have special charge of English MS collections and early printed books – the very department I should like best.

The salary starts at £400 a year rising to £800, and I could be sure All Souls would re-elect me to a £300 fellowship in addition, very soon, if not immediately.

Finally, he said 'look 20 years ahead' – which means plainly that I ought to be Bodley's Librarian in the end if I am made sub-librarian now. So there is the offer.

Well, I need hardly say that this is about as tempting an offer as I could possibly receive. I have never wanted to teach at Oxford, but this is the ideal alternative. And it wd. mean that I should start pretty well straight off at £700 p.a. (I could, and feel I should, return Daddy's allowance of £200) and live in All Souls. Since I shall probably not marry, I should be about as well off as I ever want to be (my salary rising as I grew older).

Also I am influenced to accept it by a feeling of gratitude to Craster for choosing me out and making such a splendid offer. But this, I think, *should not* influence me, and I disregard it. I may say at once that no more tempting alternative to the Bar could possibly offer itself. If I were starting life in London not at the Bar I should accept it like a shot. If I had not actually started, or if I had had a year or two and were not doing well, or were not liking the work – again, I should accept it, I think, without hesitation. Also, if I were as I am now, but hadn't the opportunities of visiting Oxford afforded by my fellowship of All Souls.

But, as it is, it has come at the worst possible moment – so that I am asked to make, not an easy choice, but the most difficult choice I could (as far as I can see) ever possibly be called upon to make.

My financial prospects on the other side must be set out.

As far as I can see, with my allowance of a little over £200, my fellowship of £50, and what I have saved from my scholarships, I ought to have a little less than £400 a year for the next five years. I asked Cyril Radcliffe about prospects of earning money at the Bar. He never takes a sanguine view. But he said he could keep me on in his chambers (allowing me, I assume, to put my name up there), that I might get a little devilling from him, and that when he took silk in seven or eight years time there was a first rate junior practice which would fall to the juniors in those chambers. He also said that he thought I had the right type of mind for the Bar. So that, allowing for the difference of expense between living in Oxford and in London, I ought with luck *in the end* to be equally well off either way. But if I chose London it means 1. I shall have to work harder for the money when it comes. 2. I shall have a hard, not an easy, time for the next six years at least.

(These two considerations seem at first sight in favour of Oxford. In the end I am not sure that it isn't just they which turn the scales in favour of London.)

As far as the two sorts of work – I should enjoy both. The Bar has no 'glamour' for me now, but offers solid intellectual attraction. The Bodleian wd. give me a lot of administrative work which I sh'dn't much care for, and I might get lazy *about the research.*

The new friends I have consulted all advise the Bar. Radcliffe because he is dead against any Oxford life, and would advise in favour of any alternative to it. I have not asked Maurice Bowra, who I know would favour Oxford – largely because he wd. like me to be there.

But in the end, I think one's friends can't decide these things for one. I should *very much* value the views of you and Daddy on this difficult choice . . .

My mind is practically made up in favour of the Bar. But I am conscious that it is largely because it would be an almost impossible effort to give up the Bar just at this point and because to be introduced to the Bar by Radcliffe is quite unlike what it wd. be to be introduced to it by anyone else.

This was just the first of many letters in which John enjoyed setting out various pros and cons, when in fact he had already made up his mind. I am certain that he never intended to accept Craster's offer. But the letter does throw light on John's state of mind at that time, particularly the intellectual pleasure he derived from working under Radcliffe. John knew many men of outstanding intellect, but outside the academic world Radcliffe's mind was the one he admired most. To leave the Bar at this stage would also have been to show grave disloyalty to a man who had given him patronage and friendship.

Apart from his work, John was – as he indicates – beginning to enjoy the pleasures of London life, where he was able to keep up with old friends and make new ones. This was the first time he had lived in London, a great change after Wolverhampton, Winchester and Oxford. London offered a lively literary scene, and John became a regular contributor to various journals, particularly the *Spectator* and *The Times Literary Supplement*. It was a good centre for book-collecting and club-collecting – the pleasures of the Reform, the Garrick and the Beefsteak standing in for the All Souls common room during the week.

And London must have provided more opportunities for his homosexual activities, though there is no evidence of these in his papers, except for a few unnamed photographs of young men, and one or two letters from which it is clear that he gave money to other young men. Years later, his great friend Sally Owen asked him if it were true that he had picked up young men in the streets and paid them for sex, and, if so, wasn't he ashamed of himself? Without remorse, and with a touch of black humour, John replied, 'Not at all. They needed the money, and I probably did them good.'

In 1931 John published four articles about John Donne; letters from Richard Jennings, and one from the writer and critic John Hayward,* suggest that he was considering writing a critical biography of Donne, a book similar to one that Hayward had already started. Hayward wrote to John:

> I am very glad indeed you are doing a book on Donne and I know it will be very good in every way. The pity is that Donne, even now, is hardly popular enough to bear the strain of two studies published within a short time of one another. And after all, it is important that a book should have a good sale – to pay in cash and credit the pains taken in writing it!

John did not proceed with the book. He may have been discouraged by the competition from Hayward, or simply lost interest in the idea.

* John Hayward, CBE (1905–65). Educated at Gresham's School and King's College, Cambridge. Anthologist and bibliophile, a close friend of T. S. Eliot.

[71]

Hayward also failed to produce his critical biography of Donne. Perhaps both writers decided that their 'pains' would not be suitably rewarded.

But in the same year John did publish his only book of classical scholarship, *Half-lines and Repetitions in Virgil*, produced by the Clarendon Press. It was a short book of only 156 pages – possibly a project John had been working on even while at Oxford – and one classicist regarded it as his most important work.

Virgil, the greatest Roman poet, left an abundance of textual problems behind him for endless scholarly debate. Some of these were caused by his unexpected death, which prevented him from revising his last poem, *The Aeneid*. There are apparent inconsistencies in the text: about fifty half-lines may or may not have been awaiting his revision. Such textual problems were ideally suited to John's scrutiny, illuminated by his appreciation of Latin verse. Whether or not his arguments were convincing is a matter of scholarly opinion. Few letters from contemporaries survive, expressing their reaction, except for a note from Gilbert Murray, who agreed with John's conclusions about the half-lines, but was less happy with his comments on the repetitions.

Late in 1930 William Hutton, Dean of Winchester, died. He wrote to John several times during the year but, enfeebled as he was by illness, his letters are nearly illegible. However, his continuing affection for John was obvious, and he begged him to make a final visit to Winchester. Hardly had this been fixed for August when John received a postcard from Freiburg explaining that the Dean's doctor had insisted on his immediate removal to a German sanatorium. It was to no avail, and the Dean died on 24 October, aged seventy. His obituary in *The Times* was unusually personal for those days, and showed that John had not been the only young person to benefit from this civilized and kindly man's patronage:

> He loved to have guests at the Deanery, and, beyond all, young people. Often, too, it was not hospitality alone that he gave them; they were drawn from all sorts and conditions, and there was scarcely any limit to the generosity with which he would supply substantial help to those whom he thought likely to profit by it.

John had not needed material help, but to the end of his life he remembered the debt he owed Dean Hutton, described in the last sentence of the obituary as 'of the deepest piety, of the most engaging charm, a staunch friend, and a great gentleman'. It is, of course, possible that John wrote the obituary.

In 1934 John published a book of literary criticism, *Sense and Poetry*. He had already told his mother in a letter dated 11 January 1932, 'Constable have agreed to publish my "Modern Poetry Book".' And in the March issue of *Life and Letters* he published one part of the book as 'Obscurity and Communication'. The book was also published in 1934 in the United States by the Yale University Press. In January 1949 Michael Sadleir wrote to John suggesting a new edition, but this came to nothing. John's own copy is covered with pencilled corrections, and he was probably unwilling to undertake the extensive rewriting necessary for a new edition.

Sense and Poetry was a critical study of contemporary poetry, and an attack on much of it. It was a surprising and unwise subject for a man who had devoted himself to the classics and seventeenth-century English literature. He had no great understanding of contemporary verse, and even less sympathy for it.

Following the publication of 'Obscurity and Communication' E. L. Woodward* of All Souls sent a copy of John's article to Christopher Cox† at New College, observing with justification:

> It is very clear, but a little obvious – the lawyer writing about poetry and missing the point. Lawyers as such, and particularly the practising lawyers, are too much given to the mistake of describing motion in terms of an infinite series of rests.
>
> Talk about literature is mostly word-spinning – dreary or disturbing as the case may be – unless it is what I might call 'historical talk'.

John did not miss all the points, and there are good things in the book, but like a lawyer giving an opinion, he allowed his analytical powers to blinker his sensitivity.

While writing the book John had sought the help of both Horace Joseph and Maurice Bowra. Joseph, while disclaiming any real know-

---

* Sir Llewellyn Woodward (1890–1971). Educated at Merchant Taylor's School and Corpus Christi College. Fellow of All Souls 1919. He had a distinguished academic career at various Oxford colleges as a modern historian.
† Sir Christopher Cox, GCMG (1899–1982). Fellow of New College. In more recent years he ran the Chalet.

ledge of modern poetry, gave him meticulous and useful criticism of
the text. After Joseph had read the article in *Life and Letters* he
wrote two long letters, offering advice. Most of his comments concerned John's own lack of clarity, even obscurity. He wrote with a
diffidence in marked contrast to his reputation as an overbearing
tutor, and showed sympathy for the most *avant-garde* poets, even
defending the writing of Gertrude Stein.

Bowra, writing about the same article, went straight to the heart
of John's problem with this subject:

I have been thinking about your critical work and have come
to a serious conclusion. I think you do not put enough of yourself
and your tastes into it . . . it seems to me that you fall between
two stools. On the one side there is the subjective criticism, full
of personal tastes and insights, which charms ultimately by the
author's character and good taste . . . This is true, I think, of
Pater, Symons and the old-fashioned critics generally.

Then there is the high and mighty kind in whom you feel that
the desire for truth is so strong that there is a great dignity and
power in the work . . .
1. You are clearly full of partial judgements – so much the better
but they consort oddly with your impartial air of demonstration.
e.g. you like Donne and dislike Auden (rightly) but do you dislike
and like them for the reasons you give? You may, but I doubt
it, and in any case you don't persuade your reader to share your
partiality.
2. Your manner is scientific, out to prove, careful, considering
all possible alternatives, studiously exact. These qualities, essential to logic, must be united to a grand manner – a real and
passionate desire to find the truth. There must be no suspicion
of partiality. Here I think you fail . . . I feel you ought to be
either more scientific and grand, or more appreciative and if you
like subjective. In the first case you must know more, in the
second you must think more imaginatively. Then you can be
either high and grand or moving and sympathetic. I feel that
your display of reason is a mask for prejudice and, if I may say
so, for some sterility of mind. Is not all this fine distinction-
drawing a cloak to hide your failure to think about the great
masters no less than the irritable moderns?

While writing this, no doubt Bowra had the influence of Joseph in mind. Ironically, had John absorbed Joseph's criticisms into the final text, it would have been a better book. Unwisely, he ignored the advice of both men, leaving himself open to attack from less friendly critics.

The book is dry, though not without humour, often irritating in its obvious prejudice, and lacking that acute sensitivity to words that characterized John's later literary criticism. He attacked what he saw as the incoherence of a group of modern English writers and poets, and the critics who admired them. Not all were condemned: John admitted the genius of Joyce and the success of some of Edith Sitwell's personal imagery. But he accused them all – even T. S. Eliot – of self-indulgence, of using images that could have no meaning for their readers. The book is well written, with a devastatingly polite attack on F. R. Leavis.*

Bowra sent him his opinion of the book in January 1934:

I read the book carefully last night, and though you must not expect me to praise it, I must admit that I found it more readable and less intolerant than I had expected . . . Your writing seemed to me generally clear, often amusing, sometimes instructive. I don't really feel that I have learned much from you but that is probably my fault. I still think the subject was bad, unworthy of you or of any serious critic . . . But since you tackled this question, you must be met on your own ground, and here I think you may be seriously attacked on several points. You set out to be clear, well informed and comparatively impartial. But I must attack you for the following faults.

1. Ignorance. You will remember that I wrote to you before and asked who are the Symbolists? . . . If you mean only Mallarmé, then you use the word in your sense. If you mean him and Rimbaud, much of what you say is grotesquely untrue of both. If you mean the search for pure poetry, then there are many aspects of the search displayed by the Symbolists themselves. Your book gives the impression that they are all ninnies . . .

2. Prejudice. Naturally there are some writers you like more than others. For instance, Virginia Woolf. I find her a bore,

* F. R. Leavis, CH (1895–1978). Educated at the Perse School and Emmanuel College, Cambridge. A distinguished if controversial literary critic.

dislike her imagery, suspect her psychology. But you put up an excellent defence of her, as a good critic should, and I am interested and feel that I am wrong about her. Excellent. But there are other writers you don't like, perhaps with justice. But when you write about them you do not try to see where they are right, but where they are wrong ... It is not really criticism but hostile argument.

3. I take it that the real defect of these poets is their lack of logical structure. Personally I don't see it as a defect. I can think of many pieces of poetry which have no such structure and yet move me a great deal.

4. Dishonesty – not deliberate but I think real. Perhaps self-deception is a better word. You give an air of explaining, and when you explain you quote, and lo it is bad ... You make your case from what you think will persuade the jury, but you try to influence them by hints and suggestions. I think this is intellectual bad manners and leaves a disagreeable impression of a lack of candour.

...I also feel that you have played into the hands of the Philistines and committed an act of treachery. Much of your Edinburgh Review style would make nonsense of Kubla Khan, why 'honey-dew'?, and a dulcimer is ridiculous. Personally the intellectual content of poetry means very little to me. I am content to be excited and can do without being informed.

In fact, to be frank, I think you were wrong to write the book. You don't know nearly enough (it is absurd to talk about Symbolism without a mention of Rilke or Blok) ... You are too sure you are right. Your approach to poetry is probably not that of a pedant, but it looks damn like one ... With philosophy and law I daresay accuracy is essential but not with poetry.

Sense and Poetry was John's first public statement on a subject which was to occupy so much of his thoughts and time, and of which he was to become such a sensitive critic. Like Bowra, I have long wondered why he wrote the book. I found a partial answer to that question, together with John's considered opinion, in a letter to William Plomer* of 18 April 1944:

* William Plomer (1903–73). Born in South Africa, and educated at St John's College, Johannesburg and Rugby School. Novelist and poet. A friend of JS.

Sense and Poetry – yes, I am in some ways ashamed of that book now: not ashamed at having written it, but ashamed of the self which any reader may be forgiven for assuming to be the only self of the writer.

Not a very good sentence, that; but what I mean is this: I was writing largely out of the exasperation aroused in me by a number of (I still think of inferior writing and writers) who were having far too good a time just then.

Exasperation makes me calm – at least, when I am lucky it does – and I was particularly calm when I wrote those essays, and of course I went much too far in the calm direction, and gave the impression of being someone who enjoyed Pope and Dr Johnson and Boileau and thought *The Ancient Mariner* improbable and inconsistent and so much the worse as poetry – which is not what I really have ever thought.

But there it is – it was meant as a corrective. To say which is, I fear, to condemn myself and defend myself in the same breath, because that is not a sphere of discussion to which correctives are appropriate.

It was an honest piece of self-criticism. Although the book was not well received by the critics, or his friends, it did much to launch him into the literary world of the thirties, leading to friendship – and some enmity – with a number of young writers and critics, such as Dylan Thomas and Geoffrey Grigson.* However, John's troubles were not over. One of the poets 'corrected' struck back. Edith Sitwell wrote her first letter to John from Paris on 14 May 1934. At that time she was battling for her own literary reputation and, in the process, determined to destroy her arch-enemy, F. R. Leavis. The restless style of this letter is typical of all those that followed, and it is a perfect example of her correspondence with John:

Dear Mr Sparrow,
    I have just read with delight, amusement, and instruction, your learned and witty book 'Sense and Poetry', and I find myself unable to resist writing to thank you for restoring some kind of order in this time of formless disorder. I think Mr Pound is a

* Geoffrey Grigson (1905–85). Educated at Leatherhead School and St Edmund Hall, Oxford. Prolific poet, critic, anthologist and man of letters, involved in the literary controversies of his time.

very fine poet – (usually, though not always) – but he is admired for all the wrong reasons, and your urbane execution of Mr Leavis has delighted me, though I doubt if it has delighted him. He seems to have been a little less noisy just lately.

I have so great a respect for your opinion, that I hope you will forgive me if I question one or two points in your book relating to my poetry . . .

My dear Sir, should you blame me for making an ugly sound, when *you* have made it for me? I did *not* write 'and why should the spired flowers' (which is hideous). I wrote 'and why should the *spined* flowers'. For the rest, the sounds are flat on purpose, to suit the boredom of the two young women.

Again, in my poem 'The Bat' you have unfortunately mis-quoted me twice, – in one instance adding a syllable, which threw the rhythm out of gear. I did *not* write –
'In his furred cloak hang headlong down from the flat wall' etc.
I wrote –
'In his furred cloak hang head down from the flat wall' and the name of the Bat was Heliogabaluscene, not Heligabaluscue – (a sound which, to my ears is wrong because it is too hard).

Then you deprive me of a syllable in 'The Owl'. You make me say –
'In their thick-*bushed* leaves were laughing like Punch.' I said 'thick-bustled', which has a definite meaning in connection with the previous line.

As for the trouble about 'pigeons smelling of gingerbread,' I can assure you that pigeons' feathers, in hot weather, *do* smell exactly like gingerbread. I don't know if all birds do, but I can vouch for the fact that pigeons do . . .

By the way, I didn't write 'Emily-coloured hands', I said 'Emily-coloured primulas', to convey that they were like pink cheeks of a country girl, – Emily being a country-sounding name.

If this sounds captious, please believe that this letter is the result, not of captiousness, but of admiration for your criticism, pleasure in your delightful book, and of a wish that you should not misunderstand me. – Believe me that, in spite of the fact that Mr Leavis says I belong 'to the history of advertisement (Leavis used the word "publicity") and not of poetry,' I am incapable of writing anything excepting what I believe to be true.

I hope you will forgive me for this inordinately long letter, and ascribe it to its true cause.

Believe me
Yours sincerely,
Edith Sitwell

I am bringing out a book on modern poetry in the autumn, which I will send you, if you will allow me.

Thus began a correspondence, prolific in the thirties, but which continued more sporadically until Edith Sitwell's death in 1964. It was also the beginning of a friendship which led to visits to Renishaw, meetings with Osbert and Sacheverell, and lunches at the Sesame Club. Without doubt, John was fond of Edith Sitwell, but he also enjoyed her as something of a curiosity. The loss of John's letters to her – both sides of the correspondence would have provided a fascinating view of the literary scene of the thirties – makes it difficult to judge their relationship, though she was always extremely loyal to him, and much concerned for his safety during the Second World War.

By the 1950s she had begun to appear in John's apocryphal stories. He liked to tell – with imitations – of her vanity about her elegant hands, and how, after she had sat down, she would take time to arrange them on her lap, or wherever they could be seen to best advantage. It should be added that John had a certain vanity about his own hands.

He had another favourite story about her: due to his wartime duties they had lost touch, but in 1946 he wrote to apologize for his long silence, hoping that they could meet. Edith Sitwell, dismissing the total disruption of the war years, wrote back on a postcard, 'I am not accustomed to being dropped, and picked up again on a moment's whim.' 'Dropped,' said John. 'She wrote of my *dropping* her as one might speak of dropping an atom bomb. To me, it was more like dropping a stitch, or dropping an "aitch"!'

In reality they had never ceased to correspond, and on one occasion he investigated a morale case for her when he was working at the War Office. Despite their lengthy correspondence and occasional meetings, I do not feel that Edith Sitwell ever knew John well. He

was her 'white knight' who leapt to her defence in her literary jous-
tings with Leavis, Herbert Read and Geoffrey Grigson, writing a
supportive review or letter to one of the journals.

John was, in fact, a friend of Grigson's and probably found his
company more congenial than Edith Sitwell's. There is a story that
John went on holiday to Ireland with Grigson and Dylan Thomas,
and that their seaside pastime was to set up large pebbles painted
with the faces of their least favourite contemporary writers, who
were then skittled out with small pebbles. One of the faces was that
of Edith Sitwell.

And as time passed John became more reluctant to accept her
invitations to Renishaw, or to her parties at the Sesame Club.* They
had one friend in common, Richard Jennings, who as literary editor
of the *Daily Mirror* had published her first poems in that newspaper
(poetry received more general attention in those days). But her world
was not John's. Once she introduced him to her adored Pavel Tcheli-
chew,† a Russian painter, 'whom they think great,' John wrote to
his mother, 'and who was, at least, the most voluble and vehement
person I have ever met'.

While there can be no doubt that John was absorbed by his work
at the Chancery Bar and enjoyed his excursions into London literary
life, now, as always, his heart was in Oxford, and he seldom failed
to spend his weekends in All Souls, though frequently he had to take
legal work with him. He was loyal to his Oxford friends, not least
to Maurice Bowra. Their relationship remained hard to fathom, as
their existing correspondence gives few clues to their real intimacy:
Bowra continued to destroy all letters from close friends; nor did he
risk writing intimate letters to them. His letter to John of 12 June
1934 was not intimate, but it was one of the rare occasions when
he discussed his feelings towards John:

> Berlin, whose judgement I trust, tells me that I am often cruel
> to you, and I have thought it over and decided that he is right,
> and I am filled with shame and humiliation, because I can't feel
> that real cruelty is justified except towards the wicked and I

* The Sesame and Imperial Pioneer Club, 49 Grosvenor St., W1, a London club
where Edith Sitwell lived in 1938 and entertained her friends.
† Pavel Tchelitchew, a Russian painter and set designer, who had worked with
Diaghilev, and for whom Edith Sitwell suffered a long period of unrequited love.

don't like to think that I show it towards my friends. However putting aside the occasion when I was drunk and mocked your article I feel there are other occasions when I have gone out of my way to hurt your feelings or not to sympathize with you. For this I am deeply sorry and would like to think that it will not occur again. If it does, you must tell me at once.

I naturally ask myself why I have done it and I think it is due to my being irritated (unreasonably perhaps) by certain things in you. I don't want to justify myself, but I think a plain analysis of the facts can do no harm.

1. I definitely find your attitude to life too ethical. This is not to say that I don't pass moral judgements as often as you do, but I feel that when you pass them a subject is closed for you but not for me and this hampers me, and I feel too that you have lots of moral standards which I do not share, especially in your notions of desert, consistency, and in regarding morality as a set of rules, whereas what I like is a good man, a unique individual who is plainly good irrespective of rules.

2. Your muddling (which you admit) is really a great source of irritation to me. For instance your unpunctuality really drives me frantic and puts me out of humour for a long time. I hate to feel that I am wasting my time waiting. The muddle (which you must admit to exist) is irritating in much the same way, and you would agree how annoying it was of Ironside not to turn up when he said he would. Of course you have usually a genuine and good excuse – but you ought not to need one, and there ought to be no muddle.

So much I feel compelled to say – not for defence but for explanation. And please if I wound your feelings in the future, tell me before you tell others . . .

The letter is typical of Bowra, reading more like a statement of self-justification than an apology for insensitivity. Bowra was cruel to his friends, and often they loved him for it. Nor does one think of John as unpunctual or a muddler. Bowra probably forgot that while he lived at the leisurely pace of an Oxford don, John often arrived for the weekend at All Souls with unfinished and urgent legal work, which had to take priority over the social round. Such a conflict of interests appears in a letter of 15 February to Isaiah Berlin:

[81]

My dear Shayah,*

Indeed I had not forgotten. Indeed, I have been, and am, looking forward to it. (You notice how that comma in line 2 makes the second 'indeed' almost a different word from the first?)

I think you'd better not ask Price for Sunday. Simply for this reason: that I have been given a piece of work to do with Wilfrid Greene, and it is urgent, and will occupy the weekend, and I had already asked Ben Nicolson (Harold N's nice weak worthy son) to dinner on Sunday (you will help, if necessary, won't you?) and I mustn't make any more engagements that day.

Perhaps John was more punctilious with Isaiah Berlin or, more likely, Bowra was more demanding, with less sympathy for John's Chancery work. The first paragraph of his letter to Berlin shows John's fascination with the use of the comma, which came to play a subtle part in his later writing.

After *Sense and Poetry* John published no further books during the thirties. The demands upon the time and energy of a rising young Chancery lawyer were considerable. He was, however, an active reviewer for various London publications. His output was large: for example, twelve reviews in 1934, ten in 1935 and nine in 1936. Many of the books he reviewed dealt with seventeenth and eighteenth-century writers, a literary world where he was thoroughly at home. But from time to time he returned to the contemporary poets, and to contemporary novelists such as Virginia Woolf, Aldous Huxley and William Plomer.

There were also articles about writers who touched his particular interests and sympathy – Donne and John Evelyn – and essays on Housman. The beginnings of his taste for controversial issues emerged in various letters to *The Times*: 'On Abyssinia and Italy' (1935); 'League Problems' and 'On Germany' (1938); and 'On a Hitler Calendar' (1939). A more mischievous controversialist was revealed in a *Spectator* article in 1936, 'What does a Socialist Woman Do?', which made waspish fun of Naomi Mitchison; and his mother

* Shayah, a diminutive of Isaiah, used from early days by family and close friends. It was not liked by Berlin and after the last war, nearly everyone acknowledged him as Isaiah.

1. The wedding of John's parents in 1905

2. A family group in 1910: Mollie, Margaret Sparrow,
Tim, John and Daphne with the nurse

8. A young Wykehamist

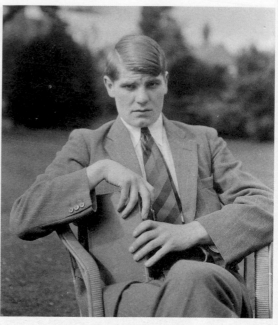

9. A old Wykehamist

10. College Prefects: Summer 1925 (back row, from left) J. McH. Willis, C. H. de Saumerez, H.C. Lewis, E.A. Radice, W. S. Tegner, P. J. Clapham (middle row) J. H. A. Sparrow, W. E. Philip, A. W. Haslett, W. G. Hayter, R. O. Wilberforce, R. H. S. Crossman (front row) A. G. White, H. P. Kingdon, W. Empson

very cross. And reviewing a book by Godfrey Winn, his distaste was not concealed in the title, 'Winsome Is as Winsome Does'.

Finally, always versatile, in the *Spectator* for 5 May 1939 he wrote his first account of a professional soccer match, the cup final, under the title, 'Impressions at Wembley'. He wrote from the heart, for his own Wolverhampton Wanderers were playing in the cup final for the first time, against Portsmouth, but were beaten 4–1. John was stoical, almost poetical, in defeat: 'They never lost heart, and they never lost their tempers ... But they have this consolation: they will be seen again at Wembley very soon.' Anyone who doubts John's passion for the game of soccer should read this article.

John occasionally lectured on English literature. Edith Sitwell mentioned a lecture he was to give on his admired Dr Samuel Parr. Many of John's lasting enthusiasms began early in his life. For some of them – Parr, Pater, Pattison – great things were planned, but as his collections of papers increased, the work involved in such projects seemed less attractive.

John gave a lecture at the British Institute in Paris in January 1939 on 'Traditions and Revolt in English Poetry'. His opening words – 'No one I think will deny that England in the present century has been poor in literature' – show that at the end of the thirties his views on modern writing remained unchanged. The lecture included a long passage considering and praising the poetry of Yeats, whom he admired so much, and whose books he collected so avidly. He considered Yeats's poetry ideal for reading aloud. When the poet came to Oxford in May 1938 John invited him to dine at All Souls. He described the occasion in a letter to his mother of 8 May:

> One news 'item' – I had W. B. Yeats to dine last night. I asked him last weekend, hearing that he was to be in Oxford.
>
> He stayed at the Mitre. I asked two other people – Roy Harrod (minus wife!) and one Hampshire,* a young Fellow of this college.
>
> W.B.Y. is much roused on the question you feel so strongly about – the necessity of restricting breeding from bad stocks

---

* Sir Stuart Hampshire. Educated at Repton and Balliol. Prize Fellow, All Souls 1936. Philosopher. Warden of Wadham College, Oxford 1970–83. A good friend of JS if stern critic.

[one of Yeats's pseudo-scientific obsessions]. He was full of Catell's book. And he wanted to find out more facts and figures from Harrod.

The evening passed off well: Yeats was in good form and talked and talked and talked. Too little about poetry, and too much about politics (he hates materialism, which for him is typified by Russia so much that he is practically pro-Nazi) and about spiritualism. He is very eloquent and very amusing. But he's getting very old, and shaky physically.

Yeats died within a few months of this meeting, on 28 January 1939.

John's letters to his mother also reveal something of his busy legal and social life in London. Typical is this letter written from All Souls on 6 October 1935:

Dearest Mummy,

Very many thanks for your letter, and for arranging about the washing, which arrived safely on Friday.

I have had a busy week, or I should have written earlier. Dinner with Richard Jennings and Edith Sitwell one evening; Woizikowaki's Ballet (W. had his own company 1935–6) another evening with Duff Dunbar; and on Thursday Betjeman took me to dine with Lord Berners,* to whom I took a great liking.

I have had bits of work to do, too, which have kept me occupied during the days.

Yesterday afternoon I saw the Arsenal play football, and I have never seen any team play much better. I got here in time for dinner. Today I attended a dull committee meeting.

The great excitement of the week came on Friday, and you will read about it about the same time as you get this letter.

I was in Cyril R's room when there was a knock on the door and Wilfrid [Greene] came in, very sunburned and calm. He asked after our holidays and told us about his, and then in a rather nervous and embarrassed and modest way said, 'I'm afraid I am deserting you fellows: I've taken a job.' 'A job?' we said,

---

* Lord Berners (1883–1950). Author, musician and artist. During the period of his life, whenever two or three eccentrics were gathered together, Berners was likely to be amongst them.

as if bewildered, though we had a shrewd suspicion what he meant. 'Yes, they've asked me to join the Court of Appeal.' He then told us how he had received a wire when in a bathing dress on the beach at Monte Carlo, offering him this post, and asking for an answer by return. It will mean (apparently) selling *both* his houses, the town house and the country house; and his salary for the next three or four years will be completely absorbed in paying off arrears of tax, or rather instalments of super-tax in respect of past years. Not an easy decision for him to come to. But it was not the drop from about £40,000 to £5,000 which seemed to affect him as much as the prospect of giving up his old life, leaving his chambers, and seeing less of his friends at the Bar.

This will affect others in the chambers in various ways: it will, I think, improve Cyril's practice, though of course he won't 'step into Wilfrid's practice' because Wilfrid Greene hadn't got a practice in the ordinary sense: people just brought him work of many different kinds. Thresher of course, is most vitally affected; he adopts the attitude of being overjoyed at Mr Greene's success, saying that as far as he himself is concerned he 'can't complain', and that he hopes Mr Radcliffe will soon be in Mr Greene's position (with equally desirable results for him, Thresher). As for Duff and me, it means that there will be no more 'little cases' into which Thresher is able to push us as Mr Greene's paid assistants – a serious financial loss.

To go straight from the Bar to the Court of Appeal is I think unprecedented; to do so at 51 or 52 (his age) is more remarkable still.

Other events of importance are the commencement of Italy's war of self-defence, and the installation of my new curtains, which I think are pleasing . . .

John was pursuing all his interests: his work, the literary world, the ballet, home comforts and football. Other letters to his mother mention meetings with Elizabeth Bowen, T. S. Eliot, Leonard and Virginia Woolf – who invited him to edit the letters of Rupert Brooke – a visit to Paris with Harold Nicolson, and

I forgot to say that I dined on Monday (alone) with Gertrude Tuckwell . . . Unfortunately she is hardly a marriageable person

for me now, since she is seventy-five years old. She is a niece of
Lady Dilke, and correspondingly, by marriage, of Mark Pattison,
and she had the most thrilling letters and pictures and books to
show me, and (above all) personal reminiscences to tell me of
Oxford in the 70's and 80's.

The gentle jibe about a 'marriageable person' touched on more personal matters which John seldom raised with his mother. However,
the letter he wrote to her on 26 May reveals something of his feelings
at that time, and is more open than any of his previous letters to
her:

I wish I were not desperately busy – so that I cd properly answer
your touching letter . . .
    I did so much enjoy our very brief holiday. I only wish you
could have come *abroad*, as I am sure that that complete change
is what you needed . . .
    As it was, as soon as you said you w'dn't come abroad I told
my clerks and an actual appointment was fixed for Tuesday
subject to cancellation. That was why I had to be back in chambers to see how things stood . . .
    I am truly sorry that I didn't let you know earlier when I sh'd
be free, but there was no question of keeping from you some
personal appointment – some 'real reason' for my return to
London and my delay in joining you – which is what I imagine
had crept into your mind as reason of it all.
    As for your 'sermon' – I can only say that I find it difficult to
know how to answer –
Tuesday evening –
    Perhaps my best answer, to allay your anxiety, is this (and I
can honestly give it):
    Though I am in some ways whimsical (I can't think of a better
word: I mean that I play at being other than I really am, and
enjoy mock-melancholy and other half-feelings or poses), and
though I am not a buoyant and superficially cheerful person –
like Tim – I am, on the whole, a happy person. My work, my
friends, my books (my 'library', I mean) and more still my love
of reading, particularly poetry, and the thought of people I am
fond of – these are enough to fill my life completely and give

me all in the way of happiness that I shd ever dream of asking for.

I think it a full, and not an empty life. I don't say that marriage (which I think is often at the back of your mind when you think of me) wdnt supply something more – but it wdnt supply anything of which, with, my life filled as I have described above, I feel the lack. There may come a time when I shall feel the lack; then will be time enough to think of marrying. To marry before that, for the sake of marrying would be a mistake – and might involve the mistake of marrying the wrong person.

As for 'souls' – I believe in souls – though I am not sure about their immortality. Or, to put it another way, I always think of people, myself included, as something more than their flesh and blood and 'reactions' – and of course that thing in, or aspect of, people – call it integrity or personality, or soul, or what you will – is what is important.

Perhaps when I was a child I was more easily moved to a *display* of feeling than I am now; and perhaps I now hide my feelings under a mask of insouciance. That does not mean that I attach less importance to soul or to people's feelings, or that I feel less deeply myself. Rather the reverse. I feel very deeply in personal matters *and* the state of the world. But I am not going to wear my heart on my sleeve, even to please you. I do not find that feeling deeply is conducive to happiness, but that is neither here nor there.

To lose the capability of feeling would be the worst thing of all, worse than any amount of unhappiness.

You must not think that because I chose the Ch-Bar instead of being Mr Eden that it means that I feel less deeply than you about international or social conditions. I won't argue about this, because if you do not understand it when it is just stated, argument will not convince you.

Another point – You say, à propos, I think, of modern cynicism and the modern outlook generally (with sex particularly in mind, I fancy) – that things are said and thought and done today as if they were the natural thing which in yr young days wd have been deemed unnameable – Well, you know I am not a radical, or much of a believer in 'progress'. You know how I loathe the Mitchisonian outlook.

[87]

But this I do think: that though the change towards broad-mindedness in sex is not all to the good (what change is?), it is on the whole for the better – and that all that one may deplore in the change is only a price one has to pay for what is on the whole an improvement. That is my considered opinion – it is far too large a subject to argue about – but I think that mine is a judicious view. (I am myself old fashioned in feeling about these things and so broadminded as to be absolutely *open-minded* in opinion.)

Well, it is sometime after midnight and I mustn't go on. But I am glad you wrote, because I should hate to think that you were worrying about me, and I honestly think that if you consider all I say in this letter you ought to come to the conclusion that *on these points* there is no need to worry. Catarrh – that is another matter; but not so important?

But one word of warning: there must be differences between the generations – however much they mean to each other, and however close they are in affection. Partic. bet. sons and mothers. Differences in outlook, in standards, in tastes. They must take each other, to a certain extent, on trust. That has always been so: it may be more obviously so now when the world is changing so fast, but it is an old thing, and doesn't alter the fundamental relationship.

I, as a matter of fact, and for reasons which I can't always fathom myself, am at my worst at home, and you see almost the worst of me. It is infuriating that this shd be so – and when you speak of my being 'wonderful' as a son I can only blush in real shame – and wish that sometimes, just for your benefit, I could wear my heart on my sleeve, so as to convince you that I am not *really* as horrid as I sometimes seem on the surface.

I certainly often feel that any good innate qualities which I have – no, not *any*, but those I value most – I have from you, apart from all you have done to bring them out and educate them. This again makes me feel ashamed.

One final thing: the refusal to believe 'ill' of one's children, the desire to defend them at all costs from others' attacks – may be natural, but it is I think wrong, and a sin against the light.

Either you are ashamed of your child or you are not. If you are you should, on proper occasions, say so: adding, if you like, that it does not affect your devotion to him or her.

If you are not, you shdnt conceal his faults – indeed, if you are not ashamed, why shd you wish to?

Of course, good sense tells one to minimise scandal, not to publish or advertise the faults of anyone one knows or cares for – that is quite another matter. What I am saying is that it is no proof of love to one's child to pretend to one's self or to others who are closely concerned that he is other than he is. You do not owe it to him to do this; rather you owe it to him not to do this.

I am not being clever or arguing to prove a point, but being quite sincere.

I will only add that if you knew how much yr letter was going to upset me during the best part of two busy days you wd probably not have written it, *not*, I mean, to spare me, but because the very fact of my being upset as I was proves how far from true a great deal of what you said about me was.

I don't say this with a sense of grievance, but rather with a sort of satisfaction – it just *proves* you needn't worry!

With love
John

I am glad you wrote –

For all its length, the letter never actually comes to the point. But it was the thirties, when certain things could be hinted at, or skated around, but not actually spelt out. It was not until the early fifties that John felt able to write to his mother more about his homosexuality, although it is hard to believe that she did not know about it long before then.

But the letter, both in its content and its style – with its effective rhetorical punctuation – presents a good self-portrait of John and his complex character, as it had developed by the mid-thirties; many traits would be recognizable to those who knew him later. The man and the lawyer are intertwined and he presents his arguments to his mother as if he were presenting them in court. Despite his unquestionable fondness for her, one feels that he wants to maintain a certain distance.

It would be misleading to end a description of John's life in the thirties on too solemn a note. His charm and his humour, so much a part of his later reputation, were already evident, as was his taste for life. His enjoyment of London was probably his most genuine reason for not staying in Oxford. Although he was certainly an active homosexual during these years – an activity easier to pursue in London – there is not a scrap of existing evidence of any romantic attachment. There are among his papers scrappy notes suggesting encounters with young men, but it was a time when the law still required extreme discretion, and allowed no record of emotional or sexual attachments with other men.

But there is plenty of evidence for his lively sense of humour, which already stretched from clever jokes in the senior common room to a love of farcical situations and pure fun, enjoyed by his friends of all ages. Nigel Nicolson looked back to his boyhood with his brother Ben, and how eagerly they anticipated John's arrival for a hilarious weekend. His gift for amusing both the young and the old was fully developed by then. It remained one of his most appealing character-istics throughout his life.

V

THE SOLDIER

1939–46

I think that the hardest thing I have had to bear
since the war began was the sight of Haydock, yesterday,
eating jam with shepherd's pie.

*John Sparrow describing life in the ranks
in a letter to his mother,
10 November 1939*

IN EARLY August 1939 John was making one of his frequent
visits to the Asquiths' home at Mells in Somerset. He had been
a close friend of the younger members of the family since his
Winchester days. He was also close to Mrs Frances Horner, a relation
and friend of the Asquiths, who as a widow lived at Mells. It was
she who equipped John with thick sweaters and oilskins before he
set off for a sailing holiday in the English Channel with Harold
Nicolson, Harold's younger son Nigel, and Duff Dunbar, friend and
colleague from 3 New Square.

In a letter of 7 August he wrote to his mother from the yacht *Mar*:
'I like the feeling of being cut off from the world – particularly when
the news from the world is not likely to be good.' This mood of
escapism continued for a few more days, and on 16 August he wrote
saying that he was thinking of stopping for a week in France.

By 24 August it was no longer possible to ignore the situation in
Europe. Dunbar had already left the yacht to join a territorial camp.
Harold Nicolson left for London, and John told his mother that he
was also 'going to London for a night to see about joining some
territorial unit'.

From 1 September to 12 January 1940 John recorded his early
experiences of army life in the only 'diary' he ever kept – a loose-leaf
notebook labelled *Wartime Notebook 1940*. It gives his impressions

of life in the ranks and a detailed account of why and how he tried to resist taking a commission.

Despite its title, the notebook begins in 1939:

> Friday (1 September) – after a week of being unsettled (cruise with Harold had ended on previous Sat. Then a week in Oxford with a visit to London – Handel St and Goronwy's [Rees] flat) called at Drill Hall on Fri morn – told to come back in afternoon – accepted that evening HQ Cy of 5th Bn (Oxford & Bucks Light Infantry) . . . in the George that evening. Prof Z [Zaehner]* champagne.
>
> Sat morning – bustle and confusion at Drill Hall – me standing in brown coat and grey flannel trousers and rather coarse brown shoes. Sitting about and waiting – herded about – . . . gradual issue of equipment and bedding (2 blankets, no sheets, no mattress or pillow for two or three days) don't remember anything distinct for first day or two except cleaning QM's belt instead of Ch. parade on first Sunday.

From 1 to 26 September John's platoon was quartered in the New College squash courts, with the cricket pavilion as the mess hall. John was in No. 2 squash court, where there were twenty beds, with about four more in the gallery. They got up at six and spent the day doing basic training in Christ Church meadow, or in Magdalen College School grounds. Their duties ended at 4.30, and the diary describes how John spent his evenings: 'Evening – usually AS in my room – letters etc, cold supper supplied by very willing servants . . . who however assumed I was aiming at and wd soon achieve a commission. Back by 10 pm, lights out 10.30.'

At that moment he was not aiming at a commission, and in the notebook he explains his initial reason for enlisting in the ranks rather than seeking a commission:

> I joined the army on 1st September 1939. It was made clear to me before I joined . . . that, if I wanted to join straight away, it was only possible to do so by enlisting as a private. This did not make me hesitate; I had assumed that this wd be so; indeed,

---

* Prof Robert Zaehner – often known as 'the Prof' –. Educated Tonbridge School and Christ Church, Oxford. Fellow of All Souls 1952. A scholar of Eastern religions.

if I had been told that I cd only join as an officer, I do not think I should have joined at all – not, anyhow, without much consideration.

On the morning of our being embodied (i.e. next day, Sept 2nd), just before I set out to present myself at the Drill Hall acc. to instructions, I was visited at All Souls by Frank Pakenham.* Something he said – to the effect that he had spoken about me (on the previous evening I suppose) to the C.O., and that I probably would not have to wait long for 'my commission' – was the first indication to me of the kind of pressure that might be brought to bear.

I could scarcely conceal my indignation, but I did what I could to remedy his interference by asking him to supper in my rooms at All Souls a few days later, when I tried to explain to him my attitude – viz that not merely had I no desire for a commission at present, but at present I had no desire for a commission.

John was right. Within a month pressure was being brought to bear from various directions, not least from his family. His brother Tim, a regular soldier, wrote, probably with tongue in cheek: 'It will be explained to those who are considered suitable for training, but are not desirous of being commissioned, that it is their duty to fit themselves to hold commissioned rank.'

John was to hear this official attitude over and over again from his commanding officer during the remaining months of 1939. He was also criticized by his father, despite the fact that *he* had enlisted in the ranks at the beginning of the First World War. Frances Horner wrapped her 'sermon' in sympathy, mittens and socks. Edith Sitwell was indignant that 'someone like you, with a wide mind as well as a strong intellect', should be forced to fight, and prayed that he would not be sent to France. The strongest criticism came from his mother, whose main complaint was that he was 'wasted' in the ranks. He replied to her on 13 September, explaining his attitude:

---

* Lord Longford, KG. Educated at Eton and New College. Distinguished political career as Labour peer.

Dearest Mummy,

Mine is a terrible fate, I seem to be condemned (like some character in Hades in Greek Mythology) to go through life explaining myself without ever being understood.

Just on the point of *waste*: of course my special abilities, such as they are, are wasted in war. But one of the awful things about war is that it entails such waste. Take artists and musicians and writers – whose gifts are perhaps the most valuable things in the world – they must be wasted in war. (If a particular artist happens to be 65 when war breaks out, that is a different matter.)

My particular intellectual gifts are for textual criticism and literary criticism of a sort, and for historical research of a kind (Dr Parr) and for Chancery things. In war, such gifts are at a discount.

If I were over 40, I might force these intellectual gifts into some channel which w'd be useful in war – but I am not, and there are plenty of people over military age just as good as I am at things like the Ministry of Information, which is over staffed. On the other hand, younger people are, I hear, flocking into the forces – and if this is to be a long war they will all be needed – the only other young colleagues here whom I have met – Davies and Hampshire – have both joined. I expect their mothers think that their genius is wasted too.

You *do* see what I mean?

This was John in a perverse mood, and unusually insensitive to his mother's feelings. Of course he was wasted as a private soldier, and it did not take the army long to find him an important job which made full use of all his 'special abilities'. But his four months in the ranks proved to be a valuable experience when he began to investigate army morale in 1942.

Why, for his first four months in the army, did John resist every attempt to send him to OCTU for officer training? His notebook reveals that he enjoyed barrack-room life and the company of his platoon. It might be argued that he shirked his duty, preferring the discomforts of the barrack-room to the burdens of responsibility. But John does not appear to have found life in the ranks so hard. He was thoroughly enjoying himself:

Attend Battalion at Drill Hall – Cookhouse fatigue with Harris – v. hot – nothing on under canvas. Drain clogged, cleaning it out

with tins – scooping in bacon fat and mud. Bathing in Parson's
Pleasure. Allowed myself to be thrown in by K Walters and
others. Banged head on wood at edge – didn't mind – credit
gained from this. Feeling of physical well being and *freedom* –
exulting feeling.

At thirty-three, John was fit and strong, still useful on the football
field, with indomitable humour and, above all else, an interest in
people and an ability to make friends with men who came from
entirely different backgrounds; he was free from social snobbery. But
it was a letter from Cyril Radcliffe, written in September, which
mischievously touched the heart of the matter: 'Thresher says that
you have "Joined the Territorials". When? how? I hope that you are
not too uncomfortable: it is the first wish for any war. I am sure that
you will have some beautiful companions.'

There were indeed 'beautiful companions'. They and their attractions were recorded in John's notebook:

S – dark curly hair, brown eyes, flat nose, full lips, good teeth,
brown skin, strong neck. A perfect example of a 'soldier boy'.
AJ would slip over and whisper with S, which puzzled me and
made me jealous.
    Canoes in river – S – Japanese bridge – perfect happiness in
canoe with him.
    G – big brown eyes, red cheeks rather ugly really but nice face.
His mock endearments – and embraces. His badinage (which I
regretted) with B. (Awfulness of B . . .)

It would be misleading to pick out these comments without emphasizing that, in the context of the notebook, they are affectionate but
not predatory. There are many more sketches of the unattractive
members of the platoon, mixed in with accounts of daily events: fire
picquet, a boxing match at St Edward's School and visits to that
'awful little café in the Iffley Road'.

But without doubt, the homosexual in John found barrack-room
life sympathetic. The platoon recognized John for what he was – one
man went round singing a ribald parody of a popular song which
dropped a heavy hint – but his companions were tolerant, and they
liked John, accepting him as a friend and one of themselves. In a
fish-and-chip shop in Banbury one of them remarked on his unwill-

ingness to take a commission: 'Perhaps you are right, John. They'd only give you the cold shoulder in the Officer's Mess – *look* how they treat the Quartermaster.'

And he was a good friend. He took an interest in their characters, the problems of their private lives, and even made notes on their 'Flowers of Speech' – the special usage of the four-letter word. He went pub-crawling with them, listened to their family troubles and helped them to write letters to their girl friends. He found army life a refreshing contrast to his previous middle-class, academic existence, and an endless source of amusement. He was, as he frequently said, 'enjoying himself'. It was not, unfortunately, a sentiment that was to carry much weight with those who thought it his duty to submit to officer training.

At the end of September 1939, John's company was moved to a temporary billet at Wykham Park, near Adderbury, and in mid-October to Greenhill House, Adderbury. John had been promoted to lance-corporal, a degree of responsibility he was determined not to exceed. His superiors, notably his commanding officer Colonel Edmunds, were equally determined that he should take a commission; as a first step he would be made a sergeant-major. There is a lively account of John's losing battle in his notebook.

John was on weak ground from the start. Colonel Edmunds was not only an Old Wykehamist, but so sympathetic that it was difficult to argue with him. John did his best. He was gaining valuable experience in the ranks, though for what he didn't explain. He wasn't cut out to be a warrant officer, and he had not had time to make up his mind about a commission: 'And I am really enjoying my time very much, and making friends whom I should be sorry to leave.'

Colonel Edmunds caught the word 'enjoying', and said: 'Enjoying yourself! That's what I can't understand. Enjoying yourself! I should have thought . . .' He remained remarkably patient through several more interviews but, having dropped the ill-conceived idea of making John a sergeant-major, eventually had him posted to Aldershot for officer training, on the understanding that he might still refuse a commission after he had completed his time at OCTU. That compromise was soon forgotten, for immediately John became as keen on becoming a good officer as he had been determined to remain in the ranks. He realized that he really had no choice and decided to make the best of it. But he never forgot his platoon, and was still corresponding regularly with some of the men years later.

A letter to his mother, written on 14 January 1940, described his new life, his companions and his attitude to both:

I reached Aldershot on Friday afternoon. Need I describe Aldershot? The town itself is pretty frightful: between it and my barracks (which are really in Farnborough) stretch miles on miles on miles of brick or wooden huts, intersected by monotonous roadways or alleys thronged with thousands and thousands of soldiers. The effect is terrifying, particularly when (as now) the whole place is frost- and fog-bound, and the blackout reigns in the evening.

My conditions of life are in a way an improvement on what I have been having – we sleep in beds, under a roof (wooden) and there is a proper washhouse (water sh'd be, but isn't always, hot), proper dining room etc, and most orderly duties, like washing up, are done for us. We are addressed as 'Sir' by the N.C.O.s and other staff and wear white bands in our hats to distinguish us from common privates: this makes me feel strange.

My companions of course are civilised: the language would scarcely offend even you; mealtime is not a scene of savagery; there is quiet in the bedrooms. But how much rather I would be with those whom I have left behind than with my fellow officer-cadets!

Some are youths from second-rate public schools, evidently trying to become officers and gentlemen simultaneously; others just the Sandhurst type, with premature moustaches. There may be nice ones among them, but so far I have only been able to form a general impression.

Throughout February, in his letters to his mother, he continued to debate the question of a commission:

. . . the commission problem no longer preys on my mind. I am clear in my mind that I should prefer to be in the ranks: I would never have come on this course if it had been left to me to apply to do so. And even if there are moral considerations in favour of taking a commission, I don't think that they are so strong as to make it in the least obligatory on me to yield to them. But I feel that I shall probably take the line of least resistance and go through with the thing, simply because I am here and it would be difficult and cause awkwardness to get out of it.

In his next letter to his mother, of 11 March, he describes another near, if different, upset to his military career:

You will be interested to hear of an interview that I had with the Commanding Officer yesterday morning.

I was sent for without warning, entered the Orderly Room, saluted, and stood smartly to attention.

'Oh Sparrow, Regimental Headquarters tell me that MI5 have been asking for you. I don't know what they want you for – probably some job which means sitting in an office all day. *Now, do you want to sit in an office all day?*'

'No, Sir.'

'I had hoped you would say that.'

John had a brief leave at the beginning of April, most of which he spent removing his possessions from Pump Court and putting them into store. For the rest of the war All Souls was to be his home. He returned to Aldershot where, as he wrote to his mother on 8 April,

... we were apprised of the King's impending visit, and Sat & Sun were spent in an orgy of cleaning scrubbing polishing – walls, ceilings, floors, belts etc etc ...

My great news is that I have heard from the Coldstream that I can *rely on being gazetted to them towards the end of May.* Col. Edwards wrote me a very nice letter. Evidently communications from Wilfrid Greene and H. A. L. Fisher had done the trick.

I am now frightfully keen on the Coldstream, and feel 'all set' that way.

John had accepted that he could not be a private soldier, and now began to see himself as a good infantry officer, looking after his men and serving alongside them. But there were further obstacles to surmount. His letter to his mother continues: 'And just at this juncture arrives a telegram from Gen de Fonblanque definitely offering me the A.D.C.'s job! I have to ring him up tonight. I don't know what to say. If I have to decide straight off, I think I shall say "No"...'

John wrote to his brother Tim on 9 April, setting out the pros and cons, and asking advice. It was a long letter, typical of John in that, despite the arguments in favour of the ADC's job, it was obvious that he had already made up his mind to refuse it, because he had now set his heart on becoming a good regimental officer: 'My own feeling is now one of great keenness about the Coldstream, and I want to go through the discipline of becoming a junior Guards officer and learn how to look after a platoon and be as smart as I can be. I am, so to speak, all keyed up for the Coldstream.'

He refused the job, much to the disappointment of his mother. He replied on 26 April, telling her that her letter had made him 'most unreasonably furious':

> Of course your strong feelings are not prompted by joy that the country has got the full use of my wonderful brains, but by relief that I might have a really safe and at the same time *nice* job. After all, would there have been scope for any brains in an A.D.C.'s job? Not at all. Any young man of tact could do it. *It is just like being a Judge's Marshal.*

John had his way – at least for the time being – and joined the Coldstream in May, describing his initiation in a letter to his mother of 23 May:

> I was received most graciously at the C. Gds H.Q. Col. Edwards was evidently delightful: clean shaven, with a worn, gentle, face and gold spectacles.
>
> I am to join the Holding Battalion at Regent's Park Barracks on Monday. Meanwhile I have to get my uniform, and most of Monday afternoon was spent in toiling round tailors and shoemakers etc. On Tuesday I had my first 'fitting' at the tailors, and the Adjutant attended (he always does, it appears)!! He was very nice, and the atmosphere of the Mess there is evidently friendly: I felt as if I was being received into a family – rather a good family, though.

John had made one good friend at OCTU, Brian Spiller, an Irishman of exceptional good sense, and with a serious interest in English poetry. They exchanged letters throughout the war; those from John give an account of his military duties together with his thoughts about the progress of the conflict. His first letter after they both left OCTU was written on 9 July 1940:

My dear Brian,

I was delighted to get your letter – letters, in fact – Strange that you should be in England, and that my old Battalion – the 5th Oxf & Bucks – should be in N. Ireland, at Antrim . . .

I was glad to hear of your experiences, on the shores of Lough Foyle & the Atlantic, and now on the English coast. I would give anything to be stationed in the country instead of town, and with a platoon that I could call my own, instead of being one among many unallocated officers in a Battalion with a constantly changing personnel. We are still doing all the odd jobs of London, from mounting guard at Buckingham Palace (*or 'Buck House', as we in the Brigade call it* –) to escorting aliens to internment camps. Our most important job is the defence of a certain sector of N. London from parachutists, but we have no time to practise that, and our ideas about the location of our positions, the way to get there, and what we do when (or if) we get there, are sketchy . . .

I wonder how soon we shall be put to the test. It is useless, of course, to talk of the future. But I do not think it can have anything in store that I haven't been through already in my mind – in so far as one can anticipate actual experience in imagination . . . What a lot we have been through since you and I parted on May 19th (was that the date?) – every disaster we could have imagined for ourselves, and a few more thrown in. And the strange thing is that one adapts one's self so quickly to each next situation, and persuades one's self that one is really more comfortable in it than one was before . . .

The rest of the letter gives some more personal news, an account of an idyllic visit to the Betjemans at Offington, the purchase of four Yeats typescripts with handwritten corrections, and the completion of his selection of Bridges's poems for the Oxford University Press. Throughout the war, slipping away to All Souls for the weekend, he managed to sustain such personal interests and to keep contact with old friends.

That year, 1940, passed for John in a miscellany of military duties.

Once or twice he was required to act as defence in courts martial. He wrote to his mother on 21 July:

> I have almost reverted to my old profession – I spent last Thursday in a police court, defending a sergeant in our Company who had got mixed up in a brawl in a public house. He was charged with stealing two sausages, value 6d, and causing grievous bodily harm to the landlady ... I advised the sergeant to elect to be tried by a jury ...

In a letter to his mother of 14 August he described the guarding of 'Buck House' which he had already mentioned to Brian Spiller:

> Since beginning this letter, I have come off the King's Guard. We mounted guard on Tuesday, and dismounted this morning (Thursday). The ceremonies passed off without disaster; we had the Regimental band and the Regimental Slow March (from Mozart's *Figaro*) was played. I enjoyed doing my (small) part.
>
> I was in charge of the Buckingham Palace Detachment. The St James' Palace Detachment is under the Captain of the Guard and the junior officer (called the Ensign). I sleep in Buckingham Palace (in a sort of under-footman's bedroom over the guard room); the others sleep in St James's Palace, where is the officers' mess.
>
> The food is good, and you are allowed to ask guests – but only male guests – to dinner.
>
> The most romantic part is visiting the B.P. sentries by night – one goes round attended by two guardsmen, a sergeant, a corporal with the key and a drummer with a lantern. The gardens of B.P. (which I had never entered before) seem very large, and, in the moonlight, romantic.

John was now the keen young officer, frustrated at being kept in a holding battalion in central London, and longing to see action. Now he had accepted that he could not remain in the barrack-room, his only wish was to have his own platoon, so that he could look after his men. He had his first experience of command in September 1940, when he and his platoon were sent to Chequers for a month to guard Churchill.

John was asked to dine with the Churchills, and described the occasion to his mother in a letter of 9 September:

Winston came down on Friday night, with Beaverbrook and Sir John Dill and Sir Alan Brooke and other important personages.

We hoped for an invitation to dinner – I did tell you, didn't I? that myself and another young officer were asked up to dine last Sunday. The company commander had lunched there, and mentioned the names of his officers, and mine was recognised by Prof. Lindemann* of Christ Church – a sort of tame scientific adviser of Winston's – hence an invitation to me and another colleague.

John Colville, private secretary to Churchill, recalls the occasion in his memoirs, and comments that Mrs Churchill only invited officers of the Coldstream Guards. Officers of the Oxford and Bucks Light Infantry were ignored. John's letter went on:

I got on well with Mrs Winston [so well that she invited him to the theatre the following December] and enjoyed listening to Winston who was in excellent and truculent form. He much admires (as I have always done) Nathaniel Gubbins' page 'Sitting on the Fence' in the Sunday Express, and read it out to us after dinner.

As I was saying, we hoped for a repetition of the invitation tonight. But this morning we heard that the P.M. was going up to London . . . He strolled up, smoking a cigar, to say goodbye to us. He seemed to be in excellent form, his spirits apparently rise higher the more serious the situation becomes.

John was far more concerned with the welfare of his platoon than with having dinner with the Churchills. One member of that platoon, Guardsman Radcliffe, in later years always sent a card to John on his birthday, although they had not met since the war. In November 1990 I persuaded Malcolm Radcliffe to visit John a few days after his eighty-third birthday. Though neither recognized the other, Radcliffe remembered John as a young officer perfectly.

'He was very popular with the men,' he said. 'When you saluted him, he not only saluted back smartly, but gave you a smile . . .

* Frederick (Lord Cherwell) Lindemann, CH (1866–1957). Educated in Germany. Scientist, elected student of Christ Church 1921. Friend and scientific adviser to Churchill during the thirties and forties.

Nothing was too much trouble for him. I have good reason to remember his help.' It seemed that Radcliffe's marriage had been in trouble. He was on sentry duty at Chequers, in the pouring rain, when his bedraggled wife suddenly arrived. She had come down from London without warning. At that moment John appeared, took in the situation at a glance and immediately found a substitute sentry. He arranged for Mrs Radcliffe to get dry and to have a cup of tea. Meanwhile, he signed the necessary papers to enable Radcliffe to take a few days' compassionate leave. The marriage was saved and Radcliffe never forgot his debt to John.

John would have made an admirable regimental officer in the field, but it was not to be. The War Office had other plans for him.

After another tour of duty at Chequers in January and February 1941 John wrote to Tim on 24 February:

This note-paper [War Office] tells its own story.

I am now 'MA to AG' – which means Military Assistant to the Adjutant General, and I have the rank of (I really feel ashamed to say 'I am') a Captain.

All this is only since last Thursday. At the end of the previous week my company returned from Chequers and on the same day I was sent for without warning by the commanding officer (we have a new commanding officer, by the way) and told that I had been asked for this job and that it was my duty to take it.

I acquiesced in this, but very reluctantly, as I was increasingly liking my job as a platoon commander – particularly since out at Chequers I had got to know my platoon intimately and had a perfect platoon sergeant with whom I got on very well indeed.

It was very hard to say goodbye to them all – the only consolation being that personnel change so quickly – particularly in a Holding Battalion – that I should probably have had to part from most of them quite soon anyhow.

As Staff jobs go, this certainly seems to be very good indeed ... It involves seeing all the Cabinet and Army Council papers that are submitted to the Adjutant General and helping him over them in ways which will presumably become more clearly defined as I get more experienced ...

What does make a difference is that the AG (Lt.-Gen. H. C. B.

Wemyss) is the most delightful man and as far as I can judge very easy to work with and for.

John gave a more detailed description of his War Office life in a letter to Brian Spiller, written in May:

You will observe that my Army life so far had divided itself into 9 months without and 9 months with a commission. The last three months have been spent at the War Office. Daily I take a bus from Albany Street [the Regent's Park barracks] to White-hall, sit (alone, I am thankful to say) in a room designed for the late Duke of Cambridge, oak-panelled, with a stately clock, two or three mahogany tables, a map of Europe, and portraits of the Adjutants-General *d'antan* on the walls. A cheerful fire burns in the grate, and when it needs replenishing I ring a bell, and the messenger comes in and puts on more coal.

John continued to live at Regent's Park barracks, lunched usually at the Reform, went to Oxford for the occasional weekend, and stayed with the Betjemans at Offington, and the Clarks, who took him to a ballet in Cheltenham. There were, of course, bombs – two uncomfortably close to his barracks.

It was at this time that he drafted his first will. He sent a copy to his mother, and another to Bowra, whom he had appointed his executor and trustee. He divided most of his property among the members of his family, but there were individual bequests. He left a small sum to each of his godchildren, and to some other children of his friends. To the friends themselves he left books, carefully matched to their particular interests: to John Betjeman 'all the books ... devoted to illustrated and other Victorian books'; surprisingly, to Lord Berners 'all my portraits of Dr Parr'.*

In the middle of May John dined in London with Maurice Bowra and Sylvester Gates, a brilliant ex-New College man of great charm, who turned his back on an academic life for a distinguished career in banking. He was also listed as one of the five major influences on

---

* Dr Samuel Parr (1747–1825), pedagogue and often called the Whig Johnson, fascinated JS for many years. He had a large Parr collection of engraved portraits, books and papers, which he eventually bequeathed to Parr's Cambridge College, Emmanuel.

John's life, although John had great difficulty in defining the gifts he had received from Gates, and it is difficult to read John's summary amongst his deletions and alterations. The basic gift appeared to be an ability to appreciate excellence in everything, from literature to food and drink.

Bowra wrote about this dinner to an American friend, Felix Frankfurter, a Justice of the Supreme Court, but did not mention that John was almost immediately leaving for Washington. A few days later there is a letter from Gates to John, which makes a passing reference to his departure, and there is a letter of 14 June from Edith Sitwell, expressing 'extreme relief at the thought of you being in America'. John first explained his new posting in a letter to his mother, written from Washington on 15 June. General Wemyss, accompanied by John, had been despatched there to join the British Military Mission, whose job was to foster American interest in the war against Germany. They crossed the Atlantic on a battleship and landed at Boston, travelling to Washington by train.

John was most unhappy with this new posting. At the War Office he had led a life of comparative ease. In Washington he was living in luxury, but he was completely removed from the real war. The letter to his mother goes on:

> He [the General] if possible grows nicer all the time. He is my one consolation – and yet an equivocal one, for I don't know how I shall ever have the face to tell him that I want to go home! That is at the back or the front of my mind the whole time, though I should find it hard to explain why, for I can't pretend that I don't enjoy the ease and luxury of life here – eating better without a sense of sin etc etc.
>
> But whenever I think of home I have a feeling (I don't mean of ordinary home and ordinary home sickness, though that plays its part too) that I should be happier there and can be happy just nowhere else. By home I mean (in this particular context,) Regent's Park Barracks with 'the lads' in the Army. I believe I can help them more than I can help the dear General W and should be happier doing it.

It was difficult because, despite these inner feelings, he could not help enjoying himself. He found old English friends, and was introduced to delightful new American ones. He went to New York, where he not only visited the ballet but met Massine. He was obviously a great success when he spoke to the Virginia State Bar Association on 'A Lawyer in Wartime', which was published the following year. There were weekends in the country, 'a real 18th century Virginian country house, with its contemporary garden. I think the whole thing is very beautiful.' As he wrote to K Clark in July, 'I have always hated noise, vulgarity, ugliness, much talk about money, and hypochondriacal old women, and at first it seemed strange to me that I should be expected to like the Americans. But I have been won over by their niceness.'

There was one guardsman John particularly missed – his soldier servant, Boynton. Boynton was on the verge of marrying a girl from Sissinghurst, and his friendship with John was based on respect, and a sharp native wit. John had a couple of pages in his army notebook devoted to 'Boynton-dicta': 'After I got my job in the War Office, and he and I were transferred from No 4 Coy, he told me he had been attached to HQ Coy.

'I said lightly, "I wonder what I am attached to – the War Office?"

'He said, "You? *You're* attached to *me*."'

On another occasion John and Boynton were discussing the usefulness of going on technical courses. Boynton said: '"I don't think it does you any good to know too much. It makes you too big for your boots. It doesn't do you any good."

'I suggested that it was different for different people; he said, "The trouble with you is you don't want to be big enough for your boots."'

In a letter written to Brian Spiller in August John wrote:

... I have a feeling – quite irrational no doubt, that I ought to be at home; and also a positive and strong desire to be back with my regiment – which desire is fed by regular letters from Boynton, signed 'Your ever devoted friend and servant'. As an afterthought, he wrote a P.S. to me the other day, 'Hurry up and come back. You make life worth living for lads in the Army.' I mention this not in pride, but because I think you of all people will understand the effect it has on me out here. That feeling is working inside me *all the time*.

Harold Nicolson reported the details of Boynton's marriage, all arranged with loving care by Vita. It was clear that for once the occasion overawed Boynton into silence. On 6 August Nicolson wrote John one of his teasing letters:

> I do not feel that sympathy for your home-sickness which I ought to feel. One of the faults of my friend John Sparrow is that he is not a very adaptable person. He became a tram at the age of 13 when he obtained a scholarship at Winchester. That tram led him quite definitely through the illuminated arches of New College, Mr Joseph and All Souls to the grand profitable tunnel of the Chancery Bar. During that sojourn in that tunnel the denizens of the Chancery Bar accumulate many strange mushrooms and fungi. They come to believe that even forensic success can only be judged by the standards of the Master of the Rolls. They come to believe that the ordinary activities and ambitions of men are as incidental to their own highly profitable careers as is a glass of kummel in the life and work of an Archbishop. In other words they come to disbelieve in everything (including the United States of America) except the Chancery Bar.
>
> It may be that certain eccentrics among them glory in the luxury of individual pirouettes, become successful in the Coldstream Guards, or the Ministry of Information, but their heart remains the philosopher's stone.
>
> All this, as you will realise, my dear John, is not meant to be applicable to yourself since I well know that your heart is as tender as a ripe plum. It is based solely on certain analogies which I recognise as between you, Duff and Cyril Radcliffe, and which explains to me why I am so fond of you all three. As I told you, America is like the children's hour and one is delighted when that finishes and one turns on to the 6 o'clock news.

If there was a slight note of bitterness, it was because Nicolson had just resigned from the government.

John's papers do not make it absolutely clear when he was recalled to England, but in a letter to his mother of 24 October he wrote: 'A cable from home is expected, dealing with my return. I fancy this will be in November or December . . . My worry now is to persuade the General not to insist on putting me on to a staff course when I get back. All I ask is to be *left alone*.'

Writing to Tim on 6 November, he gives a provisional date, and tells how he has refused the offer of three different and permanent jobs in Washington:

I must not let my stay in America pass without writing to you. And since my days here seem to be numbered (I have just heard that my provisional date of departure is *Dec 16th*.)...

I have been offered *three* jobs out here – one on the Secretariat of our Mission, one vaguely Civil Service one, and one very secret one – which could have involved being seconded out of the Army and (in the cases of the first and third, anyhow) staying out here for the duration, but I did not feel like accepting them, though I hesitated about the third.

The General recommended me for the next Staff College course at home; I have (I think) persuaded him to withdraw his recommendation. Was I right? I don't want to become a Staff Captain, or something like that, or to go back to the W.O.

John had a temporary reprieve. Back in England, most certainly to his delight, he was posted to Chequers in charge of a platoon for January and February 1942. The presence of Boynton can only have added to his pleasure. But it was a brief respite, for he wrote to his mother on 27 March to tell her of a new job, back at the War Office:

About my new job – you could not make a bigger mistake than to suppose that morale in battle is what the War Office are concerned about. No one has any doubt that the morale of the Army w'd be all right if put to *that* test. The problem is exactly the reverse – to keep up the morale of the Army during long periods of boring inactivity such as they have been undergoing for the last eighteen months – to deal with, and remove the cause of, absence without leave, desertion, apathy etc...

Reports and enquiries are being made about pay, entertainment, leave, food, accommodation, relations of officers and men, wrong men in wrong jobs etc etc – all the 1000 and 1 things which go to make the Army contented or discontented. *That's* the present morale problem, which touches every side of Army life. *Not* whether men run away in battle.

Whether these things can really be affected by action by the W.O. is doubtful. I may make a better contribution to morale myself by keeping one platoon or company happy. I *think* I shall be able to get out of this job and get back to the regiment after 3 or 4 months, and I shall try to do so unless I think I am doing real good here.

In fact, John did such a good job that his boss, the Adjutant-General Sir Ronald Adam, was trying to persuade him to postpone his demobilization as late as 1946. John never ceased writing to friends that he would be 'happier' looking after his platoon, but of course, it was this feeling for the welfare of his men which made him so good at his War Office job. He was fearless in pushing for reforms to improve the lot of the ordinary soldier; his outspokenness was not always well received by his superiors.

John kept a copy of all his reports and on a page in the front of the volume, *War Office Reports on the Morale of the Army 1942–1945*, he described this opposition:

The first two of the following reports were practically my own unaided and uncensored composition. Increasing dissatisfaction and hostility on the part of the then Secretary of State (who threatened to have the Report discontinued and the Morale Committee wound up if a more favourable or 'balanced' picture was not given) led to stricter supervision, a greater degree of toning down, and insistence on an attempt to compile the report on a 'statistical' basis, 'weighting' every conclusion by a reference to the number of times each topic was mentioned in the sources. We were told also that all comments on pay and allowances must be relegated to an Appendix.

The reports contain a mass of detail on a great variety of subjects: conditions on troopships; fears of infidelity at home; 'spit and polish'; desertion; relations between British and American troops; pay and allowances, and anything that affected the morale of the army in any way. One theme appears repeatedly, inspired no doubt by thoughts of the 'platoon': good morale is largely dependent on good relations between officers and men, particularly junior officers directly supervising the soldiers' daily life; 'the Platoon Commander should be a "father" to his own men'.

John was promoted to major in May, a fact that embarrassed him when he wrote to friends like Brian Spiller, who was on active service. He described his daily routine to his mother in a letter dated 5 June:

I sit in the beehive called Hobart House, which is part of the War Office. Fortunately I have a room to myself. I have just finished the draft of my immense and most important Quarterly Report on the Morale of the Army. I am alone and in my shirt sleeves and have just been brought a cup of tea by Miss Norton who is called a Temporary Civil Servant (3rd Grade) which means she is learning to type at the Government's (or yours and my) expense.

I have good long gaps of inactivity, which enables me to write to you, but also gives me time to wish I was back with 'the lads'. (That is how individual private soldiers normally refer to their comrades collectively.)

Being back with the lads (i.e. regimental duty) unfortunately involves also being with 'the chaps' (i.e. one's fellow officers). That's the snag. I expect I shall be back with them all in the autumn, in some God-forsaken place and under a loathsome company commander, and wishing that I was back in this ignoble job, which at least gives one the chance of walking across St James' Park to lunch with John Sutro* at one's club, of looking in at the bookshops during the luncheon-hour; of spending evenings with the few friends one has left in London; and of getting to Oxford for 24 hours most weekends and rearranging one's books on Dr Parr.

It was not a bad life, but John was already beginning to experience doubts about what it was he really wanted. He did manage, despite his War Office duties, to sustain a good deal of his private life. He stayed with the Keyneses, the Betjemans and Mrs Montagu, and visited his mother. He corresponded with several friends, and despite his slanderous story about dropping Edith Sitwell, during 1942 alone he received nine letters from her. On one occasion she wrote to him about a soldier who she thought was being badly treated. John investigated the case and dismissed the soldier's complaint as 'an abject whine'. But he did take the trouble to write her a nine-page letter in his own hand, not only dealing at length with the soldier's complaint, but setting out his philosophy of army morale. It is tantalizing to think that his letters to her of the thirties, which she

---

* John Sutro, an Oxford contemporary of Evelyn Waugh, notable for founding 'The Railway Club', a dining club which held its dinners on the move in hired restaurant cars. A friend of JS for many years.

threw away, may have been as long and as fascinating on the subject of contemporary poetry.

John did not return to regimental duties in the autumn, and throughout 1943 remained at the War Office. His military life followed the same routine, except that in October he moved to Wellington barracks, nearer to his office, but likely to separate him from Boynton. His old tutor, Horace Joseph, died on 13 November, and his friend Bevan* died earlier in the year. There is one interesting letter to his mother, written on 5 December, which describes a visit to the theatre with Mrs Churchill:

> I will give you my only bit of news: the theatre party was very pleasant. It consisted just of Mrs Montagu and her daughter, who is in the A.T.S. – a thoroughly nice girl – and Mrs Churchill.
>
> The play was amusing – 'Mr Bolfry', but not by any means first-rate . . .
>
> A car then took us to the Prime-Ministerial abode – not Downing St but a nearby 'hide-out' strongly guarded and well-appointed and comfortable inside, where we had a pleasant though not excessive dinner *à quatre*.
>
> Mrs Churchill is 'all right', and I get on well with her. But she is really, simply *a wife* and not (I think) a person in her own right. (As Mrs M most certainly *is*.)

Wartime activities had not wholly distracted John from his more academic interests. In 1941, besides publishing *A. E. Housman: an Annotated Check-list* in collaboration with the distinguished bibliographer John Carter,† he published with the Oxford University Press *Poems in Latin, together with a few Inscriptions*, a compilation of modern Latin verse written by such well-known writers as Housman. A second series appeared in 1942. John had been collecting good examples of 'modern' Latin verse for some time.

His next publication was more ambitious – a collection of Latin inscriptions, another form of Latin which interested him. Somehow,

* Edwyn Bevan (1870–1943). Educated at Monkton Combe and New College. Historian and philosopher, he had a long friendship with JS and bequeathed him some of his library.
† John Carter, CBE (1905–75). Educated at Eton and King's College, Cambridge. Distinguished bibliographer and expert on antiquarian books, which led to his friendship with JS.

he had heard of the engraver Reynolds Stone, later to become so highly regarded that he was chosen to design the lettering for Churchill's tombstone in Westminster Abbey, but less well known in the forties. Janet Stone recalled the amazement at their wartime breakfast table when Reynolds Stone opened a letter from a Major Sparrow in the War Office asking him to design a heading for the title page of *Lapidaria*, a collection of inscriptions, the book to be designed by Stanley Morison and printed by the Cambridge University Press. It was published in 1943. It was the beginning of a continuing commission, and a long friendship with the Stone family.

The following year, 1944, brought a welcome and stimulating change to John's War Office routine. Ronald Adam, who had great confidence in John, decided that his reports on army morale would carry more weight if he visited various theatres of war and was able, by meeting men of all ranks, to make an on-the-spot assessment of the needs of each area. John made three journeys during 1944–5, all recorded in detail in the second volume of his reports; more personal descriptions are given in many letters to his family and friends. To assist him in dealing with senior ranks, John was promoted to lieutenant-colonel in April 1944, and he set out on his first foreign tour to Italy, North Africa and the Middle East on 9 June.

He sailed from Glasgow to Naples on an overcrowded troopship, where he found much to disapprove of, as he made clear in his morale report, and in a letter to his mother dated 25 June:

> I arrived (at Naples) about 48 hours ago, after a perfect, and most interesting (though uneventful) voyage.
>
> I had a cabin to myself – which made all the difference. I managed to get a lot of men (Gunners) to look after – *they* were travelling in very far from cabin conditions! I was called on to give a talk to an officer audience on Anglo–US relations, which was NOT a success, and I gave another to my gunners on Demobilization which was such a success that I had to repeat it to an audience of sailors.
>
> ... there were three young Coldstream officers going out to join the regiment whom I took under my wing – all three of them nice, two exceedingly so – the nicest young officers on board I should say.

It was an exhausting tour. He travelled all over occupied Italy, flying to Cairo on 29 July. From Egypt he went on to Lebanon, Jerusalem, Baghdad and Tehran, returning to England on 10 September by air from Cairo. Everywhere, he had interviews with the C-in-C or GOC of each military command, noting his particular concerns; General Leese in Italy, General Paget in Cairo, and Lieutenant-General Sir Arthur Smithers in Iraq. Besides these generals, he talked to a wide variety of regimental soldiers of all ranks, army psychiatrists, welfare officers, education officers, editors of army newspapers, and officers involved with courts martial. But he sometimes said in his personal letters that he learned more about how the troops really felt from his RASC drivers.

John acquired a mass of detailed information, which he presented with the absolute clarity one would expect of him. The report ranges from military matters, such as the need for more reinforcements, to such common causes of morale problems as anxiety about domestic affairs, a monotonous diet, feelings of isolation and uncertainty about the future. Amongst the more common problems were lack of radios or jealousy of the better facilities enjoyed by American troops. In Iraq John found a very different cause of complaint among the Indian troops stationed in that area:

> Several Indian army officers in Paiforce told me of serious discontent arising from the fact that numbers of Hindus of higher caste were enrolled in the Indian Army as sweepers. Once they were enrolled it was impossible to alter their army status. This offended their deepest religious feelings and was a perpetual source of unhappiness to them; many went to great pains to conceal their status from their families; in some cases, I believe, this has led to suicide.
>
> The cause of the trouble was said to be excessive zeal and rapacity on the part of Indian Recruiting Officers, who enrol recruits without fully explaining to them the conditions of their service.

To friends such as Brian Spiller he occasionally described moments of his tour in more romantic terms. He wrote to him on 6 October:

> Anyhow, I had the most wonderful three months abroad. I suppose the most interesting time that I am ever likely to have.

I saw, for the first time, the Tiber, the Nile, the Tigris. I can
say, like de Quincey, that I have slept at the base of the eternal
pyramids – tho' I cannot go on to say, with him, that I have
been kissed with cancerous kisses by crocodiles.

I also saw guns fired 'in anger' for the first time. And the
goal, if not the end, of my pilgrimage – I saw *Boynton*,
with his battalion at rest in a field on the shores of Lake
Trasimene.

Meanwhile I am writing a Report on my tour and uneasily
resuming my secretarial 'morale' job. My travels have made me
restless.

A thread of literary correspondence runs through 1944. On 3 January
he received a postcard from Edmund Blunden thanking him for his
opinion, probably about a poem. In an undated letter he sent John
Betjeman a poem written by himself:

3. *The Spiritual Magnolia* – revised, I trust, in accordance with
your directions.

I think that it is beautiful – though I should not say so.

I do not think it is indecent, and you may make what use of
it you will I think Gerald [Berners] might enjoy it) – publish it
in the *Guardian* or elsewhere, over my initials, if you like, but
not over my name.

As far as I know the poem was never published, although towards
the end of his life John searched through his papers for forgotten
work from his pen. In the course of my own rather more thorough
searches 'The Spiritual Magnolia' is his only unpublished poem to
emerge:

Deep in my spine, where none suspect or see,
Grow the strong roots of an aspiring tree;
Thick through my limbs its tendrils spread their mesh,
The leaves unfold and fluctuate in my flesh;
Its urgent sap wells up in every vein,
Burdens each gland, and burns within my brain,
And at the peak of that impetuous flood
Swells an enormous, all-but-open, bud.

When will the touch of some experienced hand
Persuade those milky petals to expand,

Woo the impending blossom into bloom,
And free the flowery embryo from its womb?

For now, alas, the noon of my delight
Lies veiled in darkness and the depth of night;
Only when sleep sets all my fancies free
Comes the full spring and summer of my tree,
And in the lonely and the lightless hours
I flower and flower and still renew my flowers.

In the early forties John had met and taken a liking to the poet and
novelist William Plomer. John admired his work, and enjoyed his
sense of humour, which bubbles through so many of his letters. A
typical exchange of admiration and high camp are found first in
John's letter of 10 April, written from the Betjemans':

> I have brought into the country for quieter absorption the slim
> volume lent to me by Corporal Preston [Stuart Preston, the origi-
> nal of 'the Loot' in Evelyn Waugh's *Unconditional Surrender*.]
> and I have been deeply moved by one or two of the poems, and
> have much liked several of the others. The one which moves me
> most is *September Evening 1938*. I do admire you immensely
> for having composed it: it is perfect and deeply affecting, and
> says what hundreds and hundreds of people have tried to say
> without any success whatever.
>
> 'Did you tell him I had lent it you? Did I get the credit for
> it?' he asked me, so pathetically that I do not think you would
> quite have despised him for it.
>
> He also said, on hearing of my passion for Association foot-
> ball, 'So you're an *outdoor type*! . . . I'm *so glad*.'

William Plomer replied on 16 April: 'Dear Outdoor Type, . . . Oh,
what a lark about Master Preston. Poor little chap, good little chap.
I am horrified to hear of Lieut. Wood's obstructiveness: if I knew
him a shade better I would give him a piece of your mind.'

At the end of the year John brushed with three distinguished
literary figures. In October he received a card from T. S. Eliot
thanking him for advice concerning some litigation. In November he
visited Wilfrid Greene, and met Max Beerbohm: '. . . *he* quiet and
modest and humorous and delightful and all, in appearance and
manner, that one would wish him to be; *she* most trying: never

[115]

allowing attention to be focused on him, and fussy and without charm.'

In December there was a letter from E. M. Forster, asking if John could help him to trace a friend who had not answered his letters and might be a POW or killed in action. Judging by a second letter, John went to great lengths to trace Forster's friend.

Nineteen forty-five opened with an extraordinary event, which I had never heard mentioned until I read John's letter to his mother of 14 January. Warden Adams had just retired, and the Fellows of All Souls were to elect a new Warden:

Dearest Mummy,

I came to Oxford after all, as you see, and without paying you a visit!

There was a preliminary 'exploratory' meeting about the Wardenship today.

I wasn't sure whether I sh'd be able to get down, or whether it would be right for me to be here, since I was one of the candidates under discussion.

You will wish to hear the result of the meeting in so far as it concerned me.

A number of names were mentioned as receiving support, including mine and that of one other Fellow who was present (the others were away, through tact* or because they cdn't get down here).

* I was not tactless in being present, having taken authoritative advice on the point. My name hadn't officially come up. If it had I *might* have stayed away. The other Fellow and I were asked to withdraw into an adjoining room, where we waited a little shyly. I told my companion (whom you don't know) that we need not worry, because he would certainly be thought too old, and I too young.

The first part of my prophecy was verified in ten minutes or so, when he was recalled. But I had to wait from 11 o'clock until very nearly 1 o'clock, during which time I read all the Sunday papers, and had a very pleasant conversation with FE Hutchinson, who looked in, not himself taking part in the proceedings (he is not a Fellow).

Then, when I had really begun to think that I must be taking part in a close finish, I too received my summons – and joined in the remainder of the proceedings, my own candidature having been relegated to Limbo.

We are now left with two candidates (I may not tell you who they are), and another meeting will be called in March to decide between them. [Humphrey Sumner* was elected.]

Rees (a staunch supporter throughout) asked me whether I was disappointed – to which my answer was 'I *could* be very disappointed indeed', which is the truth.

But since I had determinedly *not* set my heart upon it, and had also decided that I had little if any chance, I was quite calm. No pang at all.

Though (as I say) if I had allowed my mind to dwell on the desirability of succeeding, and if I had begun to play with visions of success, I think I might have suffered considerably.

Altogether, I profited from my study of the Stoic doctrines of M. Aurelius!

Incidentally (but quite incidentally) I think that the college have missed the chance of a remarkably good Warden. Against that, I think they will get a quite adequate one, so one need not regret it from the College *point* of view.

I gather that my little band of supporters were true to me, but made no effort to make converts.

Now *Bodley* remains a possibility. Should I compete? I own that I am strongly tempted.

On 6 February John's relation Reginald Weaver, Master of Trinity, wrote urging him to let his name go forward for the Bodley Librarianship:

The Committee for the selection of Bodley's Librarian is meeting on 15 February. There are, at present, only 3 candidates, not one of whom is an Oxford resident, and only one of the three an Oxford man (2nd in Greats 1929 and junior to you in the Army). May I write to the U.C. and put forward your name? Please allow me to do this. I do not say that other names may not be proposed but no more candidates *can apply*. On the

---

* Humphrey Sumner (1893–1951). Educated at Winchester and Balliol. Warden of All Souls 1945–51.

present field, my private opinion is that you would certainly be offered the post, if I put forward your name. No doubt, the Committee would like an interview in any case. Let me know as soon as may be.

There is no further correspondence on the subject, and one must presume that again John decided against a career in Bodley. With regard to the wardenship, one wonders if an ambition for the future had been planted in his mind.

A large part of 1945 was taken up with two more 'morale' tours abroad. The first was to Belgium, Holland and Germany in March and April. In Germany, much to John's satisfaction, he was up at the front, with all the sights and noise of war, 'which cannot properly be conveyed by the films or otherwise reproduced, and the slight (in my case, very slight) sense of personal danger'.

> Two or three days ago I came upon Tim quite by chance. I had heard that he was with a neighbouring division, and had planned to seek him out, when I (almost literally) ran into him in the outskirts of the town above referred to.
>
> I have been with him for the past three nights, and it is (for me, anyhow) an ideal arrangement.
>
> I had an interesting day the day before yesterday – beginning with the capture of two Germans, whom Tim and I saw in the woods, continuing with a visit to a concentration camp recently 'uncovered' by us, and ending with a 'talk' which Tim invited me to give to his men – or rather a 'session' at which I answered their questions. It lasted nearly two hours!

Tim still recalls how John held his audience spellbound, with the men happy to sit and listen for another two hours.

From June to October John toured India and South-East Asia, which included visits to Ceylon and Burma. His reports cover every aspect of morale in great detail, from major issues, like pay and prospects for demobilization, to such essentials as beer, cigarettes and films, without which soldiers soon became discontented. It is obvious from the reports that John's mind was again focused on the men, and he is frequently critical of their officers for not looking after their welfare. It was also characteristic of John that these exotic travels made little impression on him. In later years he never mentioned that he had visited all these places, and throughout our long friendship I was under the impression that he had hardly travelled further than Venice.

John was still in the army at the end of 1945, but becoming increasingly tired of everything. A letter to Brian Spiller – dated 25 November – sums up his mood:

> You speak of nostalgia. Don't build too many castles in the air of England. London is most unpleasant to live in – shabby and cold and damp and unlit. Everybody is on strike and everybody (particularly the lower – Yes! the lower–classes) is bad tempered. The question of the hour is, when a bus conductress strikes you, are you allowed to strike her back? The answer, I am afraid, is that you are not.
>
> . . . I am longing to get out of the Army, but in no hurry to start civil life – and don't know whether to go back to the Bar or Oxford or what . . .
>
> You ask me how long it is since I got into the habit of calling the Japanese the Japs. I have pondered over this question, which is a fair one, and really cannot decide whether I used the aberration ironically, in (tacit) inverted commas, or whether I did become infected with the jargon of the Far East during my brief sojourn there – which leads to a general reflection:
>
> I don't know whether I suffer from being taken literally when I am whimsical, or from being thought to be joking when I am indeed in earnest, or from not being sure myself whether I am in earnest or not.

It is a reflection that throws a great deal of light on John's character. It was often difficult to separate what he really felt from his irony and his whimsy, and sometimes perhaps he was as uncertain as the person he was talking to.

The War Office were reluctant to release John. In January he did return to All Souls, but he was not demobilized, and occasionally he had to accompany the Adjutant-General on visits to various army units in the London area. In April Ronald Adam urged him to make another tour of India, but he declined. He was finally demobilized in June 1946, after spending nearly six years in the army, a military career which stretched from his days as a private soldier in the Oxford and Bucks Light Infantry to lieutenant-colonel in the Coldstream Guards. Like millions of others, John had given up six of the most important years of his life, a loss he was to feel acutely when he returned to practise at the Chancery Bar. He was honoured with an OBE for his morale work, 'your very well deserved honour,' wrote Adam, 'and my grateful thanks for all you did in the War Office for me, for which I hope this is some inadequate reward'. I suspect that John regarded it as no more than a 'handout', small consolation for those lost years.

But his time with the morale committee had been an unqualified success. He brought to this job all his talents, together with his heart, motivated by his own experiences in the ranks and his life with the 'lads'. It was an inspired appointment. But when the war was over, and he was again engaged in civilian life, he put most of the memories of his military career behind him and seldom spoke of them, unless they provided some grist for his humour.

I remember having dinner with him in a square in Padua one night in the early fifties, when he told me a long and hilarious – and almost certainly partly imaginary – story of how he was sent to investigate an army psychiatrist who was suspected of molesting his soldier patients. Now, I can remember only the crucial fact that the psychiatrist kept addressing his soldier-servant as 'darling'. John was just about to draw the obvious conclusions and, reluctantly, to consider recommending a court martial, when he realized that 'Darling' was the soldier's surname. It was a typical convoluted John story, made funny largely by the way he told it. Like so much of his humour, it evaporated on the evening air.

I was surprised, early in our acquaintance, when on a shelf in his bedroom at All Souls I saw two snapshots of his platoon football team, with John seated in the centre, dressed for the forthcoming game. Otherwise, while he reminisced far and wide across his past life, he never mentioned Washington, the War Office, or India, or Burma.

However, John never forgot his friends in the ranks, with whom he continued to correspond for years, answering their simple letters with admiration of the snapshot of the new baby, or giving a sensible bit of advice. There was nothing patronizing in this: they were his friends, and his equals, and they were the only legacy of his war that touched him. It was sad that in later years he could not give the same friendship, concern and understanding to his junior academic colleagues. But in a strange way military life combined with his homosexuality and brought out the best in John: a sense of service to others he never found again.

VI

THE CANDIDATE

1946–52

Still, as it is, the Bar is a good discipline in more ways than
one, and there are many things about it that I much enjoy.
But if you tell me to find something which does give me self-
fulfilment, to which I would willingly surrender my whole self,
I ask you, *what is it to be*? Tinker, tailor, soldier, sailor? None
of those. Librarian? No. Journalist? No. Publisher? No. 'Man
of letters'? No. No! Clergyman? No (don't believe in
the creed). Schoolmaster or college tutor? No. BBC,
Civil Servant? No, no, no!

John in a letter to his mother,
24 March 1947

And I realise that, in spite of all my superficial and short-term
doubts and indecisions, it is the thing I want and always have
wanted more than anything else in the world. I might have
been born for it, and it might have been made for me.

John on the wardenship in a letter to
Isaiah Berlin, 1 June 1951

WHEN John Sparrow was finally released from the army in
June 1946, he was also freed from the military discipline
that had compelled him to get on with the matter in hand,
whether he liked it or not. Immediately, all the doubts about his
future that had troubled him in the thirties returned – above all the
rival attractions of Oxford and the Chancery Bar. He did return to
the Bar, but during the next few years his letters are full of a possible
return to Oxford and to some kind of career at All Souls, though he
had no way of foreseeing the untimely death of Warden Sumner in
1951.

In March 1946 Geoffrey Faber*, then Estates Bursar of All Souls, suggested to John that he might be a candidate for this influential post, which involved regulating the college's finances. He wrote to his mother telling her that he would make an excellent Estates Bursar, but that he was unlikely to be appointed since he was not well regarded by Warden Sumner.

He also mentioned that a very different career had been suggested to him:

> The second conversation was with Salter [Lord Salter, Ind. MP for Oxford University with A. P. Herbert], who encouraged me to think that I might be a suitable successor to himself or AP Herbert when the time came. A month ago, he said, he would have supported Harold Nicolson, but the latter's move in joining the Labour Party has changed that – partly because it will probably remove him from the field as a possible candidate, partly because it is such a clear demonstration of his lack – not of principle, but of judgement.
>
> So you *may* see me as a member of Parliament one day, though never, I fear, a Cabinet Minister.

A parliamentary seat did attract John, appealing, one suspects, more to his sense of theatre than to his intelligence. However, the opportunity did not arise since the university seats were abolished in 1950.

With less ambition, he considered – if not too seriously – taking a £600 fellowship at All Souls and devoting himself to writing a monumental study of Mark Pattison. He had the knowledge, but he lacked the will.

Such ideas show that he remained as divided about his future as before the war. And once again, he took refuge in the disciplined practice of the law.

He returned to 3 New Square and, having lost six years of legal experience, had to work hard to keep up. Cyril Radcliffe was still head of Chambers, but was appointed a Lord of Appeal in 1949, when John found himself in charge, although still a junior. Michael (now Sir Michael) Fox joined the Chambers just before Radcliffe was promoted:

* Sir Geoffrey Faber, (1889–1961). Educated at Rugby and Christ Church. Fellow of All Souls, 1919, and Estates Bursar of the college 1923–51. Founder of publishers, Faber and Faber.

I became John Sparrow's pupil in 3 New Square in April 1949. Cyril Radcliffe was then head of Chambers. They had a flavour of their own. They were extremely shabby, not to say dirty, but they had a great reputation because of the Maugham*, Greene, Radcliffe succession; the three most eminent lawyers of their time.

The Clerk was Mr Thresher. The great years had left on him a certain glaze of prosperity. On arrival at Chambers, he went to his room and telephoned his stockbroker. It used to be said that anybody could be a successful clerk to the likes of Maugham, Greene and Radcliffe. But I think there is no doubt that he was a highly competent (and tough) clerk. He was extremely civil to me in a crushing sort of way.

When Radcliffe left, John, as the next senior member, became head of the Chambers. The other members then were Peter Foster and Raymond Walton. Alan Hopkins was a member for a time but left the Bar to go into politics.

As regards John stepping into the shoes of the Greene Radcliffe dynasty, I think the position was this:

1. There was no great difficulty about the costs of running the Chambers. The rent in those days was low. The only staff were the two clerks. The Senior Clerk simply took a percentage of the fees. In a good year he did well; in a bad year he did badly. The junior clerk was paid a salary ... There were costs of heat, light and telephone but those were easily absorbed. I do not know what John was earning by mid-1949, but I should think £4/5,000 a year. At that time the salary of a High Court Judge was £5,000.

2. As to professional status, nobody at the Bar in 1949 would have regarded John as replacing Radcliffe, who was at the very top of the Bar while John was a rising junior. But nobody was surprised that he took over the Chambers. He had a considerable reputation. I always understood that, by 1939, Richard Wilberforce, Herbert Hart and John were regarded as the likely future stars of the Chancery Bar. By 1949 John had been back at the

* Frederick (Lord) Maugham, KC, (1866–1958). Educated at Dover College and Trinity Hall, Cambridge. The first of three outstanding lawyers to be head of the 3 New Court chambers. Lord Chancellor 1938–9.

Bar for three years, he had a substantial and growing practice in very high class work. I think most people in Lincoln's Inn would have agreed that he had a bright future.

As regards advocacy, my impression was that he did not feel at ease with it and did not greatly enjoy it. That was, partly at any rate, because he did not have much experience of it. It is a problem with high class junior work of the sort that John had, that it does not give the junior much scope for advocacy. Much of it is advisory and, if it gets into Court, the issues involved are sufficiently important to justify taking in a silk.

As to 'cutting a dash' [a claim made by John in later years], John would never have been a fashionable silk of the Norman Birkett, Patrick Hastings sort. He did not have the training or, I think, the temperament for it. But I have no doubt that had he stayed at the Bar and taken silk he would have obtained a very large and remunerative practice in cases involving the analysis of difficult points of law or complex facts. He greatly enjoyed argument and, once he had gained real experience in Court work, would have become an effective advocate. At the time he left the Bar he did not have a very impressive Court presence, partly, I think, because he had a rather thin voice.

I should add that John applied for silk in 1952 and would certainly have got it (either then or in the following year) if he had not been elected Warden.

John worked hard during his last years at the Chancery Bar. When I first knew him in 1951, I felt that he lived in the shadow of tomorrow's work, often cutting short an enjoyable evening to look over his papers for the following morning. Whatever he may have written to his mother about 'self-fulfilment', at that time he gave the impression of a man stretched by his work, but enjoying it. And though he worked hard at the Bar, his letters from those days show that he still found time for his friends, and for some literary activity.

During the early summer he decided to live in Brighton, a town he had enjoyed before the war. He found a room, took his meals at the Union Club, and commuted to London each day. In August, with the end of the Law Term, he returned to All Souls to struggle with writing the regimental history of the Coldstream Guards from 1920 to 1946. It was an unlikely commission for him to undertake. Perhaps he was partly fired by a genuine pride in the regiment, but more likely, when he accepted it in late 1945, it seemed to provide a short cut out of the army and back to All Souls. It proved to be nothing but a burden, until he was rescued towards the end of 1946 by a fellow Coldstream officer with a developing taste for military history, Michael (now Sir Michael) Howard*. He has been kind enough to describe how he became involved in the history and, as it turned out, its main author:

My involvement was as follows. I met John during the war, first when we were both living in Albany Barracks in spring 1943, and then when he came through Italy on his investigatory tour in 1944. I was demobbed and went straight back to Oxford in September 1945, and of course met him again when he came back to All Souls. In October 1946 he was working on the regimental history, and talked to me about it; without great enthusiasm, it must be said. I must either explicitly or implicitly have expressed an interest in helping him, because very soon after I came down in December 1946 I received an enquiry from Regt. HQ as to whether I would be available to help him with it. Being jobless, with nothing in view until the following autumn, I happily said yes.

During all this period John was back at the Bar, and very busy. The only time we could put into our joint work was at weekends, when we had more enjoyable things to do. He had at this stage completed about a fifth of the work, dealing with the inter-war years and the campaign in France and Flanders leading up to Dunkirk. We agreed that I should produce draft chapters for the rest for his comments and correction. This I did. It involved not only constructing a narrative from the documents, but conducting a lot of very interesting interviews with participants. John went through the drafts carefully, but his corrections were almost entirely stylistic. It was a wonderful experience for me, because it taught me how to write. But I was the primary author of the bulk of the history, as he very generously insisted on recognising on the title-page.

The few occasions when we attempted direct collaboration

* Sir Michael Howard, CBE, MC, (b.1922). Educated at Wellington College and Christ Church. Expert on war studies. Fellow of All Souls.

were not a success. As you know, he was a perfectionist, and if we could not get the right word in the first sentence we could go no further. Hours would be spent wrestling with it. It did not surprise me that he never produced a major work.

That year saw the beginning of a more sympathetic literary task. John had remained close friends with John Betjeman, and he had also become an admirer of much of Betjeman's poetry. At this time Jock Murray, Betjeman's publisher, was planning to bring out a first selected poems, and John agreed to be editor and to write the introduction. John was to work closely with Jock Murray, who was himself one of the finest literary editors of his generation.

John was a severe editor, but Betjeman was shrewd enough to recognize that he was a perceptive and valuable critic of his poetry. Betjeman had a high opinion of his literary judgement, and nearly always took his advice. John's earliest surviving editorial letter to Betjeman is dated 4 February 1946, and its schoolmasterly tone is typical:

p. 38 With every breath a human dies –
for God's sake read 'a mortal dies'. I will not have 'human' as a noun. 'Mortal' is, also, a more sinister and effective word.
p. 47 Nor gives the Holy Table glance nor nod.
'or nod' sounds better and is better grammar.
So is *began* instead of *begun* five lines lower down.

Betjeman did not always agree with John's criticisms, but he never took offence: their deep mutual affection no doubt played an important part in this. Betjeman liked to cast John as the stern pedagogue in the humorous by play they wove into their long friendship, a role he often reversed into the eternal schoolboy.

Throughout 1946 and 1947 John frequently stayed with the Betjemans at Wantage, and by August 1946 there were direct references in their correspondence to the selected poems. But poetry was not the only attraction offered by the Betjeman household. Although he seldom mentioned it to anyone, John had a passion for riding horses, and Penelope Betjeman provided him with a mount. She used to say that he was the most courageous, and worst, horseman she had ever known.

The selected poems were to be published in 1948, and Betjeman wrote to John on 25 December of that year to say that he had now read 'your ADMIRABLE Preface'. However, he strongly disagreed with John's main thesis, that he was a poet of place rather than of people, arguing that his initial inspiration came from 'people first and place as an inextricable part of them'.

John had written:

> Yet, though these poems owe so much to places and their associations, they are not 'Nature poems'; though he is moved by what he sees around him in the country-side, their author indulges in no reflections upon it, still less upon the feelings it evokes in him. He is content to observe, and – however deeply he may feel – to describe only what he sees and hears. In other words, he is not a Nature poet, like Wordsworth, but a landscape poet, like Crabbe. And, like Crabbe, he is the painter of the particular, the recognizable, landscape; his trees are not merely real trees with their roots in the earth, they are conifers with their roots in the red sand of Camberley, 'feathery ash in leathery Lambourne', or forsythia in the Banbury Road. For there is a great variety of landscape in his poems; unlike most pastoral poets, each of whom has his own 'especial rural scene' – Crabbe on the Suffolk coast, Cowper on the banks of the Ouse, Barnes among the farms of Dorsetshire – this poet is equally at home in the most diverse surroundings . . .

The fact was that John admired Betjeman as a gifted landscape poet, evoking with equal sensitivity the Thames valley, the Cornish coast, the Lincolnshire fens, or an Irish churchyard. He did not admire 'Miss J. Hunter Dunn' and the suburban poems of that kind. Though they had done much to make Betjeman famous, John thought they detracted from the higher reputation he deserved as a serious poet. And like many talented artists, Betjeman was not always a good judge of his own work. On one occasion he produced an undergraduate poem he had just discovered, pressing for its inclusion. John thought it very bad, said so, and it was never heard of again.

When John returned to the Bar in the autumn of 1946, he still had nowhere to live in London. In November he wrote to his mother telling her that he had put his name down for a flat in the Temple. It had a number of drawbacks and he thought that his chances of getting it were uncertain. He was proved right, and in a letter to his mother of 2 February 1947 he revealed that he had taken rooms at 81 South Audley Street, where he remained until he moved permanently to Oxford in 1952. There is nothing in his papers to show why he chose these lodgings, nor why he suddenly decided to live so far from 3 New Square and the Inns of Court. Perhaps South Audley Street was more convenient for the Reform and the Garrick clubs, and other centres of his social life. Shortly after he had moved in during the severe winter of 1947 he wrote, '... they look after me well at 81 South Audley St, which is a blessing'.

Although John seemed firmly established at the Bar, he never ceased to question his future. His mother received a typically introspective letter, written on 24 March 1947:

Dearest Mummy,

I found your letter on returning to 81 South Audley St this evening.

Indeed you needn't apologise for lecturing – or advising – about my future: I need advice, if not a lecture – and who has a better right to give it than you, and from whom could it be more welcome?

As for the Bar: I think that that falls into your second category of jobs – jobs that one can do, or hopes to do, completely, but which don't offer complete self-fulfilment. I mean that if I gave myself up to it entirely, a good deal of myself (and I may say the better part of myself) would go unfulfilled.

This is partly a matter of *time*. A sheer question of the number of hours in the day. I know *no* law, and my chances of learning it have been put back exactly *seven years* by the war. Consequently it takes me two or three times as long as the next man to do the same thing. It is like playing chess and having to look up the moves – or anyhow the gambits – in a book.

(And of course what you say about self-fulfilment is absolutely right: that should be one's first and last aim. Personal advantage is a minor thing – or nothing – compared with that.

If personal advantage – income and comfort – were my first aim, I think I would take (if offered) the Bodleian, and other jobs (eg. British Council) as to which I have been sounded, which could certainly give me money, prestige and comfort. But I don't think I should be happy in them.)

[129]

Consequently, to be (say) a judge, or at any rate a 100% lawyer, I should, now, have to give up my whole time and mind to it, and I am not prepared to do that.

Had things been otherwise, I think I might have had a full life as a lawyer and, at the same time fulfilled my truer self on other lines, but the war stopped that.

Still, as it is, the Bar is a good discipline in more ways than one, and there are many things about it that I much enjoy.

But if you tell me to find something which does give me self-fulfilment, to which I would willingly surrender my whole self, I ask you, *what is it to be*? Tinker, tailor, soldier, sailor? None of those. Librarian? No. Journalist? No. Publisher? No. 'Man of letters'? No. No! Clergyman? No (I don't believe the creed). Schoolmaster or college tutor? No. BBC, Civil Servant? No, no, no!

Now can *you* suggest anything? You know me better, and understand me better, than anyone else in the world, so you should be able to say if anyone can.

Also you sympathise more than any other persons I think, altho' your sympathy is not always expressed as H. W. B. Joseph would have expressed it. So I think your advice is better worth having than anyone's.

But what *is* your advice?

It's no use saying – 'Do what you feel gives best scope to your highest powers' because that leaves me just where I was before.

I am not conscious of any very great powers, and least of all any very 'high' ones.

I have no illusions (thank goodness!) about any powers as a creative artist or saviour of mankind. I haven't the gifts of the one or the faith of the other.

You mention my introduction to *In Memoriam* [Nonesuch, 1933]. I think that that was quite good, and I am capable of writing a good review or introduction or essay now and again. But I have not the gifts or the impulse to be a 'writer' (like Keats or Flaubert or those who were prepared to starve in order to fulfil their genius) and I certainly don't intend to take up literature simply as a profession, without self-fulfilment in it as my main aim. As a profession, the Bar is infinitely better (and better *for* me) than Literature.

The trouble lies partly with me, partly with the world as it is today. I am not a person with any great gift or mission.

I am rather (perhaps considerably) above the common run in sensitiveness and appreciativeness of several kinds and, I dare say, in intelligence. But I have not got it in me to be a great painter or poet or philosopher or thinker.

In the old days, politics might have given me a real opening for making the most, or the best, of myself. That was one of the advantages of the old party politics: they did give scope for people like me. But I see no such scope for me now, with my views, at my age. If I were a Communist, or an idealistic socialist, or even a crusading Tory, I might be ready to throw myself heart and soul into the frightful scramble in Parliament now. But I am not.

And I can see no profession outside politics which offers the slightest inducement to me to throw myself into it heart and soul.

This is not entirely my fault: it is largely because the world at present is what it is, both inside and outside Parliament.

Strangely enough, I was perfectly happy in the Army, both in the ranks and as a platoon-commander and (at moments) in my 'morale' job. But that was because circumstances forced me to cut off all but a small part of myself and enabled me to give full play to that small part. If the War came again, I could do the same thing or something like it. But Peace neither gives the same compulsion (forcing one to limit one's self) nor the same opportunity (providing scope for that limited self).

Such gifts and desires as I have tend in two (or more) directions:

(1) a feeling for *people*, and a gift for winning their sympathy.

(2) a feeling for knowledge, or learning – accompanied by certain corresponding intellectual gifts.

I don't know of any profession which enables one to develop both those gifts simultaneously, to this greatest extent.

I think my greatest desire is to be really learned: to know all about history and literature and thought. Not to write or teach; just to know. And I think that the best thing I could make of myself could be a learned man, in accordance with the ideal of Newman or Mark Pattison.

The only way of doing that would be to take a research fellow-ship. But nowadays even research fellowships aren't meant to encourage that kind of thing: you must be *useful*, and teach, or produce theses etc etc.

I would take one, I think, all the same – but for several con-siderations – viz.

(1) I don't trust myself not to become lazy, go to seed etc (tho' I think that I could overcome this).

(2) I do feel that at the present juncture of national affairs, someone with my varied experience ought not (unless he is quite sure he is right) to cut himself off from a more direct contact with 'affairs'.

(3) It would, or might, starve the other side of myself – that which is interested in people, and in influencing them, and which is capable, I think, of doing some good (though exactly what or how I find it difficult to imagine) in that way.

There you have my reasons for thinking that such a job as the Est. B'ship [estates bursarship at All Souls] would probably give me a better chance of 'being myself' than any other. Not that I am a 'born' Estates Bursar – who is? – or that (to put it another way) that job in itself offers me 'self-fulfilment' – but that it would give me a chance of pursuing my bent in learning and letters and also give me a practical job in which my gifts of dealing with people (both in Oxford and in the job itself) would have some scope.

And it would also keep open that door into public life (Parlia-ment, if you like) which I don't want to close entirely because (as I say) I feel that I might make a contribution there, though in the present state of politics it could only be the contribution of a critic. A cross-bench is the only possible place for me in a world like the present, I fear.

To end on this priggish note which you deplore: I think that the best thing I can be certain of giving to the world is help of a personal sort to individuals.* (*This sounds like lending people £5 – it really means, I think, having a large number of friends and acquaintances, not merely for the pleasure of having them.) And that is done in off-hours, not in hours of duty, and has nothing to do with the choice of profession.

After such a scribble and scrawl as this, you need never apologize again to me for being muddled or obscure or inconsequent. But I rely on your understanding, which rarely fails.

And I hope it will convince you that I have thought – do continually think – about this problem, and that it is not an easy one.

But it is nothing to be depressed about. I think that your somewhat despairing or discontented attitude comes from the wholly false (alas!) assumption that there 'must be' some job, some profession, which offers self-fulfilment. Ideally, perhaps, yes: but you must take me as I am, and the world as it is today.

I must say goodnight and work!

Love
John

The letter shows that he continued to be restless about his future, and that in such periods of restlessness his thoughts always returned to work in Oxford, preferably to a job in All Souls. And all his arguments are rooted more in his selfishness than in laziness. He examines each possible profession in terms of what it has to give him, with little or no thought to what he might give. It seems strange that such a gifted man – clever and good with people – should refuse to see any openings where he might make use of his talents. He had proved himself to be a notable editor. He was to prove a formidable journalist and, when he bothered, a perceptive scholar. He could also be an inspiring teacher; he would have been an outstanding college tutor, had he been allowed to choose students he found sympathetic. He was marvellous with those he liked, but had no wish to help those he didn't. His mother had received many of these long, self-justifying letters and, knowing her son well, she must have become accomplished at reading between the lines; she must have known that a basically negative attitude lay behind the heartfelt debate.

Four months later, on 3 July 1947, John received a letter making him an offer, which he refused, again showing that negative attitude – and, to be fair, a marked lack of ambition. He was invited to go to the newly formed Pakistan, to advise their constituent assembly for three to six months and to help draft the constitution. It is likely that he was recommended by Cyril Radcliffe, who had been at the centre of the partition of India. John wrote across the bottom of the letter, 'Declined: too busy with my practice in Lincoln's Inn.' He gave a rather fuller explanation in a letter to his mother, written on 8 July:

> After a good deal of fuss I have turned down Mr Jinnah's offer – at least, my mind was made up for me by the Brewers [clients of his Chambers], who (very naturally, I think) would not have released me even for two months (August and September), for which I would have been prepared to go (at 1000 guineas a month plus expenses!).
>
> I think that they (I mean my Indian employers) would have insisted on my staying six months, as a matter of fact, and that was longer than I could have managed . . . so India will see me no more; perhaps a relief, all things considered.

It seems clear that John did not want to go, and was hiding behind his obligation to the Brewers. A 'good deal of fuss' implies that some pressure had been put on him by higher authorities, and had he showed enthusiasm for the job, no doubt the same authorities could have brought pressure on the Brewers to release him for the necessary length of time. There can be no doubt that he would have done the work well, and a success of that kind would have been noted both by the Bar and the government. His refusal to go must equally have caused those in authority to question his sense of public duty. But John did not nurse that sort of ambition – even at 1,000 guineas a month.

The same letter to his mother tells of the sudden death of his friend Geoffrey Madan. Madan had enjoyed a brilliant classical career at Eton and won a scholarship to Balliol. He served in the First World War, then spent a few uncongenial years working in the City. However, after an attack of meningitis in 1924, he retired and, with a comfortable private income, devoted the rest of his life to his many friends and his interest in books, wine and collecting aphorisms from his wide reading in a series of private notebooks. John's letter perfectly describes his friendship with Madan:

> I really think I have felt this [his death] more vividly, if not more deeply, than the death of anyone I have ever known.
>
> His almost physical presence has haunted me ever since. I only managed to shake it off in Court on Monday morning, and then not entirely.

It is absolutely unexpected, and infuriating, and even ridiculous. I cannot believe it.

It was not that my affection for him was so very deep (though I realise now that I was fonder of him than I thought) but that our sympathy was almost complete, and I had hardly a pleasure in life which was not increased by being shared with him.

I shall miss him intensely – though less and less, I suppose, as time goes on.

Of his many qualities, John most enjoyed his knowledge of literature, and his discriminating sense of humour. Both men revelled in their dislike of dogs, and from time to time Madan would send John amusing press cuttings on this subject.

Some time in the fifties John told me a strange story about Madan, and at the time I wondered if it were true. According to John, Madan had developed a passion for Mrs Winston Churchill, and impulsively had sent her a love letter. Within hours he regretted his action, and begged John to see Mrs Churchill, to apologize on his behalf and to retrieve the letter. When John first told me this story, I did not know that he already had some acquaintance with Mrs Churchill. Embarrassed, John went to see her, but she was discreetly charming about the incident, returned the letter and made the meeting as easy as possible for John.

Years later, when John's memory had largely gone, I reminded him of this story. He denied all knowledge of it, and was certain that I was confused. He began to get heated, as he sometimes did on such occasions. To distract him I suggested that he should read me some extracts from Madan's *Notebooks*, which he had edited with John Gere in 1981. As I took his copy from the shelf, a sheaf of letters fell out of it. The top letter was from Madan's wife, thanking John for his good offices with Mrs Churchill. John was profuse in his apologies, and I gained some confidence in my own memories of the many stories he had told me over the years.

John's life had now settled into a familiar routine. He worked hard and his practice at the Bar was growing. He wrote to his mother early in June 1948: 'Thresher has given up his rooms to me: "my practice" now demands more dignified surroundings.' But his practice did not seem to limit his social life, which now centred on the Reform and Garrick clubs during the week, and All Souls at the weekends, when he was not away from Oxford, attending occasional country house parties.

In 1948 there were various letters to John Betjeman, commenting on the favourable reviews of the selected poems, and others from such friends as Richard Jennings and William Plomer, congratulating him on his introduction. In January 1949 John wrote to Plomer to thank him:

> My dear William,
>
> Absolved! To which I may add Admired! Adored! Your praise is very gratifying to me. I was asking for it – and (having seen your letter to Betje) was sure I should get it and – best of all – sure that it would be genuine when it came.
>
> Let us meet in what Pater calls the brief interval that is allotted us – before old/middle age grips you/me; too late, I feel, even as I write the words – old age will never grip you; *you* (when the time comes, if it ever does, you will grip *it*; and middle age has had its talons on me since 1945).
>
> All the same, I don't see why we shouldn't meet, *at any age*, and I suggest that you dine with me at the Garrick . . .

The correspondence with Plomer shows how John chose friends from among creative men – writers, poets and artists.

During these years John travelled to the Continent for his annual holiday, usually alone. He went to Brussels and Bruges in 1947, and the following year, on the way to stay with his brother in Greece, he stopped briefly in Venice and Rome. This was his first visit to Venice, which from then on became his favourite city. He returned there in September 1949 and, to his delight, met Kenneth Clark, then Slade Professor of Fine Arts at Oxford, with his twins, Colin and Colette. The children left for home the next day, and John wrote to his mother:

> We saw them off next day at the station – sleepers reserved, guards and train officials handsomely tipped, and every precaution for their comfort and safety taken by K, who is, I must say, a wonderfully affectionate and solicitous parent.
>
> It was pleasant to have K himself for another 48 hours, he is an excellent companion, particularly in such a place as this – knowing everything, and imparting his knowledge easily and

amusingly, so that one *sees* ten times as much as one otherwise would. It is like going for a country walk with a naturalist.

This encounter inspired John to write to Clark after his departure:

My dear K,

Let me, while the mood is on me, put into words what I have so often felt, but in the sluggish atmosphere of England always repress: my immense feeling of gratitude to you (it came over me with especial force when you had left the other day) not only for the day to day acts of generosity and hospitality in which you abound, but for having in so many ways enriched my life. Dormant aesthetic and intellectual instincts revive after contact with you, and when I think how much of the background to which they belong would not have existed for me but for my friendship with you, I feel conscious of a debt which can be 'repaid' only by gratitude. Also, I ask myself, after spending with you an hour such as we spent among the Bellinis, whether I am not wasting my life by spending it in a métier from which all that world is necessarily shut out. Really, I hanker after that world, but since I do not have the happy gift of creation, in any line of art, nor the almost rarer gift of fruitful criticism (I am a desiccator), perhaps I am right to stick to my last. Self-knowledge at least saves me from being a not-quite-first-rate something-or-other in the world of art or letters.

But when I revisit that world with you – who did so much to introduce me to it and point out its beauties and significances – I can only say that a warm gush of gratitude wells up, which I have for once, in this letter, tried to express . . .

This warm letter typifies the freedom of spirit and expression which John found in Venice.

In the spring of 1950, with Geoffrey Faber's retirement as Estates Bursar of All Souls, the question of a new Bursar was raised once again. Any candidate needed the support of the Warden. Humphrey Sumner was an upright man, somewhat puritanical, and nicely described by Geoffrey Madan as 'not so much a fine-looking man as a charcoal sketch of one'.

After a conversation with Sumner in the middle of May, John came to regret having given the impression that he did not wish to stand – he had assumed, probably correctly, that Sumner did not approve of him – and he wrote a long letter to the Warden attempting to retrieve the situation. The letter was, as much as anything, another statement analysing the conflict in his career:

My dear Warden,

Thinking over the conversation we had an evening or two ago about the Bursarships, I have come to the conclusion that I ought to remove any possible misunderstanding about my position in the matter.

When I told Geoffrey Faber that I no longer wished to be considered as a possible candidate my reason was not (as I think you very naturally assumed) that I was set on continuing my career at the Bar. You put it to me more than once during our talk that I was destined to become a judge and that in any event my success was so assured that I would be foolish to give up my prospects at the Bar. I wish I could think that this was so. But I can say quite definitely that I shall not become a judge – this would be confirmed by Cyril Radcliffe and anyone who really knows the measure of my qualifications as a lawyer. I myself think it doubtful whether I shall ever be justified even in taking silk.* (*I expect I shall – but when and with what success must be very doubtful.) My work is a perpetual struggle – a pleasurable and a stimulating one, but still a struggle; I feel all the time that I am skating on the thinnest of ice.

And even if success in the rude sense were assured, I am not at all sure that the prospect of it would be enough to keep me at the Bar. At the end of the 'successful' career, what has one to show for it? Has one ever 'possessed one's soul'? I want, before I die, to have time really to 'cultivate' myself – not necessarily to write, still less to publish, but to read, to study, to think – to turn myself from a half educated into an educated person. The Bar gives no hope of this. The comparative leisure of a college office would do so. And of course the temptation to seize an opportunity of doing this in the surroundings of All Souls, which I regard in every sense as my home, is very great. But whether it would really be for my ultimate good, or for the ultimate good of the College, for me to make the change, I am not sure. I might just become lazy and diffuse. The Bar at least concentrates me, tho' on an unworthy object. And it is questionable whether one should seek a position for the sake of the leisure it affords rather than the work it entails.

These were the conflicting consideration which perplexed me for about a year, until a few months ago I told Geoffrey Faber that I did not wish my name to be considered. My reason for doing this was not (as the above will have made plain) any prospect of success at the Bar; it was simply that Geoffrey Faber had indicated to me, in the most tactful way possible, that he thought that you doubted whether I was altogether the right person to succeed him. So far from being upset by this, I seized upon it with a feeling of relief, and for the last month or two I have been happy to think that a problem which had for some time been a perpetual worry no longer existed for me.

If Geoffrey Faber rightly interpreted your feeling, I can only say that I accept it without question and without demur. Apart from my personal feeling of relief, I am sure that it is essential that a Domestic or Estates Bursar (still more, one who combines both offices) should have the complete confidence of the Warden. I can even say that I hope that Geoffrey rightly interpreted you, since if I were pressed to offer myself I should, for the reasons which I have tried to explain above, be in a great difficulty how I ought to decide.

You may say that the upshot of this letter is, as far as I am concerned, to leave things where they were when we parted the other evening; but even if this is so, it is better, I think, that there should be no misunderstanding about the underlying considerations, to which justice would not be done by the assumption that I had withdrawn simply because I was sure of success at the Bar and set upon attaining it.

It was a clever letter, if somewhat contrived, but it is hard to believe that it did anything to serve his cause with the Warden. John sent a copy of the letter to Geoffrey Faber, who wrote an amusing answer:

I am glad to have seen your letter to H.S. If I may say so, it is a remarkable letter – the kind of document which your future biographer will rub his hands over. 'Note', he will perhaps say, 'the confident denial of the future Lord Passerine that his abilities would ever lead him to judicial office.' Seriously, John, it is a very good letter – honest and eloquent – two qualities not often going together.

And having said that, I don't know that I have anything more to say. I am sad that there is no prospect of my being succeeded in the Bursarship by that one of the Fellows whom I know and like the best – but then I knew that already. I hope that H.S. won't think ill of me for having told you what he said about you in this connection; but I think I was right to repeat it, and I don't in the least blame you for using it in order to clear up an otherwise cloudy situation.

Forgive a short note . . .

John's letter to Sumner is not quite as startling biographically as it seemed to Geoffrey Faber, taken in the context of so many similar letters, and with the knowledge of what lay in the future. The letter does show, however, that John's eyes were still firmly fixed on All Souls, whatever future he may have predicted for himself at the Bar. But one thing is certain: in the spring of 1950 he had no idea of the dramatic events that lay one year ahead.

John wrote to his mother on 22 April 1951: 'I was only in College for a few waking hours – the chief news was that the Warden had been taken ill again, and has had to have another operation. But by all accounts it was a minor one, and was successful. I feel very sorry for him.'

John misjudged the situation. Humphrey Sumner died on 25 April, and immediately speculation began about the election of a new warden of All Souls. Isaiah Berlin has told me that John swore to him repeatedly that he did not want the wardenship. I saw a great deal of John during 1951, and it was clear to me that he had set his heart on it, although he liked to pretend that the inner conflict between All Souls and the Bar continued to rage. Fortunately, his own part in the elections and his personal feeling about them are well-documented in the letters he wrote – many to Isaiah Berlin – during the campaign.

The course of the elections – there were to be two in the year following Sumner's death – was complicated and is now difficult to unravel in every detail. Even those who took some part, and are still alive, at times seem uncertain of the exact course of events, and their accounts do not always agree. The process of electing a new Warden of All Souls is an internal affair, following its own rules and traditions; there is no requirement to give any public account of how the result is reached. That is not to deny that there was considerable public interest, particularly in Oxford, and contemporary gossip to some extent clouded the facts. The most celebrated saying to come out of the first election – 'one Sparrow does not make a Sumner' – has long been attributed to John. But a letter he wrote to Isaiah Berlin credits *him* with the quip. A. L. Rowse gives an interesting and detailed account of the elections in his *All Souls in My Time*, but fails to list Isaiah Berlin among the candidates for the first election.

It is hardly surprising that memory fails after all these years: All Souls' method of choosing the final list of candidates was anything but clear-cut; one might say that the final candidates *emerged*, rather than being *selected* in the way of more public elections. In meetings and discussions possible candidates were considered, some from within the college, some former Fellows, then outside the college. There was endless speculative counting of votes: possible candidates could not canvas directly, though Rowse says that John had a 'whipper in' working for him both within the college – Lionel Butler* – and in London – Goronwy Rees. As many people have observed, the election of a Warden reminds one of C. P. Snow's Cambridge novels. John's letters written during the elections would have provided that author with excellent raw material.

John's first mention of the forthcoming election appeared in a letter to his mother on 7 May 1951:

> It was very nice seeing you and talking to you – not that there was much time to talk properly. And I was a little upset by the unsympathetic and even apparently hostile attitude of Daddy at a time which is for me a very worrying one. Still, I expect he does not see the situation quite as I see it.
>
> As a matter of fact, I think that circumstances may decide for me – and decide against me.
>
> Maurice Bowra and Isaiah Berlin – both shrewd and friendly

* Lionel Butler. Educated at Dudley Grammar School and Magdalen College, Oxford. Fellow of All Souls 1946. Professor of Medieval History in the University of St Andrews 1955. One of JS's closest supporters during the elections for the wardenship.

[141]

observers – went into the question very thoroughly with me on Sunday evening – and it appears on an analysis of voters that the anti-me vote slightly exceeds the pro-me vote (strange to think that a collection of men chosen, supposedly, for their intelligence should be so wrong-headed!) – and in any case, it appears that Donald Somervell* will probably stand – in which case he will, I think, sweep the board. So all my pangs and doubts have (in all probability) been superfluous.

And I ought to be grateful that choices between such desirable alternatives present themselves – instead of complaining that the choices are so difficult. Few are, after all, so lucky.

Two days later John put his problems to his old army friend Brian Spiller:

If I am asked to become Warden of All Souls, ought I to accept?

This may become an urgent question, and I should value your opinion on it. It might vitally influence my decision, if I have to decide.

Should I, if I took it, miss too painfully the opportunity which the Bar gives me of exercising (in Court and with clients) a certain histrionic gift, throwing (in a mild way) my weight about, which fulfils a need in my nature that has no other outlet?

Of course, the compensations for the loss of that would be immense. But – again – would I rust – and go limp? Also I like being incognito, just myself – not 'the' something ('What name shall I say Sir?' '*The Warden* of AS'. I couldn't bear that . . .).

But . . . but . . . but . . . the compensations would be immense. *And a book about Pattison might really get written* – but, again, *would it*?

Of course, if the opportunity had come in, say, 7 years time – when I had rounded off my time (I don't call it, because I don't mean, my 'career') at the Bar, I shouldn't have hesitated. *One never gets what one wants when one wants it.* I suppose the right advice is 'Take it when you can get it'?

---

* Rt. Hon. Lord Somervell (1889–1960), lawyer (KC, 1929), Conservative MP (1931–45), Attorney General (1936), Home Secretary (1945), Lord of Appeal in Ordinary and life peer (1954–60), Fellow of All Souls (1915).

Anyone close to John, friend or colleague, during the time of the elections was to hear all these arguments from him over and over again. I never doubted that he wanted the wardenship, and his arguments in favour of his life at the Bar seemed no more than a safety net should he fail to be elected. His letters, particularly those to Isaiah Berlin, suggest a determination that he should not fail to achieve his ambition. How well I remember Lionel Butler hurrying in and out of his rooms at this time to report a possible vote gained, or a suspected vote lost. John was fighting his corner, as far as the traditions of All Souls allowed. All of this is immediately apparent in John's first letter to Isaiah Berlin about the inner politics of the election:

My dear Isaiah,
   Your brilliant proverb about one Sp. not making a S—r has been replaced in my mind by one still more sinister, to the effect that one Sp. does not make a *Somervell*.
   Perhaps we have been alarming ourselves unnecessarily ... I saw yesterday evening
   (1) Old Dougie,* who told me to stay away *from the College* next week-end – advice given in good faith, which I shall follow:
   (2) Donald (Somervell) who walked home with me after dinner. He has not been asked to stay away, evidently to his surprise, and I think to his chagrin. I said that I had heard rumours that he might stand, and I encouraged him, but not pressingly, to do so. I also told him, in reply to his direct enquiry, that I would take the position if it were offered me. He was (like all of us) above all things anti-Rowse.
   In reply to my faint encouragement, he said that he was very happy in his work, and enlarged (rather sourly – the sourness, perhaps, of sour grapes still on his tongue?) on the boredom of the duties, the committees, university business, etc etc; and he said that he was less of an Oxford person than I was. We parted on good terms.
   (3) M.G.R. [Goronwy Rees] – we drank in a pub and intrigued. Not intrigued, really, but exchanged information and speculated on votes and voters – nothing more ...

* Sir Dougal Malcolm (1877–1955), scholar and imperialist, Fellow of All Souls (1899).

Perhaps you would let me know, if you can do so without betraying confidences, what happens at Sunday's meeting.

This letter crossed with a letter from Isaiah Berlin which must have reported on the situation at All Souls before 'Sunday's meeting', to which John replied on 10 May:

My dear Isaiah,

Many thanks for your report, which, delayed in transit at All Souls, must have crossed a letter which I wrote to you yesterday.

I don't know that I have much to add to what I wrote yesterday – except (yes indeed!) that I was bidden to lunch yesterday at the House of Lords with the Senior Fellow [Lord Simon*], who duly ascertained that I would accept the position if it was offered me and that I was anxious for my name to go forward.

He behaved with perfect propriety, and I couldn't blame him for anything he said or didn't say. He gave nothing away – but I derived the impression that he would support me unless the College evinced a desire for some totally different kind of candidate – eg. an Elder Statesman.

'It likes me not', this tendency to look outside the ranks of existing Fellows ... Bridges† I regard as a *dry stick*, a worse genus to my mind than the *cold fish*. Also there is an odious aura of sanctity about him, created by the admiration of high minded persons.

I should prefer Donald, who represents to me butter, it is true, but the kind that wouldn't melt in one's mouth, not the rancid kind. Yes, if we must go outside, I'd as soon have him as anyone else. But why go outside?

I trust you to send me a report on Sunday's meeting – without, of course, violating confidences, or decencies, or telling me anything I want to hear ...

Writing to his mother on the same day, he recalled how one of his heroes had lived through the uncertainties of an Oxford college election:

* Rt. Hon. Viscount Simon (1873–1954), statesman and Lord Chancellor; Fellow of All Souls (1897).
† Rt. Hon. Lord Bridges (1892–1969), son of Robert Bridges, Poet Laureate; public servant; Permanent Secretary to the Treasury (1945–56); Fellow of All Souls (1920–27).

Your letters remind me of the stream of communications which reached Oxford from Hauxwell, Yorks, in October 1851 (just 100 years ago!), when Mark Pattison's mother and sisters followed with anxiety the ins and outs of intrigue which preceded the election of the Rector of Lincoln. History repeats *itself*. It will not, however, repeat itself by my suffering all the anguish which poor M.P. felt on his failure or his terrible bitterness.

Whatever happens, I shall have something to regret, but *much more to be thankful for*. Perhaps that is illogical, but that is how I feel about it . . .

I hear today from Berlin that there is talk in College of trying to persuade some big wig from outside – e.g. Edward Bridges – to stand.

My own reading of the situation is that it will be a close run thing between Jacob* and me, and that if it really *is* close, the College uniting and get a candidate from outside on whom all agree.

If that outsider were someone aged 60 that might suit me very well – (or should I go through the same processes of doubt all over again in 10 years' time?!) –

A letter of 14 May to Brian Spiller repeats a number of the arguments:

Many thanks indeed. None of my friends could have written me a better letter, and very few as good and understanding a one. It has helped.

But it looks as if the problem would be solved – or cease to exist – because they are sure to ask Sir Edward Bridges (a man whom I am tired of hearing called 'The Just': no one has a bad word to say for him, and he seems to me the dullest and driest of dogs and logs) and I suppose he'll accept.

So I shall plod on here . . .

As for being 'The W of AS' – it is the being, 'The *anything of anything*' that is distasteful to me . . . it labels, defines, destroys the personality. Above all, let me not be The Devil of a Nuisance – as I fear I am being to you.

John was being a 'nuisance' or, at least, an obsessive questioner of all his close friends. The continual 'Shall I? Shan't I?' became

---

* Ernest Jacob (1894–1971), historian; Fellow of All Souls (1921–71).

monotonous, as one struggled to find meaningful answers to a meaningless question. But a letter written to Isaiah Berlin on 18 May – at this point Berlin was also a candidate in the election – shows that John was not only concerned with his own candidature:

My dear old friend –

(How my dear old friends must tremble at that exordium!) Reflection suggests, and honesty compels, this *éclaircissement*.

I believe I have allowed you to assume – and have myself assumed – that each of us, if he himself were entirely out of the field, would vote for the other against all comers. This assumption, I think, underlay our discussions of the last 48 hours.

I don't think it much matters, as I don't suppose that the situation will arise in which either of us is called upon to vote. But, on reflection (and, believe me, I've not reflected on it till just now), I can't say that I should be certain to vote for you against all comers. Against Rowse – against X, against Y, against Z – I won't insult you by producing a list: yes. But against Wheare,* against Bridges, against Ernest [Jacob] even – well, I don't know. I think 'yes', but I don't know. It is only in the last few days that I have come to think of you as a possible Warden (since you tell me that you yourself were until recently in the same state of mind you won't, perhaps, be affronted by this). P.M.; yes; President of the U.S.; yes; but Warden – out of the question. That really was my frame of mind until the other day.

You won't do me the injustice of attributing to me a series of judgements about you, and your merits as compared with E.F.J.'s [Jacob] and others', to account for this. It is rather my conception of the job that differs, perhaps, from yours. It is one in which your plus qualities, and Ernest's *minus* ones, are largely, I think, irrelevant. I have a strong *formal* conception of a Warden (based on Pember,† who had all Ernest's weaknesses), and I probably let it influence me too much. This is not to say that I wouldn't in the end say that the best man (which is you) is also the best man for the job.

* Sir Kenneth Wheare, Fellow of All Souls, Gladstone Professor of Government and Public Administration.
† F. W. Pember, Warden of All Souls (1914–33).

11. An Oxford reading party

12. John and Maurice Bowra staying with
Piers Synott in Ireland

13. Harold Nicholson's impression of the relationship between Horace Joseph and his
favourite pupil

14. Geoffrey Keynes in 1929

15. Riding with Penelope Betjeman at Uffington in the 1930s

16. The young lawyer - 1930s

17. On Harold Nicholson's yacht in August 1939

18. John newly commissioned

19. John with his platoon guarding Winston Churchill at Chequers

20. The Warden at All Souls Encaenia

What I will not allow myself to be influenced by is personal considerations and personal affection.

This is probably a doubly unnecessary letter, because (probably) I shall vote for you if I do.

Stuart [Hampshire] – who fainted away and had to be revived with inferior brandy when I put my attitude to him – tells me not to send it. It won't offend you; your magnanimity is great enough for that; but you may like me a tiny little bit less for it.

I think I can say, my dear Isaiah, that if you reply in kind and tell me that you for your part would certainly put E.F.J. (or Wheare, or who you will) in front of me, it would not alter my feelings towards you the very least little bit.

Why do I write? Honesty. Really, just that. In a situation where personal and 'political' considerations are mixed as they are here, nothing must be based on a misconception. Nay more – the words come naturally off the pen – there must be no possibility of a misconception on which any thing might be based.

I am NOT sending a copy of this letter to the press; but you may certainly show it to Stuart or any other persons in whose eyes it is not likely to damage my character irreparably.

'affectionately'

John

Perhaps, we'd both be happier together on this staircase ... I wish the whole thing had never arisen.

This is not what you would call a 'noble' letter. But the more you think about it, the less you will despise the writer.

I don't think I *could* vote for Bridges, whoever else was in the field. Nor for Ernest, if it meant government by Rowse. All I am telling you is that the tacit assumption that I would certainly vote for you is not justified as an assumption.

In fact, Isaiah Berlin did later, for various personal reasons, withdraw his candidature shortly after he received this letter, but it was not a direct influence on his decision. However, his action was related to the key sentence in John's letter. 'It is rather my conception of the job that differs, perhaps, from yours.' That was indisputable, but John did not then, or on any other occasion, make clear his own 'conception of the job'. It was interesting that he should cite F. W.

Pember as his kind of Warden. During those nineteen years when Pember was head of the college his main achievement was to maintain the status quo. Those who knew John well suspected that he nursed a similar ambition and feared that Isaiah Berlin might, in one way or another, disrupt their favourite club.

Unfortunately, John kept none of Berlin's replies to his letters, but his own letters confirm that there were replies.

My dear Isaiah,

What am I to say? Really after such a letter as yours there is nothing more to be said, and anything that I do say must be pure self-indulgence – the expression, or under-lining, of feelings of mine of which your head and heart will have informed you already.

Unlike you, I can't write even a letter – even a letter like this – *straight*; I must revise, amend, re-touch, until there is a danger that the words (as you put it) will speak for themselves and not for me. And this is so natural to me, or so deeply ingrained, (those alternatives are significant, and perhaps themselves prove the very point I am making) that I often doubt about the existence of any definite *me* behind the words I use. Could I ever write a *noble* letter? If I were suddenly and violently hurt – physically, even – could I content myself with a cry of pain, an utterance? I am like the man who said on his death-bed (I misquote, no doubt) 'Je m'en vais ou je m'en va: l'un et l'autre se dire ou se disent' –

This present letter, however, is written in circumstances which preclude much revision, so it may attain a little more nearly to the ideal of spontaneity.

But I think you do me too much credit in saying that my last letter was 'uncalculating' – of course it wasn't written as a means to an end – at least not to any other end than that which you so sympathetically recognised, the end of enlightenment and a true understanding between us. But I can never do anything without reflecting and wondering and assessing reactions etc etc etc – so that I am condemned to be numbered for ever among those who are incapable of the noble or the heroic, and I begin at times (this is morbid, no doubt) to wonder whether I can even be 'sincere'. I am, indeed, capable of impulsive action eg. for friends and, of course, when in love. And, on a larger scale, joining the Army on the outbreak of war. But having so acted, I begin to analyse, and prove to myself that what seemed impulsive really was not so.

All this – I mean, the saying of it – is, as I say, pure self-indulgence; but you will allow me to go on; it is a great relief to me.

I don't in fact doubt the complete 'sincerity' of the letter I wrote you, the single-mindedness with which it was written. And as for this present letter, it is as you perceive written without any aim at all. It interests me, however, to analyse further my own attitude in the whole election business, and I think I detect two selfish strands which ought to be exposed: first, I postulate a situation in which I myself am out of the question entirely. But how far is that a valid postulate? Because I really would like this post in something like 10 years' time; therefore – hopelessly uncertain as all such future calculations are – it would suit me better for an older man than you to be elected. Therefore even if I were out of the running this time, I or my interests wouldn't be out of the *question*. How far would this consideration influence my vote? I can only say: I *hope* not at all.

One other similar consideration, and a rather more interesting one: I mind much less, in any contest, being beaten by an outsider than by a rival, being decided against for bad reasons than for good ones. Has this, subconsciously (blessed word!) something to do with my attitude vis-à-vis you and other admittedly inferior competition? I think that it probably has – but (I firmly and defiantly repeat) *subconsciously*.

For personal reasons – we needn't say this again – clearly I should like you to succeed, and after your letter I should find it difficult to vote against you – not because of anything you said in it, not out of gratitude, nothing like that, but because it shows you to be as good a person as your greatest admirers claim.

Indeed, most of your votes will be given for inadequate reasons by people who think they appreciate you but have no conception of your true quality, who only know your brilliance, and support you because you are the opposite of the sort of thing they dislike –

Likewise many (not all, not by any means all) of the votes cast against you will be given for degrading reasons of a kind I needn't attempt to describe.

[149]

Since writing the first 4 sheets of this letter I have heard from L. Butler that Bridges is not standing. This brings to a focus my own feelings in the matter, for it certainly increases my chances. And I begin to have a strong deepening of fears and doubts. My nature is in several ways perverse: the nearer a thing is, the less I want it; the further off, the more. And I begin to think how much happier we all are as at present! When I began this letter, not knowing about Bridges, I was going to suggest that we might consider both of us standing down in his favour. I was influenced (far too much) by the pleasant thought of you and me on that staircase together ... But of course we can't stand down for E.F.J. (at least, I suppose not; you certainly wouldn't – and I – well, not I either). And I do not think that either of us should stand down for the other, or that either of us wants the other to stand down for him. Most certainly I do not want you to stand down for me – and I only think it necessary to say that in case you should misinterpret, in that sense, anything I say. Particularly lest you should misinterpret me when I say 'Don't be disappointed if you don't get it.' I have, entre nous, a dread conviction that you won't. I have a dread conviction that I will. The best, or a lot of them, will vote for you; but too many of the *mediums* will vote for me. (We yet may smile together over these prognostications of mine.) If I don't get it, I shall instantly repress that in me which is disappointed, instantly, and so effectively that no one else, and perhaps hardly myself, will know that I am disappointed. A large measure of genuine belief will mask my disappointment – and how lucky I shall be to have my work and my life here to fall back on ...

As some one said in the Lincoln election of 1851 (you really MUST read Pattison while this is on) – by showing this letter to the right people you could determine the election.

Well! I've become flippant: I always do. You won't make the very general mistake of supposing that it argues an absence of deep feeling. Your letter moved and moves me deeply, and makes me very happy that I wrote to you as I did.

Yours affly
John

Don't feel you need even acknowledge this – I shall understand.

These long, introspective letters were written from 3 New Square, where John struggled to keep his mind on his work. In his obsessive state he needed someone, and someone with intimate knowledge of all that was going on in All Souls, with whom to share his thoughts. It was ironical that the recipient of his confidences should be his rival.

The next letter is dated 1 June:

My dear Isaiah,

I must tell you – but don't repeat this, please – what happened to me the night before last, when I went to a party given on a launch on the Thames, 'to view the illuminations'. All the world – the Betjeman world – and his wife were there, including Denis* and Mrs Rickett and – Miss Sumner!

She was evidently in good form, but I had no contact with her until the moment of disembarkation, then – in front of a little crowd of people – she pressed my hand and said, intensely: 'Your *proverb*!' I was at a loss. 'Your proverb', she repeated, 'about "one s . . ."' I was aghast! 'Oh' she said, with double intensity, 'you must disprove it; you must make it not true.' I didn't know what to say. 'I am keeping it warm for you,' she continued. 'What a good housekeeper your sister will be! Good luck . . .' I was quite – and quite genuinely – overcome.

It occurred to me afterwards that perhaps she treats all the candidates so. But I put the thought from me. I don't believe it.

Don't tell that (except to old Stuart). Alas! she has no vote. The porters, I am told, are on my side. But they have no votes either. My supporters are in the wrong places. I have never made friends unto myself of the mammon of righteousness.

I am heartily glad that the period of suspense is drawing to a close. I have no one here to whom I can talk intimately about it, so the thing gets bottled up and preys on me. It is in my mind night and day. I can't concentrate properly on my work. I cannot say that I *think* about it all the time, but it occupies my mind: a different thing. And I realise that, in spite of all my superficial and short-term doubts and indecisions, it is the thing I want and

---

* Sir Denis Rickett, KCMG. Educated at Rugby and Balliol. Prize Fellow, All Souls, 1929: elected with JS. Distinguished Civil Service career, ending as second Secretary to the Treasury 1960–68.

always have wanted more than anything else in the world. I might have been born for it, and it might have been made for me. Don't misunderstand me: I don't think that my wants (or anyone else's) should be a factor in the situation. I mention it only because (introspective as ever) it interests me to realise that it is so, and it is ironical but characteristic that it is only when the thing is out of my grasp that I should realise that it is so.

For it is, I think, out of my grasp. Alone in chambers last night I made calculations (to what will one not descend! – see M. Pattison, for what one can descend to) of the votes. And I concluded that you can never get a majority in a straight fight, either with me or with Ernest, and that I would get a majority in a straight fight with you and probably in a straight fight with Ernest; and that if Ernest's votes are eliminated you will probably get one over me.

Stuart wisely says that one should treat the situation as ruled by impersonal forces – chances, destiny, fortune; I think that that is right – and I see your candidature as an impersonal force – a side wind that has blown my poor bark (which has always been – it occurs to me as I write, and I cannot refrain from saying it – worse than my bite) on the rocks.

It would be ironical if the only effect of your candidature was to let in Ernest (made of paper, you say. Surely *cotton-wool*? Or is there not some stuff called *rag-pulp*.

Whatever the outcome, nothing that happens or has happened can alter my feelings for you – and you know (don't you) what they are.

Before allowing John to continue his account of the first election, two points need clarification. It seems likely that John was over optimistic about his chances. Isaiah Berlin told me that as far as he can remember, John was never certain of more than five or, at the most, six votes in this first election, and that that number did not increase until the last moment of the second election. It was obvious that the mood of the college was volatile, with a division of opinion between the old guard and the younger fellows. That must have made it impossible for anyone to make exact calculations.

John writes continually as if the election was between himself,

Isaiah Berlin and Ernest Jacob. But Rowse, Sub-Warden of the college
and with increased influence after the death of Sumner, persuaded
Eric Beckett* to stand, notionally as a distinguished compromise
candidate but, in the eyes of the fellows, as Rowse's man. Beckett
appears in John's next letter of 3 June to Isaiah Berlin:

> Perhaps the last link in our long chain of correspondence?
>
> I think I know what the Landsberg war criminals are feeling
> like just now, don't you?
>
> And I am not sure that I want to feel what Lazarus must have
> felt nearly 2000 years ago . . .
>
> My feeling this morning was that the bitterness of death was
> indeed past; and relief that a decision had been reached which it
> seemed one must accept as final was the predominating emotion.
>
> To be frank, I hated the atmosphere that prevailed in the room
> after we ceased to be alone together last night. I find Goronwy
> quite irresponsible, and John Cooper† (for whom I have a genu-
> ine and not shallow affection) pathological. But no word escaped
> you which I would not have wished you to utter. I tried to be
> calm, detached, charitable and I thought I succeeded – perhaps
> to the extent of seeming smug.
>
> (Stuart told me that John C. was in a bad way – hysterical –
> this afternoon. So I had him in my room for ¾ of an hour,
> soothed him, amused him, rallied him, talked to him about other
> things, was a little bit stern about his mad behaviour (Stuart
> tells me grim details about his conduct at the meeting) and told
> him – in a dozen indirect ways – how very much I liked him.
> No doubt anyone who saw us together thought that another bit
> of intrigue was going on!)
>
> As for Goronwy, he referred to Beckett (addressing me) as
> 'your candidate' which I thought in the circs. unkind. He also
> said he had read my letters to you, and criticised me for writing
> them; they gave you pain, he said, and weakened your resolve
> to stand. This, coming on top of that I had gone through during
> the day, seemed to me a trifle thick. But I did NOT rise! He

* Sir (William) Eric Beckett (1896–1966), head of Legal Dept, Foreign Office; Fellow
of All Souls (1921–8).
† John Cooper. Educated at Magdalen. Prize Fellow, All Souls 1948. He left All
Souls for Trinity College in the Fifties.

also said that he had not answered my letter and revealed his transfer of his vote for fear of 'adding to my irritations'.

However, he can't bear parting on a discordant note any more than I can, so he saw me to bed, was gay and charming, and I suppose he thinks that all can be thus laughed off . . . He is not a villain, of course, but he is not made of very high quality stuff. And he is a most irresponsible adviser.

Now for practical matters – The feelings described at the very beginning of this letter impel me to withdraw. I don't want to revive in myself hopes which I have gently buried and which would again be disappointed.

And I can see no point in an attempt being made to re-open (or, strictly, 'prolong') discussion unless there is a real prospect of a change of decision. Indeed, it would be wrong to re-open for the mere sake of re-opening (that would go far to justify a charge of 'dividing the College').

And there can be no hope of a change unless some of the majority come over, and your voters and mine coalesce – in your favour, or mine, or a third party's. And frankly I see no prospect of this.

These are matters that the voters must decide for themselves, and I am only too glad to have no part in the discussions.

However, I see no need to withdraw, and I think it is right to give supporters the chance of supporting again if they wish to. So I have written to Lionel B. saying that if the matter is re-opened, I am willing that my name should come up again, but that he and any supporters of mine are (of course) absolutely free to transfer their votes elsewhere.

I daresay you will feel inclined to do the same. It seems to me the right and reasonable attitude. But I shall not criticise (except perhaps to you) *any* step you take.

One practical point: The claim to re-open ought to be put forward by a member of the *majority*, who feels that he wants, or might want, to change his vote. It does not come half so forcibly from the minority. G. M. Young* *might* in view of things he said to me this morning.

* GM Young, (1822–1959). Educated at St Paul's and Balliol. Prize Fellow, All Souls 1905. Distinguished historian.

But frankly I am, as I was last night, defeatist. Perhaps I am too ready, too glad, to be a defeatist. (Perhaps, so Goronwy said to me nicely and not nastily, this morning, I *enjoy* defeat. If so, I've been having some rare times lately.)

I like to think of you and me on this staircase together. It is better so . . .

Would Beckett be as bad as all that? I don't know . . . I don't think I can vote against you; in certain circumstances I might vote blank. The feeling of admiration, respect, and affection which deserves a shorter name is too strong – apart from more relevant reasons which might as against X or Y impel me in your favour.

I am becoming disjointed. Forgive! The grammar, if not the tone, of the correspondence is being inevitably lowered.

It is obvious from this letter that the college meeting to which it refers had resulted in an impasse. Neither John nor Isaiah Berlin had received a clear majority; nor had Beckett received the support that Rowse had hoped for. John's next letter to Berlin, of 4 June, throws a little more light on the feelings of and divisions among the fellows, particularly over Rowse's promotion of Beckett:

'More last words' – Lionel Butler has described to me last night in a few hasty words certain proposed *démarches*, about which all I could say was 'Those concerned must make up their minds how they act: I must stand aside from all this', repeating any warnings about not 'reopening' merely for the sake of re-opening, and the desirability of getting the proposal suggested – or at least supported, as soon as it is made – by a member of the majority. The only such member I could think of was G.M.Y. It would seem necessary to ascertain how many such there were, and whether they were prepared, as an alternative to Beckett, to support you, or me. or E.F.J.

I had written to Lionel, before he explained to me the desperate remedies proposed, to tell him that *I was quite ready to be put up again, and that I was of course ready to be withdrawn by my supporters if they wished to support some other agreed candidate. That stands.* I think that that is the right and proper course for me to take.

I don't want to take part, or seem to take part, in plot or

counterplot; but perhaps I owe it to those concerned to say that if the alternative presented to me were Beckett or E.F.J. I should vote for E.F.J., and if they were Beckett and you I should certainly not vote for Beckett. The personal 'pull' inducing me to vote for you is strong indeed, and I expect I should yield to it. But as you know I won't vote for you just because you are you or against Beckett just because he is Rowse's candidate (though there is a pull towards doing that, also). I should like to hear a little more about Beckett. I suspect him to be a very poor candidate – but the Rees–Cooper opposition is to a large extent merely re-active.

P.S. Forgive the 'business' tone of this letter – it's written in a great hurry and no time for heart-opening.

The more I think of the Rowse–Beckett business, the more indignant I am, and I begin to share the feelings of the conspirators, and their desire to fight it. But much harm and no good will be done if the proposal is put forward in the wrong way – in J.P.C.'s sort of way – or with no chance of success.

There was to be one last-minute surprise. A few days before the final election meeting Isaiah Berlin decided to withdraw. Perhaps John's letters, and the experience of so much lobbying and dissension among the fellows, had made him aware that in All Souls, as it was then, it would have been extremely difficult for him to achieve the ambitions he had for the college, and that he would have been frustrated by the power of the older fellows. And realistically, he no doubt saw that his chances of being elected at that time were small. John wrote, on the Friday before the Sunday meeting:

Dear Isaiah,

What can I say?

Perhaps the many things I feel can best be summed up by saying that I pray that you aren't, and never will be, sorry for the step you've taken. A tinge of regret there must be – all that you feel I feel.

John

I do trust it was taken on calculated (in the *best* sense, calculated!) motives and not from the general impulse of which I know you are capable.

The final meeting and election of the new Warden took place on Sunday 10 June. Once again there was an impasse, and neither Beckett nor the other candidates in the field attracted the necessary support, which led to the election of a compromise candidate, Sir Hubert Henderson, a Cambridge man who had been a Fellow of All Souls since 1934. Henderson was an economist, for some years editor of the *Nation*, and joint secretary of the Economic Advisory Council. He accepted the office of Warden reluctantly, but with that modesty which docs not resist the wishes of his friends and colleagues. The college must have breathed a collective sigh of relief, and John wrote to Isaiah Berlin on 13 June:

> My dear Isaiah, . . .
>
> If you are coming through London on Friday, what about lunching with me – away from the smoke of the battle-field? . . .
>
> And I have several things to tell you, and I dare say you have several for me in exchange.
>
> After it all, we remain on the same staircase, and that to me is far from being the least of the consolations.
>
> Another was a letter from L.B. which I shall put beside your letters – and there are few that deserve that place.

Maurice Bowra, writing to a friend at Harvard, summed up the excitement of the election: 'Our term was almost entirely occupied with the election of a new Warden at All Souls. The highly confidential proceedings were relayed on a vast net-work, and for a fortnight we witnessed an enthralling struggle which ended in the defeat of our enemies but not in the victory of our friends.'

And on 14 June John wrote to Brian Spiller: 'I've taken it like a man – like a gentleman, even. Like a philosopher, too. The suspense was prolonged, the excitement intense, and I had lived through the disappointment and digested it long before it arrived. I find it easy to be consoled by the consolations.'

The calm after the battle was to last precisely ten days. On 20 June Hubert Henderson had a stroke during the Encaenia ceremonies in the Sheldonian and was taken to hospital. Again, All Souls was left in a difficult position, without an effective Warden, and not knowing if Henderson would recover; a situation which was to continue until the end of 1951. While Henderson lay on his sick bed any obvious move for another election would have been in bad taste, though no doubt the thought was present in a number of heads.

In his own mind John was still reckoning the odds, and he wrote to his mother while on holiday in Venice in September: 'I pray we don't have another Wardenship election in the near future. My chances, I think would be strong if we did – but I don't want it all over again just now!' I stayed with John in Venice for ten days that autumn, and I noticed that he talked very little of the election which had recently taken place, or the likelihood of another in the near future.

Hubert Henderson was still a sick man in December, and more and more the Fellows of All Souls must have wondered if he would ever be able to take up the office of Warden. On 15 December John sent another startling letter to Isaiah Berlin, then in the United States:

And now I must tell you, my dear Isaiah, that it is not in order to retail gossip of this kind that I write to you – not (I am ashamed to say) in order to renew our affectionate intercourse and to convince you of the truth that I miss you. I am afraid that I am impelled by a much more practical motive. But one not without interest to us both. Now listen.

Today is Sunday morning. Yesterday at noon I was sitting writing here in my room when there entered 'to me' (as they say in plays) the Manciple.

After a little talk about the proposed College laundry and kindred matters I asked, quite casually, whether there was any other College news.

The Manciple's face assumed an extremely grave expression, and he said that 'yesterday' (i.e. Friday) he had heard some very serious news. Since I was (he was kind enough to say) his oldest friend, he thought it right to tell me, though he did not think it proper, really, that I should hear the news from him. It has embarrassed him, he said, to be told the news (as he had been) before the Sub-Warden [A. L. Rowse]. *Sir Hubert Henderson had decided that he could not become Warden.* Lady Henderson had told the Manciple this on Friday; it was the result of the doctor's verdict after a 'slight' relapse on Sir H's part.

I said (in effect) that it might not be a final verdict, and that I believed and hoped that the Fellows would try to persuade Sir

H to reconsider his decision. (I was, as you will appreciate, quite sincere in this.) But Lady H. had evidently left the Manciple in no doubt that the doctor's, and Sir H's, verdict was final.

Thus was I put in possession of this huge, horrible, time-bomb.

I promised the Manciple that when the Sub-Warden told me (and I must say that I expected to be told in the course of the day) I would give no indication that I already knew. This was out of concern for the Manciple's sense of propriety: he did not tell me, or leave me with the impression, that Lady H had told him in confidence. It was just that he felt the Fellows ought to know first.

To this limited extent, I feel that I am in the confidence of the Manciple. I mustn't let him personally down.

I breathed not a word to a soul. But after dinner I asked A.L.R. if I might have a word with him alone in the Coffee Room. This was a masterly and legitimate (and, indeed, in a very positive sense, a *proper*) move.

I said 'I wanted to have a word about the Warden and his arrangements for living in the lodgings' – and proceeded – with due pauses to allow him every opportunity to say what he might well – and perhaps ought to – have said – to discuss some amendments which I had been asked to draft to the By-law about the payment of the Warden's servants.* (*This of course was of immediate concern to Sir H, but only on the assumption that he was going to occupy the Lodgings.) No word from A.L.R. Not a word. Should I, I suggested, discuss it with the Warden? 'Oh, no; I shouldn't do that; it would worry him.' 'I might perhaps drop him a line?' 'Yes, if you like; but don't go round there – he isn't well; he has had a slight relapse. *I shouldn't go round there until about a week before the beginning of next term.*'

Well, we had five or ten minutes of this, and then I changed the subject . . . and the interview was at an end.

(I forgot to add that I gathered from the Manciple that the D.B. [short for Dumb Babin] and also been told.)

Now I am clear in my mind that A.L.R. will keep this news secret until he has 'fixed' things in such a way that he can say that he has persuaded Bridges – or, failing Bridges, some other candidate – to stand; that that candidate is assured of majority support; that above all things another contested election is to be avoided; and that is that. A *fait accompli*.

He seems to be in a very strong position – if Bridges will indeed stand, perhaps an invincible one. But I am not as sure now as I was last time that Bridges is a certainty. And Bridges leaves for the U.S. immediately after Christmas. And the arguments for Bridges refusing are as strong as, or stronger than, they were last time.

(I dare say A.L.R. will persuade Sir H to defer a final decision, or publication of his decision, until Bridges returns.)

I am sure that A.L.R. has already written to Bridges – I dare say the old letter to Beckett came in useful . . .

If Bridges declines, who then? Possibly Wheare, more likely *Hodson* – by far the most-to-be-feared candidate.

That is my reading of the situation.

And now I must tell you that I thought it no breach of my duty to the Manciple to go round last night to the Vice-Chancellor [Maurice Bowra] and in strictest confidence inform him of the situation. After all, it concerns the Head of one of his Colleges. What the Manciple knows, I think he has a right to know. Indeed, I can see no call for secrecy – except in order to allow A.L.R. to mature his plans unimpeded.

Our old friend rose splendidly to the occasion: sage, sympathetic, practical.

We agreed that you ought to be informed, immediately. We also both hoped that you would return – whether as a rival, a supporter, a counsellor, an observer. Simply, if need be, as a *presence*. (I like also to think of A.L.R.'s face when he sees you, unannounced, and unexpected, arriving in the nick of time . . .)

But I can see that there would be no point in coming (a) if it were a false alarm about Sir H – I am sure it isn't – or (b) if Bridges (i) accepts, and (ii) is a certainty.

I suppose you might 'contact' Bridges in U.S.A. about (a) (i) *supra*.

But the idea of an immediate return for a week or two, for an unspecified reason, has its attractions. You need Oxford air, my dear boy . . .

I don't know that I can add any more – except that I have

just, two days ago, signed the lease of very expensive rooms in London, and decided to apply for 'silk' in March. But I am not publicizing these (most inopportune) steps, or A.L.R. will put it about that I have decided on a London career and do not wish to be considered as a candidate . . .

I repeat, I want you back because I want you back – whether as a supporter or a critic or a rival candidate.

The first whiff of a renewed electoral battle seems, in an instant, to have revived John's ambitions. While he was busy breaking the Manciple's confidence here, there and everywhere, it never occurred to him that Rowse was silenced by a more binding pledge of secrecy laid on him, not by a 'college servant', but by the Senior Fellow, Lord Simon. Rowse, in *All Souls in My Time*, gives a different account of Henderson's resignation, which might well explain why he was not in a position to discuss it with John at that moment. The 'hiatus' was making life difficult for Rowse who, as Sub-Warden, had to keep the college running. But he did not feel that that office entitled him to persuade Henderson to resign. The situation was becoming intolerable, and at last Simon, with the authority of the Senior Fellow, intervened. He visited Henderson and returned with his letter of resignation. This was not officially notified to the college until the Stated General Meeting the following January, but Henderson may have given his resignation to Simon in December, and he may have told Rowse, asking him to keep the news to himself until it could be announced officially at the meeting in January.

There is certainly no evidence that Rowse, or anyone else, approached Bridges, or any other outside candidate. That was all part of John's imaginings that another plot was being mounted against him, a campaign contrived by Rowse. In a letter to his mother dated 13 January 1952, before Henderson's resignation had been officially announced, he wrote:

Talking of the 'Front' [he had been describing his stay at Brighton] reminds me of the battlefront at All Souls; no news from it has reached me, but I expect intrigue is raging.

Never (of course) has my Bar practice seemed more attractive to me than it does at this moment – but that is just the perversity of my nature.

Also in January, John was preparing to apply for silk. As with most decisions, he was full of doubts. Was it too early? Did he want it? Would he get it? It had strong echoes of the arguments for and against the wardenship. One thing was certain: John wanted it very much. Cyril Radcliffe, who agreed to sponsor John's application, was optimistic.

Yes, certainly. I will gladly be your sponsor.

I do not think that Gavin [the Lord Chancellor] will fail to come up to scratch over this. Constitutionally, he regards my junior on the Chancery side as superior to any leader from elsewhere. It is something to do with the keen wind that blows there, I believe.

I shall say nothing to encourage you about All Souls: merely that I shall think better of you if 51% of its fellows do not.

Hubert Henderson's resignation was officially announced to the Stated General Meeting of All Souls on 26 January, at the same time opening official proceedings for the election of a new Warden. Once again there were various divisions of opinion and lobbying among the fellows; but the decisive event was A. L. Rowse offering himself as a candidate. The previous election had shown that many fellows did not favour a Rowse candidate. Even fewer favoured Rowse himself, and a majority of votes moved in support of John. He had a number of friends among the senior Fellows, and considerable support among the junior Fellows, including the more radical. John was elected the thirty-sixth Warden of All Souls College, but the news was not officially announced until 1 March.

A letter to Isaiah Berlin of 26 February, summing up his reactions to his election, shows that he knew the result some time before the official announcement:

My dear old friend –

I think that circumstances justify – indeed, call for – the time-honoured appellation. Don't misinterpret my silence. It was due to a mixture of causes (hardly a conception that would have appealed to H. W. B. Joseph) – and if the most obvious of these were the usual old pair, busy-ness and laziness, the deepest was the feeling that there was no practical need for me to write, because others were supplying you with bulletins (how false and fantastic and unbalanced these were I, being out of things, didn't realise), and that the time for the real, right letter hadn't arrived, and couldn't till things were, one way or the other, settled. Now I think it has arrived.

Let me strike at the outset, never to be repeated, the note of egotism and self-praise. How right all through my judgement has been! I do not think that I have made a false analysis or a false inference at any stage. All has gone as I from the outset* (*rather from the moment of A.L.R.'s decision to stand. My prophecies of what would have happened had he not stood would likewise, in that event, have been fulfilled – tho' they were less confident), quickly, insistently, *despairingly*, said it would. While the others were having convulsions (behind my back) and cabling and caballing and being *wrong*, I, whom it all concerned, the football in the midst of the milling scrum, was calm and consistent and correct.

On the other hand, I have done less than anyone else to bring about this result. A.L.R., of course, has done most. Lionel B, who (I'm inclined to think) has done most on the positive side, told me that the persons to whom I owed most besides himself – and must accordingly reward (presumably by an occasional smile and gracious inclination of the head) – were Raymond Carr*, Goronwy, and Amery†. I think this another example of Lionel's real good sense and judgement: I register the truth of his observation, and shall not forget it when I think of, and converse with the persons concerned. In particular Goronwy has, as you say, been at his best – or, I fear, at better than his best.

To their names yours would undoubtedly have been added had you been here on the scene. And you have, even at a distance, been a support in the way that those others have not been. Deep (I venture perilously near the pompous) has spoken to deep, and in an assuring voice. What I mean is that your passionate interest in it all, and the superb letters you sent me after Damascus, have

---

* Sir Raymond Carr. Educated Brockenhurst School and Christ Church. Fellow of All Souls and New College, and from 1968 to 1987 Warden of St Anthony's College.
† L.S. Amery, CH, (1873–1955). Educated at Harrow and Balliol. Prize Fellow, All Souls 1897. Statesman and writer who occupied many political posts, several of which reflected his interest in British imperialism.

meant (and I say this deliberately) more to me than anything that has happened throughout. That you believe in me, that you should be delighted, that you should think possible the kind of future that you paint – all that *reassures* me, and reassurance (believe me) is what I need.

In a way you think too highly of me, and in a less important way not highly enough. By the 'less important way' I mean in relation to the actual office. I shall be much better than you think when it comes to decisions on policy and relations with the common and the ugly and the miserable and the statistical and social scientists. Remember my wonderful work for Sir Ronald Adam and the psychiatrists and welfare and A.B.C.A. I know about enlightenment; I have a private tap.

But on the side where you are optimistic, I am the reverse. I wish indeed that I could write you the happy, serene, confident letter that you long for. I ought to be in that mood; I am told that by not being in it I am letting down my supporters. But candour, as you say, is all, and to you at least I must be sincere.

Ever since it has become apparent to me that I should be elected I have been unhappy in the prospect. I am giving up something (not, as you well know, money, success, a 'name' etc etc; all that – I think you believe me – is little enough to me; but something) that occupies me, tests me, keeps me at a stretch, prevents me from becoming loose and lazy and depressed and all over the place; something, too, that fascinates me and gives me the chance of the one thing that (in my perversity) has always meant most to me: succeeding in what I was not meant to succeed in. Also, I like the life, and I have friends and a framework, and (what I need most of all) a discipline imposed from without. And that I am to give up overnight, for what? Sir Walter Mober-ley and Mrs Macartney and dons and domestic bursars and administrative business which will bore me, in aid of ideals that I don't believe in. And the long, long hours of vacancy and depression, and longing for London and for life (and, let me add, the bore – to me so personal as myself – of filling a position, being 'the Warden' – and the consequent restraints in freedom of action. Was I not mad even to contemplate it?).

I have had my moments of panic, when I half-resolved to withdraw. And I really think it was only the thought of Lionel

Butler's inevitable nervous breakdown that restrained me . . .

Well, there it is. This is a mood, I suppose, and it will pass, and I shall settle down, and be happy with you, Stuart and Maurice and Mark Pattison and Dr Parr. I shall have to impose a discipline on myself: Bodley 3 hours every morning: German lessons twice a week etc etc. And, final doubt, can I write? have I any creative ability whatever? I think not – and if not I ought to have stayed on at the Bar which exercises the cross-word puzzle and histrionic talents which I *have*.

No time for more now. I must catch the 11.45 a.m. at Paddington for – think of it! – Henderson's funeral (he died on 22 February), poor, dear, poor, *really* dear, Henderson. Back this evening. Elections [AS was always holding various elections for various fellowships] on Saturday. I wish you were here. Not as a voter, but as you.

What can one say, except that it was so characteristic of John to continue to fight the battle after the war had been won. In all things he preferred the debate to the decision. But despite the endless musings on his reluctance to give up his life at the Bar, John took up his new office immediately following the official announcement of his appointment on 1 March.

His moment of triumph, for in reality that is what it was, was marred by one disappointment: his application for silk was turned down. He wrote to his mother on 11 April saying that only his surprise was greater than his disappointment. Some say Gavin Simonds, the Lord Chancellor, was following the precedent that silk was not given to a barrister retiring from practice, however distinguished his new employment, unless he had made some outstanding academic contribution to the law. Other legal contemporaries of John's think that it was simply an act of meanness on Simonds's part. John wrote to his mother, 'It would have been a pleasant ornament.'

VII

THE WARDEN

1952–62

It was very interesting seeing the Lodgings on Sunday. I feel
a little as if you were a bird soaring on high and caught
to peep into a wonderful nest.
The pleasure and affection your friends have shown is the
most wonderful revelation – to me at any rate. It seems to me
that you will have the making of your own life as Warden and
the influencing of other people's – both great responsibilities –
I cannot moralize but I sympathize. I hate responsibility. Don't
let all the congratulations spoil you but I know you won't.

A letter of congratulation from John's mother, March 1952

JOHN SPARROW started his wardenship in March 1952, and
retired twenty-five years later in November 1977. He was forty-
five when elected Warden, and just seventy-one when he retired.
But to understand his wardenship one must remember that he
had already been a devoted Fellow of the college since he gained his
prize fellowship in 1929. For the previous twenty-three years the
college had been his home and his favourite club.

If he was disappointed that he was not granted silk, he must have
been gratified by the large number of letters of congratulation he
received from friends and legal and academic colleagues; some were
from strangers who admired him as a distinguished Latin scholar.

There was a characteristic telegram from the Betjemans: 'OUR
THOUGHTS ARE WITH YOU DURING THIS TRYING TIME. JOHN
AND PENELOPE.' There were letters expressing personal delight
from such friends as Maurice Bowra, David Cecil, Harold Nicolson,
Edith Sitwell, William Plomer and Leslie Hartley. And there were
warm but more formal good wishes from Gilbert Murray, Francis
Meynell, T. S. Eliot, Vita Sackville-West and other distinguished
people.

John kept all these letters. And now, as Warden, with secretarial help and more space, he began to keep more letters and papers than he had in the past. His wardenship is well-documented.

Very few of the letters of congratulation expressed any reservations about John's future as Warden. His mother was a shrewd woman who knew him better than most people. While not wishing to spoil the occasion of his election by moralizing, she did point out [see the head of this chapter] the two main responsibilities that he must face as Warden, to himself and to others. Her gentle warning went unheeded.

There was a typically equivocal letter from Cyril Radcliffe:

Dearest John,

As an abstract proposition I would rather have had you stay in London some time longer. I know how much fascination the Bar has for you (I do not say that it does not secrete one or two Dougies [Dougal Malcolm, a senior Fellow of All Souls] of its own), and I would have liked you to have enjoyed more of its fruits. But there it is – Wardens of All Souls make their entrances and take their exits to what is at best a casual time schedule, and you had to take your opportunity when it came. All I can feel at the moment is my delight that you should have had so eminent a post put in your hands, for it's a great honour, and my most true wish is that it will bring you happiness and a sense of establishment.

When I saw you lunching with John Simon the other day, I thought that you were taking your decision the hard way, for you looked to me pale and I thought, not entirely able to look after yourself. Well, now you must pull their noses (not John Simon's – I have become, though belatedly, rather fond of him) and stamp on their toes, and I hope that you will. If later on, you let Antonia and me come down and stay with you for a night, I shall try to make sure that you are carrying out my programme . . .

Stuart Hampshire, who knew John exceptionally well, wrote him a more penetrating letter:

Dear John,

I think you will be unhappy in Oxford – if you are in any way like me, as in one way I think you are – unless you do find time to read the things for which you came here: under any other conditions Oxford is trivial and insipid, a great Gothic nursery where everybody seems to fidget. To read what you came here to read, and to enable others to do the same, is the only way to be happily Warden of anything. I do not know why you do not find the time, since you so extraordinarily found the time for many things in London. That is why I asked whether you really believed in people finding the time for just this: not because, as you say, you do not yourself find it, but because you seem not to want to say without qualification that people finding such time is the first object of policy in Oxford; in All Souls; in any university at any time. The rest I think is half dining club and half borough council, or so it seems to me. But if anyone whom you like says this in any practical contingency, you give the impression – and you have so cultivated giving the impression as to make it a form of action in itself – of moving in the opposite direction, in case it should seem that you have your friends behind you – as though this were the most ignoble of all scenes in which to be caught – acting in accordance with your beliefs and with the support of your friends. And your friends are left to fight their way through to your real intentions through a whole forest of impressions given, knowing that they will arrive, scratched and torn, in the end, after losing their way, or doubting even whether there was a way during some weeks. It is as if you thought simplicity in deciding must be dishonesty, and agreement must be conspiracy, and that the most painful method of reaching agreement must be the right one.

But I think you will be a good, long-lived, restless, difficult, encouraging Warden, surrounded by torn and exhausted friends, still peering through the false impressions which you give as a fire gives heat.

Did the solicitors never complain? The judges? The clients? Perhaps it was a world in which reality just is the impression given.

Happiness is too large a subject – but I think you are at the moment happy – and I *hope* you are.

Stuart

No doubt John read this astringent letter with pleasure, and ignored its truth and implicit advice; advice not dissimilar to his mother's hints. As he first sat at his desk in All Souls in March 1952, he probably looked forward to a quiet reign as Warden. He would maintain the status quo, encouraging some debate in college meetings, but using his considerable skills to frustrate radical innovations by the younger Fellows. He had no plans for the academic future of the college since he had no interest in the academic life.

He could not foresee the storms that lay in the future, when the reformers led by Franks and Bridges were to rock the status quo to its foundations, and to compel All Souls to make changes.

In the early years of his wardenship college life went quietly on its way. The distinguished London Fellows remained the leaders of college opinion and policy – an influence they had enjoyed since the twenties and thirties, when they numbered a former viceroy of India, senior politicians, the editor of *The Times* and an archbishop of Canterbury.

John was always conscientious in attending college meetings, partly perhaps because he wished to be certain that nothing undesirable happened behind his back. His correspondence at this time does show that he was busy with college and university business: meetings, elections, official guests and the affairs of Bodley. He had been drafting statutes for the newly founded St Antony's College, and one letter mentions writing a report for Winchester College about the Nathan Report on the reform of the law governing charities.

My main memory of John in the months following his election was his delight at being in possession of the Warden's lodgings. It was, after all, the first proper home he had had since leaving his parents' house in Wolverhampton. Breaking with tradition, he established himself in a study lined with books on the first floor, overlooking the Warden's garden. I also remember feeling that he was giving more time to entertaining undergraduates, of whom I was one, and his non-academic friends than to spending time with his colleagues. In the summer of 1952 there were hilarious tea parties in the garden, when noisy undergraduate laughter must have spilt over the garden wall and jangled the nerves of the more sensitive Fellows. On one of these occasions I found myself sitting next to John Betjeman, who was, no doubt, the cause of the laughter. After we had finished tea he invited me to walk round the garden. It was our first meeting, but he was so genial that I risked enquiring if I might ask a naive question.

'Certainly,' he said. 'I love naive questions.'

'How did you become a poet?'

'Ah,' he exhaled, as he turned his memorable moon-face towards me. 'You see, I was a failed schoolmaster.'

They were wonderful afternoons for the invited, but they must have generated less pleasing feelings in the uninvited on the other side of the wall.

If John's public life, following his election, was uneventful, his private life was not, and is best introduced by a long letter he wrote to his mother on 1 June 1953 – the frankest he ever wrote to her:

Dearest Mummy,

I am in a rush – for the Coronation! – so you must forgive what will be a breathless and not very coherent letter. But I feel I have to write before I go, because my letter will, I hope, have the effect of dissipating quite unnecessary worries from your mind. First, let me say that you overwhelm me with emotions which almost reduce me to tears when you speak of my being a good son, and when you suggest that I might be 'angry' at your letter. There has been an undercurrent of unhappiness in me of recent years caused by the consciousness *not* that my feelings for you have undergone a change – and no son has ever loved *or admired* his mother more, or owed more to her – but that somehow I have grown less able to express those feelings, or even to show them, than I used to be, and I have thought that you may have therefore begun to doubt their existence. Well! there's no ground for the doubts: the feelings are there, strong as ever, and deep – deep also in the sense that they are buried; but buried does not mean dead. Someday perhaps I shall write a book which will explain what I owe you; but it won't be a poetry book and I don't quite see what form of prose would do it – autobiography, I suppose. I do not think the reader would feel that I had been a very good son, but he would have no doubt about your perfection as a mother. Your only defect is *worrying too much* – and that leads me to the subject of your letter. Of course I couldn't be angry with you for expressing concern on my behalf, or the other feelings which you express in your letter. I have often thought that, being a feminist, you lack sympathy with the 'anti-feminist' in me, and find it difficult to understand my point of view. But I don't think that that is really fair to you; I think that you are wonderfully understanding, and when you talk of friendship taking the place of marriage in my life I think you state exactly my emotional position. Whether a friendship, however deep and intense, can really take the place of marriage, I doubt. I think that the happily married must be the happiest of all. In friendship, sex is 'sublimated' (that is the word, I think), but it may well be that nothing makes up for the absence of that element, and that lives which do without it (e.g. the monastic life) are incomplete and even unnatural. If so, I accept that as applying to my life. A long time ago I was faced with this, when adolescent; and I have a horror (I don't think that's too strong a word) of the sheer, unadulterated physical side of sex, in *any* of its manifestations (perhaps that accounts in part for the anti-feminist in me; women seem to me to exist for sex far more than men do: it is a greater part of their lives, and I don't like it).

But I confess that I am 'modernist' enough to be, so to say, more broad minded in my attitude than you: I don't feel inclined to lay down laws for others, except the very general law that *all* sensuality is bad. I don't like to contemplate, e.g. the sheerly sexual side of married life, but I don't therefore condemn marriage; others must decide for themselves.

The emotions which others link with sex are with me put into art (including literature) and friendship, which are sometimes deeply romantic – I think the 'romance' on my side takes a sort of protective form – I mean that I think I have a real genius for understanding and helping the simple, the weak, and the young. Hence my feeling for the private soldier when I was in the Army: I almost loved my platoon (I mean, some of the men in it), and always liked most those who most craved help. Hence also, I think my natural affection for children (nice, well behaved, *un*precocious, children!).

Such feelings are easily misconstrued by the world in general, who think that there is something unnatural about any deep affection between persons of the same sex. I bear these misconstructions with equanimity – except when it leads people to condemn my friends – of whatever age or class. And I will not surrender my friends because of such misconstructions.

[171]

I do indeed bear in mind the fact that when one has an official position one can less easily afford to snap one's fingers at public opinion, however wrong the public opinion may be. And I think it wise not to parade e.g. my friendships with humble members of society like my dear friend in Lancashire, or John Nolan; and not to *parade* friendships with undergraduates, like John Lowe or Colin. People who do not begin to understand these things (like Daddy – unlike you) may well drag in 'sex' and innocence is not altogether its own protection. But I think you can trust my shrewdness as well as my innocence. In this world alas! one needs *both*. But if you *must* worry, worry about my car-driving, where the perils (however remote) have a real foundation, and not one which exists only in your imagination. – Now I really must go to the Coronation.

All my love,
John

I wish we could have a holiday *alone together*.

As in all his letters to his mother which skirted around the edges of his sexuality, he never gave her the unadulterated truth. She, in turn, an intelligent woman, never attempted to corner him on this subject. From time to time, as on this occasion, she had suggested the possibility of marriage, but in her heart, and her wise head, she must have known that her son was a homosexual, and not a celibate one. The fact that John did not come out into the open with his mother – and this letter is about as far as he ever went – does not negate his deep and genuine affection for her: he may simply have wished to spare her feelings by not spelling out all the facts.

John never wished to share this aspect of his life with his mother. I stayed with him for ten days in Venice in August 1951. Years later, reading his papers for this book, I found a letter that he had written to her the evening I left. Our holiday could not have been more innocent or enjoyable, but he told her that he had spent the last ten days alone, working and reading: talking and laughing would have been more accurate. In the long letter quoted above he named undergraduate friends to her for the first time. I never met his mother, but the Colin he refers to here became a friend of the family.

For all the apparent soul-searching expressed in John's letter to his mother, when he wrote it, he was already deeply involved in a romantic friendship with Colin – a friendship which at about that time had ceased to be celibate. Their love affair is minutely documented by a vast number of letters between them, with the exception of those from Colin in 1952 and 1953, which it seems John did not keep. There are many love letters from John starting in 1953, and from Colin to John from 1954 onwards.

I tell their story not from any prurience, but because it shows John's romantic side, which remained hidden from most people, and also because both he and Colin come out of the relationship so well, particularly John. Colin later married but died tragically young in the 1980s. John wanted the story included, and it cannot harm Colin.

John must have met Colin either in late 1951 or early in 1952. Colin, an undergraduate reading history, wrote a rather formal letter to John on 27 January 1952, beginning 'Dear Mr Sparrow', and thanking him for a nice afternoon. There is, possibly, a slight tremor of flirtation between the lines – Colin was already a practising homosexual – which John would have recognized and enjoyed. As the year progressed, the letters became more intimate.

Colin was extremely good looking, intelligent, charming and had the most perfect manners. Some years later, after his first visit to us, my first wife remarked that he was the most charming friend I had ever brought home. In 1952 Colin was in his final year at Oxford, and thinking about his future. John was full of unrealistic plans – anything to keep Colin in Oxford – at one point even suggesting that he should live somewhere in the upper reaches of the lodgings. Colin, who at this early stage remained slightly reserved in the face of John's emotional enthusiasm, was considering the post of tutor to the son of a rajah in India: indeed, he went for an interview with this royal person in London.

John was dismayed by this prospect and, to undermine the project, persuaded Colin to take him to meet his parents. John exercised his considerable charms on both Colin's father and mother. He conquered Colin's mother so successfully that, the same evening, she told Colin that 'Mr Sparrow is your nicest friend'. The father was a little suspicious at first, but by the end of the month was writing to Colin, 'You must follow Mr Sparrow's advice, for he is a person of great experience.' The Indian venture was dead, but any solution was made more difficult when Colin got a third, which destroyed his

[173]

chances of remaining in Oxford. Eventually, he got a job with a well-known company and was sent to Bristol.

In some quarters John has had the reputation of being predatory with young men, and there are undergraduates of those days who claim that he made unwelcome advances. He certainly enjoyed the company of young men, but sex was not his only purpose, particularly when attraction developed into friendship. Colin had been an active homosexual at Marlborough and continued to sleep with his friends at Oxford. In fact, Colin was by nature a great deal more predatory than John, and on more than one occasion John warned him to be careful in these casual affairs. John had certainly not acquired an innocent friend, and could not be accused of corrupting Colin.

John was almost certainly aware that Colin was sleeping with his contemporaries, but at no time did he show any jealousy; nor did Colin make any attempt to conceal the fact. Throughout their long friendship John was protective, generous, kind and loving. He was romantically and sentimentally in love, as his letters to Colin demonstrate:

July 1953

Colin,

It gives me a strange thrill to write your name in full, as it did to see it written in full at the end of the letter which I opened this morning. I only wish I could form the letters, and the whole word, as you do.

How could you write me such a letter – giving me joy beyond anything I have deserved, and making the scrawl I sent you last night so pitiful by comparison?

And the poem – I seem to know it, but I can't 'place' it. It seems to breathe the very spirit of you ('I know you only as my need' is surely you speaking). Did you write it? It is not impossible that you should be a poet (as you certainly are if you wrote that), there are springs in you that are yet untapped. Anyhow, you can imagine my gratitude to you for sending it to me.

I had this thought last night about us (and it should strengthen our happiness, if it's true): most people fall in love with their idea of the other person; then, as they get to know each other better, the reality displaces the idea and their feeling therefore weakens; perhaps they are lucky if it survives at all. Fortunate are those who after a year of ever increasing intimacy still love each other as deeply as at first. And what of those who love each other more deeply still? As for us: 'How sweet love seemed . . .' at a time when each knew practically nothing of the other; for more than a year we have been increasing our knowledge and our closeness; and the 'summer flood' is deeper and stronger than anything we could then have imagined possible. It is founded on fact and not on illusion – on many facts, among them my strength which I draw from you and give back to you in increased measure. I feel that I am with you, just as you are with me (I don't need the token of that little red label any longer, though it still glances at me from your tree across the garden), all the time: in the retail department, and on your way to work early in the morning, and at the interviews in London, and alone in your room at night.

No, no; I'm not perfect: how far from perfect, I know well; but I do think (and this isn't sentimental optimism) that we are perfect for each other: we even correct and supply each other's weaknesses: if we aren't perfect, we have just the necessary imperfections. I have such plans for your future! But you must apply yourself, and be hard on yourself, out of, as well as inside, working hours.

This is becoming like a sermon: I must break – or you will send me in return a lecture about laziness and procrastination, which I well deserve.

I don't see how we can very well ever be happier than we were last weekend (except that we might have been alone together more); and any happiness was countlessly increased by seeing you happy, and watching others (grown-ups as well as children) coming to love you . . .

I wonder where and when, and if, I shall see you this weekend. Sometimes I feel I cannot do without you, and charades are no substitute. Indeed, I am learning to do without them. Thoughts of you, and imagined conversations with you, and readings aloud to you, are quite enough. But your actual presence is better still.

I mustn't go on. I ought to write you an amusing, or at least an *interesting* letter. For don't let's forget that we each possess

the invaluable gift of being able to make the other laugh – and
the no less valuable gift of sharing each other's interests – both
of them valuable constituents of friendship, and even of love.
Yes: our foundations grow deeper every day: strength and calm,
and understanding. On that can be built an endless superstruc-
ture of delight and pure joy – and *fun*.

I wonder if you have any idea of the strength I have in store
for you – or of the joy your last letter gave me.

AT
John

There will be many who only knew the sterner, more abrasive sides
of John's character, who will be surprised that he could write such
a letter, or entertain such sentimental feelings. The letter suggests an
element of 'being in love with love', and a failure to keep his emotions
in balance with his intelligence, a fault he often admitted to in later
life. In the earlier stages of their friendship Colin was slightly in awe
of John's cleverness, but he gained confidence as he realized that,
clever as John was, he was not always right. In 1955, for example,
during the great debate on the Oxford Road Scheme, John adopted
in public a superficial and selfish attitude, for which Colin took him
roundly to task.

But in 1953 Colin's uncertainties were focused on the question of
going to bed with John. John misinterpreted his hesitancy as some kind
of fear or shyness. However, Colin had shown no inhibitions with his
school and Oxford contemporaries, relationships in which he was
almost certainly the dominant partner. Throughout his friendship with
John he was always worried that people would see him as the 'female'
side of the relationship. Some years later, when he and John were living
in the Nicolson flat in Albany, Harold suddenly announced with
unusual insensitivity to the assembled homosexual company, 'We must
give a coming-out ball for Colin.' The implication of the remark deeply
wounded Colin's pride. He stormed out of the flat and did not return
that night. John himself did not always appreciate that his protec-
tiveness might be interpreted as a desire to dominate his younger and
weaker partner, a role quite at odds with Colin's nature.

But speculation on this subject is hardly necessary, as it is fully
dealt with in a letter from John to Colin, written on 8 July 1953,
not long after the barrier had been broken:

[176]

My darling Colin,

This is written on the 4.45 on the way back from the N.P.I. I'll post it when I get to Oxford.

Your letter made a glory for my morning. It was full of YOU – and such an interesting you; you need to be loved and re-assured and encouraged and admired (as you *deserve*) in so many different ways!

Yes: perfection becomes, every time we meet more perfect for us. I think Barbury Camp (that's its name; I've looked it up) was the best, but all was lovely. And your misgivings and qualms and fears are all absurd! Everyone likes you. The only danger is that my friends will like you too much – no; that isn't meant seriously; but I am serious in saying that I know you are a success, and just the very success that you want to be, with all the people I like. Dadi [Rylands] is frightening, I agree; 'finished' is just the word. But *he* had nothing but praise for you. As for spilling of coffee and forgetting of suitcases (both of which were just as much me as you) – well; you're being like me: inventing things to worry about. I'd soon show you how silly you are if I had you with me now as I write. As for your fears about our not suiting each other in a particular way: I've never really explained about that; but I think I can, and I think your worries (it's really *I* who ought to worry; you are perfect: I'll explain) will vanish. And it doesn't matter. It's a luxury, when it comes off perfectly – and more a matter of technique than emotions! Oh Colin! wait till we take a camp bed to Barbury Camp, and watch the moon rise and the dawn break. That sounds sentimen-tal: but there's no reason why it shouldn't actually happen. I'll teach you something about perfection then!

You say you 'become confused' sexually, as you used to do socially. In both things it's only self confidence or serenity you need – and that will come when you are convinced, as you are gradually becoming convinced, of your own adequacy (itself, what an inad-equate word! substitute 'perfection') – So will you promise not to worry? You will deserve words of punishment if you do . . .

John was, of course, aware of the romantic feelings that overcame him, and able to laugh at them, as is shown in another letter to Colin, dated 12 July 1953:

My d

You say that I help you sometimes – now will you help me by listening sympathetically and sweetly (I can see you sitting in the chair over there, even as I write) while I pour myself out to you? I've nothing to say – no confession to make – no awful news to recount – but I am brimming over with something, I can't describe it, as if an unspent force of longing or desire or strength or sweetness was welling up within me; and I want to give it, to confer it, to spend it, to pour it out; and 'it' is simply *myself*, my being and my strength. It reminds me of the beginning of a poem I once wrote

Deep in my spine, where none suspect or see
Grow the strong roots of an aspiring tree.

This mood is discharging itself in a letter, and my fear is that you will recoil from it as pure sentimentality – as if I were to empty over you a cup of very strong sweet tea – you'd want to wash it off! But I think I can rely on you to understand; for it isn't sentimentality at all: it is *me*, and you must take *me* for better or worse ('I'm quite a satisfactory, sensible person, really', I want to say in my most ordinary voice).

It is all mixed up (you see this is me being introspective and self-analytical) with the rain which is pouring down outside among the leaves of the chestnut trees and beating down the poor roses, and a heavy sky with promise of more rain still – and I want to write a POEM – 'Ah to whom?' as Shelley (I think) says. I gush on (like the rain): I wouldn't do it to anyone but you. And if there weren't you to help me, to understand me, to *receive*, what should I do? But perhaps that isn't a real question, because I think if it weren't for you this mood would not have come over me: it is due largely to the joy which flooded me when you rang this morning and something which had been pent up for three days, since we last spoke on the telephone, was suddenly released, and I felt free and strong and happy – but with a strange empty feeling too: I wanted to wrestle with someone and there was no one there to wrestle with. And how would I put my feelings into my telephoning voice? and if I could, how would they have struck you in the middle of the hotel lounge? So, instead, I write this letter, relying on you, you, you, to understand. It ought, of course, to be a poem; for it is of moods such as this that poems are born; but to write poems, alas! one has to be a poet – and I am not.

I can't even write reviews – or books – or anything. I say that the cause is my perfectionism – that nothing short of the best, in the way of literary productions, is good enough for me. I wish you were here to goad me on to working, to tell me that it is NOT perfectionism but simply LAZINESS that prevents me from getting on with my job.

That's a digression. But it is not altogether irrelevant, because it is in you that I now find my chief incentive to work; I want to prove to you that I can do something good, even if it is only a note in the Times Lit. Supp.

One cannot resist smiling at John's ardour and his sentimental expression of his feelings; it is obvious that he was able to smile at himself. There is no doubt that he was deeply in love with Colin, and although there is no definite evidence, it would seem to be the first love affair of such intensity in his life, though it was not to be the last. Colin was soon drawn more deeply and more contentedly into the affair; it developed into a friendship which continued until Colin's death.

Their immediate problem was how to see more of each other. Colin moved to his company's London office, and Harold Nicolson provided a partial solution. John was already using Nicolson's flat in Albany as his London *pied-à-terre*, and in August 1953 Nicolson wrote to him suggesting that Colin could move into the attic room: 'Anyhow, about C.1. [Albany] Your attic bed will be moved down to N's room [his son Nigel had been the original tenant] and all that will be wanted is a bed (truckle???) for Colin in the attic.'

Colin moved in and, through his kindness and consideration, soon established a warm relationship with Harold Nicolson, who teased his lodgers endlessly and referred to them as the 'love birds'. This arrangement enabled John and Colin to spend most weekends together, and they usually saw each other during the week, when Colin was not away on business.

John introduced Colin to all his personal friends, notably Reynolds Stone's family, the Betjemans, William Plomer and Rupert Hart-Davis. Colin also met John's parents and his brother and two sisters. Colin did not as a rule mix in his All Souls or more general life. John was protecting not only Colin's reputation, but also his own.

[179]

John was skilful at dividing his life into separate compartments and keeping his colleagues and his close friends apart. Colin stayed with John in Venice in September in 1953 and, when he left, John was joined by John Bryson, both an Oxford colleague and a close friend. Bryson was a tutor in English literature at Balliol; one of those rare Englishmen who had a deep understanding and love of both English literature and the fine arts. On first acquaintance he was a forbidding man, but as one got to know him better, his protective shyness melted and one discovered a kind and exceptionally cultivated person. Since they saw each other frequently in Oxford, there is no surviving correspondence between them, but they must have been very close. On his desk at Beechwood House, in his retirement, John always kept photographs of two friends: Dean Hutton from Winchester and John Bryson.

It is strange to think of John solemnly conducting his daily life, chairing college meetings, attending Herbert Hart's inaugural lecture, and dashing off notes to Isaiah Berlin, while all the time at least half of his mind must have been on Colin. But John enjoyed deception; he was good at it.

Although the years of his wardenship, in both his official and his private life, are well-documented in his papers, much of this material is repetitive trivia, and reveals more about John's personal affairs than the daily routine of All Souls. Sedentary lives always present the biographer with a problem; a chain of small incidents and personal exchanges are no substitute for a strong narrative. There are moments of drama, but in the intervals one can only select the more interesting or amusing incidents in John's career.

An annual stay in Venice had now become an important fixture in John's life, and he was there again in September 1954, this time renting rooms in the Palazzo Polignac, overlooking the Grand Canal. He was far from alone on this occasion. First, Isaiah Berlin was there for a few days, and John wrote to his mother: 'I should like to estimate how many words he had uttered in conversation with me before he left, or how many topics we discussed.' Another friend, Judy Montagu, was also in Venice, but the real invasion began with the arrival of the Stone family, accompanied by John's favourite sister, Penn, and Colin. The Stones and their guests were staying in a rented cottage outside Venice, in the grounds of the

Villa Malcontenta. As is the way with these family holidays, they needed a base in Venice, and John's apartment was ideally placed. I think it would be true to say that John adored the Stone family (he had after all introduced them to Penn and Colin), but despite his deep affection for them, he could not help reflecting in the same letter to his mother that 'They ruined my holiday, but I enjoyed sharing theirs!'

Old friends surfaced now and then. He wrote to congratulate Edith Sitwell after she was made a Dame, adding apologetically that he had long been a silent correspondent, but must now break his Trappist vow. Edith Sitwell marked this sentence in his letter with an asterisk, and wrote at the bottom of the letter, 'Trappist in invisibility as well as in silence. Why do I never see you?' The sad fact was that John had grown tired of her.

At the end of the year he wrote a melancholy 'epitaph' for 1954 to K Clark: 'As for me, I drag on, harried and beset by trivialities and family worries [his mother had been seriously ill] . . . I don't get anything done that I want to do, and am tempted at times to regret the Bar.'

There are two slightly enigmatic letters from Lionel Butler, who had been one of John's most enthusiastic supporters during the elections, which suggest that he was being 'harried' by a number of younger Fellows in the college – a body of opposition which was to grow as his conservative wardenship proceeded. Butler's letters are not dated, but must have been written in 1954, as he left All Souls for St Andrews in 1955. The first letter catches the highly charged atmosphere in which these two friends used to conduct their relationship:

My dear John,

This is the third draft of a letter intended to be self-justifying, explanatory, and apologetic. I can't manage to write it. All I want to say is that I am unconditionally sorry for all that I said that was hurtful to you, unreasonable to your ears and Isaiah's, splenetic, and violent, and nasty. There was (there must have been) *much*. I now believe that I would prefer rats in my room to wounds, inflicted by me, upon your heart and feelings: but it is too late, this time. Isaiah says that our 'midnight scenes' (yours and mine, or mine with you, if you think that is more accurate) are a form of *flirtation*. He is shrewd, but wide of the mark there. I have long gone beyond the flirting stage with you. Was there ever that stage? I love you too much to want to flirt with you or play cruel games with your emotions. I think I set absurd and unrealistic standards for you and me and the College and then distress myself about them. Well, as Queen Victoria said, I will be good, or try to be. No more nonsense, no more violence of speech, I promise, and if I don't give you the support and comfort you need, shame on me. You said on Monday (or about then) 'you are a great comfort to me,' and you could hardly have said that tonight. So I feel very bad.

I may become eccentric and bring a mop, a broom, and a scrubbing brush and use them myself. The dirt is thick and sticky. But believe me I am resolved not to fret you and myself and others further about these ghastly bursarial questions. This is a poor letter, but I hope it conveys to you that I am attempting to turn over a new leaf and give you a little more peace and in a positive and fruitful way more love.

Lionel

All Souls is a democratic institution, run by a series of committees. John was accustomed to this form of college government, but there were times when he found the system irksome, especially when he was opposed by the more radical Fellows. The second letter from Lionel Butler refers to such a passage of arms:

My dear J, . . .

I hope that you will not allow the follies and the BIGOTRY of Dummett*, Carr, and even of dear J.P.C. [John Cooper] (for whom I have much affection) to worry YOU. There is no doubt in my mind who 'comes out of' the recent hurly-burly with credit and who doesn't. (And should anyone say I am your yes-man, I can tell them that I disagree with you quite often but always openly and at College meetings unhesitatingly – where their *blind mouths* rarely do and rarely did (in the case of two of them) utter. I wish they would all grow up but I fancy they won't.)

* Prof Michael Dummett. Educated Winchester and Christ Church. Prize Fellow, All Souls 1950. Wykeham Professor of Logic at Oxford 1979.

John was a fearless man, and he was more likely to have been irritated than seriously worried by the opposition he met in the committee meetings.

In 1955 John became involved in the Oxford Road Scheme debate, in a letter to *The Times* and elsewhere, arguing vociferously in favour of removing every possible vehicle from Oxford's High Street, which by coincidence passed the Warden's front door. His arguments bristled with his personal interests. The next year he campaigned for Harold Nicolson to be the Professor of Poetry at Oxford, but Nicolson was defeated, not surprisingly, by W. H. Auden. That summer he gave up his annual visit to Venice to go with Colin to Spain and Portugal.

Towards the end of 1958 he faced a difficult decision. The important post of Vice-Chancellor rotated among the heads of Oxford colleges and in 1959 it was the turn of the Warden of All Souls. A decision was required by the beginning of that year. As usual, John prevaricated, and although he had almost certainly made up his mind to refuse this onerous and committee-ridden job, he still sought advice from friends and colleagues. Most of them, I am told, were praying that he would refuse. They thought him in every way unsuited to the post.

The situation, and John's thoughts on the subject, are fully explained by a letter he wrote to Edward, Earl of Halifax, Chancellor of Oxford University, whom he chose as his confessor in this matter. It was written on 25 December 1958:

Dear Edward,

It is Christmas Day, and I am alone in a closed and empty College. (I take my Christmas fare with my family, two miles out of Oxford, but sleep under my own roof.)

I am too late to wish you a Merry Christmas, but not too late to wish you a Happy New Year.

I am also shockingly late in answering your invitation to come to Garrowby after Christmas. Of course I am sorely tempted, and I am particularly anxious to see you just now, for a reason which will presently appear. But I am tied up with visits which I long ago promised to make: to Kenneth Clark in a couple of days' time, and to Dorset (an annual fixture, this) for Jan 2nd–5th – and on 7th the redoubtable Freya Stark comes to stay with me for three days. On Jan 11th I have a College committee meeting; Full Term begins on the 17th, and I leave for Jamaica on 21st [see pp. 189–90].

I inflict this calendar upon you only to show you how difficult it is for me to get away – unless perhaps for a night or so during my last ten days in England. Are you by any chance going to be in London at any time during January? I should dearly like to talk with you – in London, or perhaps, if you will not be in London, at Garrowby – about the Vice-Chancellorship.

The matter has become urgent because Christie of Jesus has been told by his doctor that he must stand down. It seems therefore that I must make up my mind before next term – i.e. before I leave for Jamaica.

The question has been causing me anxiety – I may say, agony of mind – for some weeks past.

When we last met I explained to you my own feelings, though I don't think I conveyed to you how strong they are. The principal persons I have since consulted reinforce my conviction that I ought not to take on the job. These are Maurice Bowra, Pickering, the new Regius Professor of Medicine, and the present V-C.

M.B. feels strongly the necessity of having had experience of the needs of an undergraduate college. (It is not simply that All Souls has no undergraduates; that might not matter if, like Sumner, I had been a Fellow of an undergraduate College. Pember, it is true, shared this disability; but in his day things were utterly different.)

Pickering (who was himself for years on the Univ. Grants Committee) was still more strongly of the same opinion. Experience of the workings of University Depts (and of their finances) he regarded as an absolute necessity, and some sympathy with or understanding of the claims of Science.

Boase [President of Magdalen] did not commit himself so decidedly, but he reassured me on what one may call the University aspect. I would not, he thought, be 'letting down' the University if I stood aside, since my successors (or substitutes) would be more experienced than I. Oakeshott [Lincoln] and Wheare [Exeter] would, he agreed, be in every way better than myself. MacCallum [Pembroke], who is next in succession, might not be as good as me in some ways, but has the necessary experience (and he has the advantage of being a son-in-law of Veale).

Boase warned me that such persons in the University as are interested would probably expect me to take it on; but he did not suggest that a refusal would be thought to reflect in any way on All Souls. Nor do I think that it would conceivably do so, at any rate among those who appreciate the considerations involved.

What the College itself would feel it is hard to say; those who know me best would support me in my refusal (and I think not merely out of complaisance); others would, I suspect, *assume* that I would (and perhaps also that I ought to) take it; but I can't attach weight to assumptions on the part of those who do not fully understand the issues.

I have talked to Waldock, who is what is called a University politician; he did not seem to feel strongly one way or the other.

I am writing to Isaiah, who is (together with Bowra) the person of all those in Oxford whose judgement in such a matter I should most trust.

I need hardly say that your judgement and your approval are things by which I set the greatest store. I have all the time borne in mind our talk on the matter and what you said in a recent letter to me – that you would not be happy if you thought that I was making a mistake.

I, for my part, would be unhappy to feel that you thought I was making a mistake. But then I think that the mistake would be to take on an office for which I have no inclination, in which I feel no interest, and for which I lack vital qualifications. I am out of sympathy with and indeed antipathetic to much that I should be called upon to pay lip service. To decline gracefully would attract no attention – or merely passing comment. To accept would be . . .

And so continued the 'ritual dance' that John performed when he felt bound to consult all his friends on a decision he had obviously already made. Maurice Bowra, who had been an outstanding Vice-Chancellor from 1951 to 1954, wrote to John on 1 December, advising him not to accept:

My dear John,

You asked me to send you a few lines about various aspects of the Vice-Chancellorship, and I am very glad to do so. I will not worry you about the ceremonial and social aspects, which will be well known to you. But perhaps I can stress a few other points.

1. Much of the work is bound to be strange to you, as it was to me. This is specially the case with the whole science world, including the medical; with anything that involves dealings with government departments; with the financial troubles of the women's colleges; with the Vice-Chancellor's Committee and the U.G.C. [University Grants Committee]. You will have no difficulty in picking this up, and the Registry staff is extremely efficient and helpful.

2. You will find that there are other matters which may be known to you but on which you find yourself in disagreement with Council or even Congregation, as Smith did on the question of the roads. In these the V-C is at a disadvantage as he is not allowed to speak in Congregation and has to rely on others putting forward his point of view. This happened to me once, and the results were not what I would have wished or might even have secured if I had been free to act myself. But this is perhaps a minor matter about which one need not worry too much.

3. I don't know how far you have kept in touch with new movements in the University. They have been many and various, and some of them require a good deal of knowledge, personal and particular, which cannot be got fully from documents or even from the Registry officials. This is especially the case with the expansion of science, but of course may be found elsewhere.

4. It is clear that the Colleges and their affairs are becoming, despite everything, more and more the concern of the University. It can't be helped, since the University has to act for them in such vital matters as scholarships, grants for building (so far rather in the air), changes of statutes etc. In such matters I found it invaluable, I almost would say indispensable, to have a good knowledge of undergraduate affairs. I don't mean personal relations and so on, but how the system works from their end. This is primarily a College matter but the University acts as a

go-between, and the V.C. is in the not too happy position of being shot at from all sides by College heads and tutors who know such things inside out and have their own well informed and well argued cases which have to be met. I imagine that this might be very difficult indeed for someone who has not been a College tutor or other officer used to undergraduate affairs. I think this is a matter of some importance, and no doubt you will have given thought to it. I feel that if you had had Sumner's experience at Balliol or elsewhere, there would be no problem, but you may well find it very difficult to pick up the threads of highly complex College business and to speak with authority and give a lead on them. If you do not give a lead, chaos usually follows, and there are as many opinions as there are people present.

I hope this is what you wished to know. I have written with complete frankness, as this is what I think you wished.

yours ever,
Maurice

The letter gives an interesting glimpse of the university's government at that time, and shows that Bowra had all the common sense that John lacked. His advice to John, though not actually stated, is obvious enough. In fact, of all the people in Oxford whom John consulted, only Walter Oakeshott, President of Lincoln College and former headmaster of Winchester, urged him to accept the vice-chancellorship, writing: '. . . You've got the qualities to make a great Vice-Chancellor. It's most important that from time to time – as at present – the outside world should be aware that there are a few distinguished scholars, in administrative positions, even in the highest offices at Oxford. You are uniquely placed to show this. Don't turn it down.' Perhaps Oakeshott was trying to kindle a little Wyke-hamical sense of public duty but he was wasting his time. It seems certain that John never intended to accept the post. And his close friends were worried not only about his lack of experience of the needs of science and the affairs of undergraduates but, worse, that his intransigent attitude to change in the university might lead to what Isaiah Berlin described as 'scenes'. On 11 January 1959 he wrote to the university registrar to decline the office. Nobody was surprised, and quite a few were greatly relieved, particularly those who knew him best.

It may seem strange to those who did not know him that a man who was so clever and, judging by his wartime service, so competent, should refuse to serve the university. But perhaps he was right. A Professorial Fellow of All Souls recalled the occasion:

... my view of John was that he was essentially a private person and a delightful one, who did not have the temperamental qualifications for the positions that his enormous abilities seemed to deserve – certainly not for any position carrying major administrative responsibilities ... All Souls he saw as an agreeable gentlemen's club, and he devoted all his enormous talents to keeping it that way. It never occurred to him that the College perhaps had wider responsibilities to the university, or indeed to the country. I shall never forget his reply when I expressed mild regret that he had passed up his chance – some would say his duty – to take on the Vice-Chancellorship, which then went in strict rotation among the colleges. 'But why should I?' he asked; 'I am not an educationist!' And into the word he put a degree of bitterness and contempt that was almost frightening.

Like so many of his generation, John hated the modern world. The trouble was, he did not do anything to make it any better. In his old age he once said, 'I mean, if you were offered the wardenship of All Souls, how could you possibly turn it down?' I felt tempted to reply, 'Yet you turned down the Vice-Chancellorship,' but he was past such arguments. He had never been an 'educationist', and a concern for education had nothing to do with his acceptance of the wardenship, or with the way in which he presided over the college for twenty-five years.

In June 1958 John received an invitation to give six lectures on a subject of his own choosing at the University College of the West Indies, in Jamaica, in February 1959. He accepted and wrote suggesting a possible subject:

Can you help me at all with any suggestions as to the kind of lectures that you have in mind? My own studies have lain in two fields: first, I was for twenty years a practising lawyer; second, I have always been interested in problems of literature and literary history. Neither of these seems to offer any very suitable topic.

A possibility that has occurred to me is that I might devise a series of lectures taking as my starting point Sir William Blackstone (1723–1780), who was a Fellow of this College. I might then develop the question of Blackstone's influence on the common law and so upon the constitution of the United States. This would give scope for reflections upon the problems of constitution-making for peoples who are newly attaining independence, and upon the principles to be observed in solving them.

Everything was agreed, and at the last minute single lectures at Antigua and St Kitts were added to the programme, through their university extramural department. John himself added another visit to his journey. Christopher Codrington (1668–1710), scholar and soldier, and a wealthy landowner in Barbados, where he was born, had also been a Fellow of All Souls. On his death, he bequeathed his books and money to found the college's Codrington Library, but also left his estates in Barbados to found Codrington College, a religious and educational institution which was taken over by the Community of the Resurrection, a well-known Anglican order, in 1955. John wrote to the Principal of Codrington College in Barbados on 10 October:

I have been invited to deliver a series of lectures at the University of the West Indies, Kingston, Jamaica, next February . . .

I am telling you all this, because I hope, if it is convenient to you, that this might afford me an opportunity of paying a visit to Codrington College. It would seem appropriate, considering the links between our two Colleges, that the Warden of All Souls, if he found himself in the West Indies, should pay his respects to Codrington's foundation out there.

The Principal, Father Anselm Genders, replied immediately: 'Your letter this evening was very exciting: it would be splendid if you could pay a visit here, and any time would of course suit us.'

John's visit to the West Indies was evidently a success; he was always at his best on such occasions. The lectures and his visit to the University of the West Indies in Kingston were reported with enthusiasm in the *Pelican*, a university publication. It was thought that seminars might have been more useful than general lectures, but his personal success among the staff and students was unqualified.

Six weeks is too short a time to spend in such an attractive place as the West Indies, felt Mr Sparrow. The UCWI fascinates him by its progress over a short ten years. He took every opportunity he could of meeting the undergraduates and it was really a pleasure to see him chatting interestedly with various students on the topics which interested them, whether it was advice on a legal career, discussion about the impact of the war and the H-Bomb, or religious feeling in England, or argument on the impact of education on the working class. We were impressed by his memory for names, his ability at dinner in hall or at the Union to make everyone relax, his interest in our attitudes to the administration, his readiness to discuss with different students means of getting into Oxford or into Chambers in England, and his willingness to offer his help when he thought it would be of use.

Mr Sparrow has made an impact on many students whom he has met which they will not easily forget, and we hope that he will fulfil his desire to return to the UCWI and the West Indies some time in the not too distant future. We say thank you and *au revoir* to a most interesting and stimulating man.

The visit to Codrington College was equally successful. Anselm Genders wrote to John on 3 April 1959:

My dear Warden,

It was very good indeed to have your letter, and to know that you thought well of this College and its rather mixed bag of inhabitants. The open-air service in Messiah-street followed by kitchen cocoa is a far cry from All Souls SCR! I did not have any doubt, while you were here, that you were evidently enjoying it.

In the post there are some photographs of you and me, which young Bernard Hodge so relentlessly took. It appears that you are more photogenic.

We are most grateful indeed for the generous grant voted by your College, and it will be a great help. Will you please, at your next meeting, convey our warmest thanks to the Fellows? Your letter came just before term ended, and I mentioned the general contents of it to the students, who received it with enthusiasm. And of course I speak also for the Brethren of the Community.

How young John still looks in the photographs, and how his success with everyone on this West Indian tour echoes his success with soldiers of every rank on his wartime morale tours. In both cases his attention was focused on what really engaged his attention – people.

John's letters written during the fifties – particularly those to Colin – are full of comments on his daily life. In May 1953 he reported that he was taking both Italian and driving lessons. There must have been some confusion since he became a good 'Italian' driver, but learnt little Italian. Somehow he passed his driving test and acquired a car, but the basic skills evaded him. Stuart Hampshire wrote: 'I remember being driven by John, terrifyingly, to the Bear in Woodstock for a celebration lunch . . . John was among the worst drivers of a car I have known . . . He had very little experience of fear and regretted missing the opportunity in the war.' In the same year he also sat for Derek Hill for the first of four portraits by that painter: 'and the resulting sketch (just like me, I think, very fierce and worried) glares at me from the bookcase.' And he liked to report the occasional joke:

At the Club [a historic London dining club]:-
    Lord X (justifying good humouredly the Government's attitude to commercial TV): 'After all, we *are* "the stupid party".'
    JS: 'Yes, but need we prove it so often?'

Following John's letter of February 1940 commending William Plomer on his editing of Francis Kilvert's diary, a lively correspondence was sparked off between the two men which continued for years. Plomer's letters were extremely amusing, and he would search out absurd picture postcards to which he added bizarre captions. John enjoyed his wit and admired his poetry; he and Colin visited Plomer in Sussex in June 1954. Shortly afterwards John wrote to Colin explaining that he had taken so long to write the introduction to the book on Robert Bridges because he could think of nothing to say.

He was a little hard on himself. Between 1952 and 1959 he published fifty-eight essays, reviews and letters, not forgetting three memorable accounts of football matches for the *Observer*, each featuring Wolves. His long reports show a sure grasp of the game.

In 1952 he published with his friend, the distinguished bibliographer, John Carter, 'an annotated Hand-list' of A. E. Housman's work, which appeared as the second volume in the series, the Soho Bibliographies. Amidst the cut and thrust of literary debate there were letters to *The Times* about the Oxford Road Scheme, on telephone tapping, and cruelty to animals. John was sharpening his knife for bigger controversies that lay ahead. His interest in Latin verse and inscriptions continued, and in 1958 he published privately *Lapidaria Quarta*, his fourth volume of Latin inscriptions. In various articles and reviews his interest in English poetry ranged from Donne to Ralph Hodgson and John Betjeman.

In 1960, probably through Geoffrey Faber, a senior fellow of All Souls, Faber & Faber asked John if he would consider the publication of a collection of his essays. John wrote to Harold Nicolson in June 1960, asking if he thought that such a collection 'would make a book'. The answer must have been favourable, and *Independent Essays* was published in 1963.

VIII

THE WARDEN

1963–77

Infirmity of purpose.
*The Franks Commission report
on All Souls College*

IT WAS during the sixties that John Sparrow faced the gravest problem of his wardenship. In what has become known as the 'All Souls crisis', the academic purpose of the college and its future, in addition to its finances, came under the scrutiny not only of the Fellows, but also of the university as a whole and, to some extent, through the media, of the world at large. The *club* that was the essence of the college to John Sparrow was threatened with extinction, to be replaced by academic reforms which he found wholly unsympathetic, even abhorrent.

In all that followed it is easy to criticize John, even to accuse him of dishonesty with his colleagues and the authorities – notably the university's Franks Commission – but it should be allowed that he was fighting for something he genuinely believed in, even if his belief was tarnished by a certain selfishness. He was the most conservative of men, subscribing to Lord Eldon's statement that 'any change, for any reason, is to be deprecated'. I discussed this attitude with him towards the end of his life, and he confirmed that he had a deep-seated mistrust of change. So often the results were undesirable, and worse, irrevocable. This belief may have been wrong, but it was sincerely held.

By 1963 John had been Warden of All Souls for twelve years. It is difficult to gauge his popularity in the college at that time. He was certainly liked by the 'London Fellows', for he and they were in agreement about the college. At the other end of the scale, he was disliked, or at least mistrusted, by some of the younger Fellows, who were eager for change and saw his innate conservatism as an obstruction to even their most modest ambitions for reform. And the Academic Fellows as a whole were hurt by his lack of interest in their studies, though many of them continued to enjoy his company and his wit as a dining companion. There were also some whom John openly disliked, and treated badly. He never learned that the head of a college, or any other organization, could not enjoy the personal luxury of displaying likes and dislikes. Even-handedness was not something that John understood.

The All Souls crisis lasted for three years, from 1963 to 1965, though its origins went back much further, and the results are still working themselves out. It struck at the fundamental purpose of All Souls, and opinions were sharply divided within the college. Thirty years later it is difficult to obtain a balanced account of all that took place during the long debate, even from those who took part. The events were complicated, created by a network of college meetings and, no doubt, by an even more complicated mesh of private meetings. The pro- and anti-Sparrow factions have different stories to tell, and the biographer, who was not present, must do his best to assemble the truth.

There are two differing accounts of what went on in All Souls during those troubled years. The first is the published account by David Caute – an involved eyewitness – *Crisis in All Souls*, which appeared in the March 1966 issue of *Encounter*, shortly after he had resigned his fellowship of All Souls in despair at the conduct of the college business. I once asked a senior and fair-minded fellow of the college how accurate he considered Caute's account. He thought for a moment and replied, 'It represents the hot end of the debate.' One might be forgiven for thinking that the nature of the debate justified a good deal of heat.

The other, unpublished, account was written by Charles Wenden, who became the first full-time joint Bursar (combining the former duties held by separate Fellows as Estates Bursar and Domestic Bursar) in 1970, a post he held until 1990. He had been Bursar of St Catherine's College since its foundation, and had worked to establish the college with Alan Bullock (later Lord Bullock). John Sparrow made two excellent professional appointments: Wenden he engaged in effect as the administrator of All Souls; John Simmons as the first professional Librarian of the Codrington – precedents which were not maintained.

Wenden became interested in the history of All Souls, and had access to all its archives and business papers. Following his researches, after his retirement in 1991 he gave four lectures on the college; the fourth was largely devoted to the finances of All Souls since the Second World War. I had a long talk with Wenden, at which time he gave me the text of his fourth lecture, saying that I could make what use of it I wished, with the proviso that I did not show it to John Sparrow, then still alive. I did not meet Wenden again as he died suddenly in 1992.

It is a long document, but I have decided to quote from it at length, for it is essential background reading for anyone who wishes to understand the intricacies – many of them financial – of the All Souls crisis. It also gives an objective account of what happened, and objectivity is a rare commodity in this episode of Oxford history. And it makes a good background to the more personal account of David Caute, which I will come to later. Let Wenden speak first:

In assessing the post-war story my first observation is the extent to which John Sparrow was a dominant personality, Warden from 1952–77, a significant figure before then, and a stimulating dinner companion for many years thereafter. It is difficult to sum up John's role, for good and occasionally for less good. An artist *manqué*, he read Greats and practised at the Chancery Bar, but he was essentially a cultivated man of letters, and above all a talker of subtle wit and charm. Almost invariably, he preferred the past to the present (and certainly to the future), men to women, and clever men to mere scholarly men. In College meetings, he would rather conduct business than reach decisions and tried to perpetuate a concept of the College that was slowly becoming *ancien régime*. He was responsible for part of the partially justified Franks condemnation of All Souls 'Infirmity of purpose'. But he was also responsible for a style of living that was civilised, generous and humane, especially in the late 1960s when academics with those qualities seemed an endangered species. Nobody examining the history of All Souls since 1945 can ignore the Sparrow factor.

John, however, had comparatively little impact on its finances. Perhaps he did not *want* the College to prosper unduly since additional money might force change. He agreed with Kingsley

Amis's dictum that 'more means worse'. He practised what he preached. I can give two examples. The Warden's stipend remained unchanged from a comfortable level in 1956 to an excessively modest figure in 1962. In the 1960s a female of the very rare species, a would-be benefactress appeared, Miss Wentworth Kelly. She expressed a wish to leave all her money to All Souls, since her hero T. E. Lawrence had been a Fellow of the College. John hastened to point out that T.E. had an earlier and stronger attachment to Jesus College. Miss Kelly showed interest. John suggested that the money ought to be shared with Jesus. To strengthen his point his point he added 'And Jesus, unlike All Souls, is a poor College.' To which Miss Kelly replied 'In that case I shall leave it all to All Souls.' Inevitably, John did manage to restrain her urge to reinforce success and persuade Miss K. to divide her inheritance between the two Colleges. Happily she is still with us and the will remains unconsummated.

College finances were guided by the [Estate] Bursars. The long reign of Geoffrey Faber lasted from 1923 to 1950. A succession of Estate Bursars followed until I was appointed the first contemporary full-time All Souls joint Bursar in 1970. I was relieved of my duties in January this year [1991] . . .

By the twentieth century All Souls was regarded as a wealthy College, both absolutely and in relation to its commitments. The College was and is wealthy, but alas not on the scale portrayed in academic folklore. But having been for many years the Oxford College with the third largest endowment income, in 1987–8 it moved ahead to record the highest net endowment income available for College purposes and repeated that last year, £2·463m compared with £2·276m for Christ Church and £1·977m for St John's. All Oxford income figures, however, are dwarfed by Trinity and King's in Cambridge. Uniquely, we were also the largest contributor to the College Contributions Fund, paying £183,000 compared with £176,000 and £168,000. This compulsory levy to the inter-collegiate system is now augmented by our voluntary contribution to the University Appeal by paying the stipends of three Professors, for the Director of the Institute of Theoretical Sciences and a Lecturer in Human Demography, a total gift of £150,000 a year, which will rise as stipends, superannuation, etc., increase. This produces a total transfer of £180,000 + £150,000 + £330,000 p.a., 14% of the College's net income. Among Oxbridge colleges, All Souls has no commitment to house and teach students, receives no fees, no income from conferences and has an appreciably smaller turnover. Endowment income that is not matched by unavoidable expenditure is free income and provides a good, but not precise, measure of a college's wealth. By that measure, All Souls is rich, although not as rich as some legends suggesting that the All Souls Bursar can walk on College land from Oxford to Cambridge ...

The College emerged from the [Second World] war with little bomb damage to its property, with agriculture revived, but with a regime of restrictions on urban and agricultural rents. Gross Endowment Revenue for 1945 was £75,947, 16% up on 1938. Unfortunately the Retail Price Index had risen by 48%. This total of £76,000 compares with £3·4m in 1988–9, a *thirty-nine-fold* increase compared with a less than seventeen-fold rise in the Retail Price Index. Of the £76,000, 30% came from farmland, 60% from urban property (mainly ground rents on housing), and 8% on interest and dividends. In 1988–9 however, urban estates produced 13.3%, farm rents 24% and interest and dividends 60% of gross income. The net figures have changed even more since interest and dividends cost little to manage compared with expenses of managing and maintaining property ...

Expenditure on Fellows in 1945 was £4,514, less than the £19,247 given to good causes and the University, the latter receiving £18,125. The Fellows received only twice as much as the Head of House, £2,318. The picture is one of a College whose real income has been severely eroded, with a depleted academic body, even from the comparatively modest level in 1938. The College faced a backlog of maintenance and repairs on its Oxford and other properties. Its multitude of leasehold rents were at fixed figures for 99 year agreements ... In 1946 the Bursar uttered the first of several warnings repeated over the next fifteen years, that 'today we cannot anticipate any large future additions to our income' ...

By the early 1950s the pessimism, national and College, was receding. The Tories were back in power. In March 1955, spurred on by John Foster*, the best-natured of all Bursarial scourges, the College made its first investment in equities, now that the definition of Trustee Stocks had been loosened. Soon £150,000 out of about £500,000 General Endowment cash and securities was committed to the market . . . Dividends and Interest yielded £6,000 in 1945, £48,000 by 1960, £125,000 in 1970, £490,000 in 1980 and over £2m in 1988–9, bounding well ahead of the rise in the cost of living, and producing a twentyfold increase in real terms. The process was helped in 1957 when the dreaded Town and Country Planning Act, that for a brief moment threatened the end of capital gains from the sale of land for building, gave All Souls compensation of nearly £550,000 . . .

A few years later even a modest growth in income was larger than the College chose to spend. In March 1959 John Hicks† called attention to the rising affluence and suggested that the College should use the money to support research and help the university. The famous, or infamous, College Committee on the Surplus, chastised in the Franks Report, was established. The name was ill-chosen and invited unmerited hostility. However, the choice can be explained. The College had traditionally operated its finances on the basis that after collecting a Gross Revenue, the cost in taxes, capital investment and management was deducted to produce a Net Income. Against this were then offset the cost of the known commitments of the College buildings and services (including the Library), and obligations to the University. Under the old system the residue, known as the surplus, was available for new ventures selected by the Governing Body. This was a relic of the pre-1877 financial arrangements when the surplus was the dividend to be distributed among the Fellows as their remuneration. But after Fellows moved to fixed stipends the surplus was available, not as a dividend to be split between the Fellows, but as a resource for new activities. In 1960 it was still called a surplus and the Committee to examine its use was

* Sir John Foster, KBE,QC, (1904–82). Educated at Eton and New College. Prize Fellow, All Souls 1924. Successful Common Law practice, becoming Recorder of Dudley in 1936. Conservative member for Northwich, Cheshire 1945–74. He remained a Fellow of All Souls throughout his life.
† Sir John Hicks, (1904–89). Educated Clifton College and Balliol. Fellow of All Souls 1952. Drummond Professor of Political Economy, Oxford 1952–65.

called a Committee on the Surplus, not a Planning Committee, for All Souls in the 1960s. The name and the College's perplexity aroused the curiosity of the Franks Committee, including that of Maurice Shock, then Bursar of University College, who had seen his proposal in 1961 for the richer colleges to help the poorer colleges rejected by All Souls.

But even before the Franks Committee met, the College began to take cautious action to use the surplus creatively. This caution, easy to criticise now, was understandable in the early 1960s, when the disruption of the war and the agony of the immediate post-war crisis were close. No one could foresee the world-wide economic boom that began in the mid-1950s and has continued for over thirty years, the most spectacular expansion of wealth in human history, or have envisaged that if such an expansion should come, Britain would share in, rather than be destroyed by it. In June 1961 it was decided to recruit more Senior Research Fellows ... In 1961 the College agreed to increase its already substantial payments to the University for Chairs, Readerships, the Bodleian Library, the Extra Mural Delegacy and the Common University Fund. Almost £59,000 (39% of its net income) was given or taken away in 1965. It promised substantial grants to new graduate societies (St Cross, Linacre and Iffley), £58,000 in all and £30,000 over six years to St Antony's. For the moment, the College offered the surplus to others in greater need. But they asked the Committee on the Surplus and the College Harrison Committee [for the election of additional fellows] to consider a more coherent strategy for the 1960s and 70s ...

Three plans were discussed initially. They were to elect further Harrison [entitled] Fellows; to contribute to a new graduate college; to help existing graduate societies.

In March 1964 the College 'expressed itself as favouring' grants to St Antony's, and also to other graduate institutions; and, subject to that, of electing six to eight more Research Fellows in the next three to four years; and finally, of putting up a building for College purposes on a site in the College. The first priority was to help St Antony's by supporting Research Fellowships. Within two months, however, another idea had emerged. In May 1964, Warden Sparrow queried the decision to elect more Research Fellows, which he thought would not win the approval of the Franks* Commission. He supported the idea of enrolling graduate students. To the Vice-Chancellor, Kenneth Wheare†, he wrote enquiring, 'Would All Souls help the University more by taking up to thirty graduate students, or by simply continuing or expanding its existing, traditional activities?' [Elsewhere, John talked of 'not less than twenty, and not more than thirty.'] The Vice-Chancellor replied, 'If All Souls could do something for graduate students it would not only help the University, but would help it more than by devoting the whole of its surplus to the expansion of its existing, traditional activities.' He also suggested other possible directions in which All Souls might contribute, should it find itself unable to adopt a graduate scheme. These were, to help fund a new building for the newly emerging St Cross Society, or an extension for the Radcliffe Science Library, or the provision of an Arts Faculty Building in Merton Street. The University although not exactly encouraging All Souls to be infirm was not helping a body chaired by John Sparrow to be prompt and decisive. The College's Harrison Committee raised Warden Sparrow's proposed number to not less than thirty, and added that they should be confined to the Humanities; that a hostel should be built; and that meals other than breakfast should be taken in All Souls. Graduates were creeping nearer to the heart of the College. In November 1964 no vote was taken since no costings were available but Fellows urged that any graduate scheme should be at least as good as those of Nuffield and St Antony's; and that, given the Vice-Chancellor's letter, such a scheme was 'the least that the College could do'; and that the Vice-Chancellor's

---

* Oliver (Lord) Franks, GCMG, (1905–92). Educated Bristol Grammar School and Worcester College, Oxford. He held many important academic, civil service and diplomatic posts: Permanent Secretary, Ministry of Supply 1945; Provost of Queen's College, Oxford; British Ambassador at Washington 1948; Provost of Worcester College. Chairman of the Commission of Inquiry into Oxford University, which proved such a thorn in the side of All Souls, demanding an account of finances and its use of its wealth. JS thought Franks a cold bureaucrat.

† Sir Kenneth Wheare, CMG, (1907–79). Educated at Scotch College, Melbourne, Melbourne University, and Rhodes scholar at Oriel 1929. Gladstone Professor of government and public administration, and Fellow of All Souls 1944. Rector of Exeter College 1956–72. Chancellor Liverpool University 1972.

alternatives should be rejected since they risked All Souls becoming the 'milch cow' of Oxford.

By this time All Souls had already committed itself to a programme of electing Research Fellows, had taken its three Harrison entitled Fellows, was pledged to pay £5,000 p.a. for ten years to the University for new graduate institutions, and £6,000 p.a. for five years to St Antony's. It was weaving an academic robe of many colours. Given these commitments, the Estates Bursar, Harry Fisher*, estimated that after paying for a hostel, the College could think in terms of having only £10,000 p.a. available for a graduate scheme. He added, plaintively, 'but I do not think that the College would be believed if it says that it cannot afford a graduate scheme'.

The College was deeply divided. In January 1965 fly sheets were circulated by different groups of Fellows. Southern† and Berlin signed a paper which declared that, given the expected expansion of graduates in the University from about 1,800 to twice that figure, the suggestion of thirty graduates at All Souls would make the College look ridiculous. On the other hand, accepting that a hostel for ninety or more would exceed the available means, they favoured 'complete union with St Antony's', one College with 67 Fellows and 110 graduates. A desperate remedy like Britain's offer of complete union with France in 1940.

Thirteen academic Fellows signed a circular a few days later advocating more Research Fellows. The Estates Bursar and another non-academic Fellow sent round a paper urging the College to invite applications from prospective graduate members without waiting to learn the ultimate numbers to be admitted, or for information respecting the site and scale of a hostel.

On 26th January, 1965, the College Harrison Committee, by 9 votes to 2 with one abstention, recommended that a declar-

---

* Hon. Sir Henry Fisher. Educated at Marlborough and Christ Church. Fellow of All Souls 1946; Estates Bursar and Sub-Warden 1965–67. Judge of the High Court of Justice 1968–70.
† Richard Southern. Educated at Royal Grammar School, Newcastle upon Tyne, Balliol. Chichele Professor of Modern History, Oxford 1961–69, and Fellow of All Souls. President of St John's College, Oxford 1969.

ation of intent be made to the Franks Commission in early February. Endorsed by the College by 31 votes for and 15 against (with two abstentions), the message was: 'The College recognises the increased importance of graduate studies in the University, and it is College policy to play a part in the development and support of graduate work. We propose to incorporate graduate students, *in one way or another*, in our College body, without delay.'

The College set up *two* working parties to explore the possibilities of implementing a graduate programme in co-operation with one or another College partner. They laboured under uncertainty both about available funds for, and the actual costs of, a graduate scheme, and especially about the possibility of All Souls making subventions to its graduates. This question was seen as very much affecting the type of intake the College might attract: without subventions, Oxford graduates might not be prepared to leave their undergraduate colleges, and the possibility of a selective intake would be undermined. They did not consider that if subventions were given Colleges might resent the poaching. The Estates Bursar's financial feet were rapidly becoming somewhat colder.

By the end of May, St Antony's, like France in 1940, had rejected the plan for total union. Nonetheless, the Committee urged that All Souls should press on and admit at least ten graduates in October, 1966, and not wait for the erection of a building. The College, less sanguine, decided by a large majority in June, not to admit any graduates before October 1967 and not to announce its decision to do so at this juncture. At this stage, it appeared that St Antony's hoped that All Souls might contribute £250,000 towards a new building on a St Antony's site, and would offer subventions to its graduates matching those offered by St Antony's, at a cost of not less than £14,000 p.a. The Estates Bursar, a vigorous advocate of a graduate scheme, reported 'It is not certain that All Souls can afford at present to build (either alone or in conjunction with another College) a hall of residence.' He feared that a joint scheme with St Antony's might lead to All Souls graduates becoming integrated with *that* College rather than with All Souls (and perhaps he recognised that for some in All Souls that would have been a not altogether unwelcome development). It was beginning to be appreciated that graduates might have wives, and that graduates and wives might between them produce children, a further complication. Most seriously of all, he suggested that to finance a graduate scheme, All Souls might have to cut back on other expenditures.

On June 19th, the Harrison Committee jammed on the brakes. A building scheme with Hertford, and parallel negotiations with Wadham, should be discontinued. The St Antony's scheme still had advocates, but neither it nor the prospect of another possible venture with Corpus, was likely to command a majority of the Committee. A final decision was put off until the Michaelmas Term.

During the summer vacation a completely new horse came up fast on the rails. An idea was put to Warden Sparrow who was, as always, considerate, encouraging, and cautious. He showed consummate skill, even joy, in keeping a variety of balls in the air. The new entrant was initially called a scheme for Associate Fellows, later to become Visiting Fellows. At meetings in October and November (All Souls even with half of its Fellows resident in London was now in almost permanent session) it became apparent that a revised scheme with St Antony's still required £50,000 more than the Estates Bursar thought could be afforded. The project with Corpus lacked a vigorous advocate. Not without acrimony, it was decided that the College should consider a Visiting Fellowships programme as its major objective and abandon graduate students.

In late November, the College rescinded its decision to admit graduate students. A large majority of the College had come to realise that All Souls was not likely to handle graduates effectively. It lacked adequate accommodation in College: there were no spare rooms, and the existing common rooms, dining facilities, and recreational areas were very limited. Its financial resources, though greater than its immediate needs, were insufficient to pay for a hostel, its upkeep, and grants to graduate students. Without such grants, All Souls would be offering less than Nuffield and St Antony's. Most academic Fellows wanted to concentrate on their own research. Those who were interested in supervising graduates were already doing so. The only benefit All Souls would be making to the University would be in the provision of a hostel, and perhaps not a very good one. The majority of Fellows engaged in graduate teaching opposed the scheme. Its strongest supporters were precisely those – three professors excepted – who might do least to make it a success. Of the 22 votes eventually cast in favour of graduates, 10 came from the eleven Prize Fellows, and a further 8 from the seventeen non-academic Fellows . . .

The College endorsed by 35 votes to 22 a Visiting Fellows operation. There was a genuine need to provide a base in Oxford for overseas scholars. All Souls could offer a social base with studies next to Bodley. Academics in other British universities would welcome sabbatical leave in Oxford. The College would be expanding traditional activities that it understood. The scheme would be flexible, and could be readily adjusted to any change in resources. A site at Beechwood House in Iffley was available for housing, and on that site ten flats were erected. (A house in Crick Road was bought subsequently for larger families.) The tale has a happy ending.

The Visiting Fellowship scheme has become an integral part of All Souls and Oxford life. It has introduced a wider range of disciplines to the College – from Oriental Antiquities to Crystallography and Engineering – but at the same time it has reinvigorated and reinforced the College's traditional concerns in history and law. It has opened up the social life of All Souls. Since the war, All Souls has played a less significant part in the nation's political life: it has become more clearly an academic institution, as a centre of research and as a venue for seminars and lectures. The Visiting Fellowships have been a not unimportant part of that process.

The Franks Commission was not impressed by the College's sudden conversation to the joys of Visiting Fellows while more than half way on the road to Damascus of graduate students. It coined a memorable phrase 'infirmity of purpose'. The phrase was an echo from Shakespeare. I like to think of Lord Franks, while contemplating the report he had to write, casting John Sparrow as Macbeth:

'I'll go no more. I am afraid to think what I have done.

Look on't again, I dare not.'

And Franks, as Lady Macbeth, replying:

'Infirm of purpose. Give me the daggers.' ...

Infirmity of purpose was not the only crime laid by the Franks Commission at the gate of All Souls. Others were:

(1) The dilution of the Governing Body by voting Fellows from outside the academic community. This criticism was rejected and the College and, in some ways the University, continues to benefit from these links with the outside world ...

(2) Failure to maximise its income and accepting a low return on its assets.

(3) Raising an inadequate income, and then being too ready to give some of it away to other institutions, rather than putting it to work within the College.

(4) Its high level of domestic expenditure. As a bursar arriving in 1970 from another College, rated as one of the poorest, I found then, and still find now, this criticism difficult to understand. The one College feast, the Chichele Dinner, did not appear until 1961. It was not until 1953 that Fellows ceased to pay a College window cleaning charge; and several other similar levies, including a charge for every sheet of College writing paper used, lasted until 1970 long after they had vanished, if they ever existed, in other colleges. The College's grandest occasion, the Encaenia Lunch, is produced and offered by the College, to University Honorands, Officials, Heads of Houses and their wives. Fellows pay a substantial price for their own guests. In this, as in some other areas, All Souls may have been and may still be guilty of hiding its candle under a bushel.

Reeling under the internal and external turbulence, the College began to move closer to the University and to respond to criticism. It accepted the new College Contributions arrangements that augmented the endowments of poorer colleges, and welcomed the University decision to take over the whole burden of Chairs and Readerships, so long funded by All Souls. Acting on Franks' advice, All Souls gave away less of its income to outside bodies. But in recent years, All Souls has understood the current dilemma of the less well-endowed Colleges and, along with Merton, took a lead in a second large programme of Endowment Grants under the College Contribution Committee ...

The College has regularly re-examined the make-up of its Fellowship body. Traditionally, an Arts College with special interest in Law and History, the number of subjects in which Prize Fellowships are offered has been increased. The vigorous growth in Oxford's scientific faculties since 1950 has not passed unnoticed. All Souls debated the College's attitude to science in 1956. In 1958 it elected the geneticist Edmund Ford to an Extraordinary Research Fellowship. The College has, I think understandably, jibbed at attempting to build up a scientific presence equal to that in the Arts – . . . The Visiting Fellowship Scheme has given the College an alternative avenue for its limited scientific ambitions and numerous elections have been made. Research Fellowships have been taken up by a Mathematical Logician, an Astrophysicist and now we have a small group of Mathematicians. At some stage the College may wish to consider the role science should play in any future expansion . . .

I must close this cursory glance back at College developments since 1945. There is much more work to be done, much more could be recounted even from the investigations I have made. My final summary is to say that I see the College story thus. In the early post-war years an attempt was made to reinstate the pre-1939 pattern in a society that had changed substantially during the war, when money was tight and the labour supply even tighter. In the Fifties and early Sixties we enjoyed a move to comparative affluence and recovery of style under Warden Sparrow. By this time many of the grand figures of the old College had gone: Amery, Bridges, Dawson, Faber, Halifax, Simon, Henderson and Sumner. The way was open for a new image of All Souls. The Franks investigation stimulated a re-assessment of its role, ending with the decision to elect Visiting Fellows, emphasising All Souls' increasing commitment to research, predominantly in the Arts. This commitment was under-lined in the following twenty years and was accompanied by a much greater participation by College Fellows in the academic and administrative life of the University . . . In the year 2001 the cir-cumnavigation of the College roofs in search of a mythical mallard should be made by a greatly augmented body of Fellows.*

---

* Every hundred years (next in 2001) the Fellows of All Souls at night clamber over the roofs of the college, singing the doggerel verse of the Mallard Song, in search of a mythical duck, for centuries a totem of the college.

Wenden's account of the All Souls crisis leans more heavily on figures than on people. He avoided personalities almost entirely, and there is little hint of the strife, often bitter, at abortive committee meetings. Of course, he had not witnessed the events, nor felt the heat of the conflict. Beyond that, when he wrote this public lecture, he had very recently ceased to be a Fellow of All Souls, and one of its most important officers. His loyalty to the college was strong, and his interpretation of the college's finances tended to cast a favourable light on them. He saw *generosity* to other needy Oxford institutions, where others saw a 'milch cow'.

The figures are interesting since as Bursar he had an unrivalled opportunity to study them. It is true that the college's wealth sparked off the controversy that caused such internal dissension among the Fellows from 1963 to 1965, but at the time the debate concerned the development of the college, and on what new academic purpose that wealth should be spent. Charles Wenden's account is bland and uncritical. Some might view it as 'the cool end of the debate'. I have read it several times, and I have always wondered why he was so insistent that I should not show it to John Sparrow.

David Caute's extremely well-written account of the crisis, published in *Encounter*, though burning with indignation, has the ring of truth, particularly to anyone familiar with John's intransigence when he wished to get his own way. Caute was a Prize Fellow in 1959, and therefore quite a junior member of the college when the crisis broke out in 1963. He was strongly left wing and, throughout the debate, one of the leaders among the younger Fellows demanding radical changes in the academic structure of All Souls. He opposed the dominance of the non-academic Fellows and supported the move to introduce graduate students into the college. Everything that John favoured, or seemed momentarily to favour, must have been anathema to Caute and all those Fellows who shared his opinions.

The progress of the crisis was complicated, but the starting point was John's reluctance to admit any change to the college, even if this required, as Wenden points out, giving away All Souls' surplus income. But the times were against him. Reform was in the Oxford air, and deliberate charity was no longer accepted as an excuse for inertia. Reforms had to be made, but whatever reforms were introduced should be allowed to disturb the college as little as possible.

The college was divided. Some Fellows, particularly the older ones, were in agreement with John, willing to support only those changes which would not disrupt their familiar routine. Another faction was more willing to compromise with the general demands of the university. And then there were the more radical fellows who saw this as the moment to introduce fundamental changes to the nature of the college.

Suggested reforms evolved gradually, from the appointment of more Research Fellows – harmless enough if men of suitable intellectual stature could be agreed upon – to the introduction of some thirty graduate students into the college. The number tended to vary according to the Warden's preferred scheme at any given moment. The admission of more Research Fellows *and* graduate students would present an acute problem of accommodation in a college where the existing sixty Fellows amply filled all private and social facilities.

It was then resolved that new accommodation for the additional Research Fellows should be provided in a building to be erected on the east side of the Warden's garden. This was agreed, though according to Caute, John reminded the meeting that the Warden had the legal right to object to a building within the bounds of the lodgings. Nevertheless plans did go ahead. The first architect's plans were rejected, but new ones were commissioned. Although the project was abandoned, Caute maintains that the resolution was never annulled.

John confounded his enemies, within and without the college, mainly through delaying tactics which allowed enthusiasm to cool and majorities to wither away. He was, in his own way, courageous in such affairs, and though he must have been genuinely worried that undesirable changes would be forced on him, particularly by the University Commission headed by Lord Franks, he kept all at bay with a useful Machiavellian skill which he had honed at the Chancery Bar. If on certain occasions he appeared to manipulate the truth, he would no doubt have replied that all is fair in love and war, particularly a war to preserve the integrity of All Souls.

Extra research fellows, a building in his garden, and a growing enthusiasm for the admission of graduate students – John must have found all these proposals equally unsympathetic, but in June 1964 he seemed to favour the graduate scheme, no doubt trying to draw away support from the other projects and even hoping that enthusiasm for the graduates would fade. He misjudged the situation. By the autumn support for the scheme had increased.

He fell back on procrastination, a process facilitated by the infrequency of even important committee meetings – meetings that sometimes got no further than electing a sub-committee to look into what to others might have seemed urgent business. There was no doubt that the graduate scheme raised many practical difficulties, and John played for time by making the most of these.

John was not only withstanding pressures from within the college, but also those from the university. He had written to the Vice-Chancellor asking how the college could best help the university. The Vice-Chancellor replied that an intake of graduate students would be helpful, and that anything would be better than All Souls continuing to expand its 'traditional activities'. Worse, the college was due to appear before the Franks Commission in February 1965 to make its intentions plain. Conservative members of the college were worried, their only consolation being that All Souls had managed to escape the interference of previous commissions as far back as the Royal Commission of 1852 and, more recently, of a Royal Commission of 1922. The meeting with the Commission on 11 February was an uncomfortable one for the representatives of the college, the overall criticism being that it had 'the appearance of exclusiveness of a club'. John wrote after the meeting, 'Our treatment at the hands of the Commission would have been very different had the policy decision taken at our meeting of 30th January been other than what it was.' At that meeting it was resolved by 31 votes to 15 'to incorporate graduate students in one way or another, in our College body without delay'.

One answer to the problem of housing a significant number of graduates in All Souls was to form an alliance with an existing graduate college which could provide certain facilities, and had experience of integrating graduate students with a senior common room. Negotiations started with St Antony's, which had already proved its success as a graduate college and, equally important, had land where a new building, funded by All Souls, could be built. But the passing of time again changed the weight of opinion in All Souls, and on 6 November 1965 the college voted by 35 to 22 against the graduate scheme; those who had supported it with such enthusiasm saw that it was dead. David Caute resigned his fellowship.

However, John realized that the Franks Commission must be offered another project in place of the graduate scheme. This was the Visiting Fellows scheme which, for the Warden, was certainly a lesser evil. The scheme was adopted, possibly with a general sigh of relief. A handsome eighteenth-century house was bought at Iffley, and an ugly block of flats built in the grounds. Another block of flats was built in Crick Road.

The Visiting Fellows scheme was a compromise: according to A. L. Rowse, it had been promoted by Bryan Wilson, a sociologist and Research Fellow, who apparently advised John Sparrow on such academic matters. No doubt several Fellows welcomed the scheme as a means to extend the facilities of Oxford to serious academics from around the world. Some Fellows embraced it as an alternative to the threatened incursion of a number of Research Fellows, the disruption of a new building within the college or, worse, the invasion of some thirty graduate students into their quiet lives. One or two of these Fellows have confessed to me in confidence that while they went along with the Visiting Fellows scheme, privately they thought it a dilution of the true purposes of the college. John put a brave face on it, for at least it freed him from the future attentions of the Franks Commission and the university authorities. He had no desire for any change, but at least the Visiting Fellows meant that he was no longer threatened by a building in his garden or by the many problems posed by the graduate student scheme. Moreover John could, from time to time, get old friends elected Visiting Fellows, whose company he could enjoy for a year.

The Visiting Fellows scheme has now been running for a long time. There have been certain practical problems in integrating these visitors into such a tightly knit society; the acute shortage of rooms in college meant that they had to be accommodated at Beechwood House, some distance from All Souls. However, the new Sparrow building behind New College Lane has alleviated this situation. The Visiting Fellows are now a part of All Souls life, and soon there will be few Fellows left who lived through the fierce debate from which the scheme sprang.

It is difficult for an outsider to express an informed opinion on the daily life of All Souls. However, during my researches in Oxford for this book, All Souls kindly allowed me to stay at Beechwood House. I have met a wide range of Visiting Fellows at the communal breakfast table, and not only were they extremely interesting men and women; it was obvious that their studies were benefiting from their stay in Oxford.

21. John visiting Codrington College, Barbados, in 1959

22. A more raffish Warden (one of John's favourite photographs)

23. The book-collector relaxing among a collection of Victorian poetry

31. John Betjeman

32. John with Edward Hussey

33. The last visit to Venice in 1985

34. John's last days at Beechwood House

Throughout the crisis John must have suffered great anxiety as he saw All Souls threatened with change of one undesirable kind or another; early on he must have realized that he could not maintain the status quo. During most crises in his life he discussed his predicament in letters to friends. I have not found a single letter from him discussing the threatened changes at All Souls. Perhaps he was so absorbed by the inner politics of the college that he had no energy left to discuss them with friends outside.

However, in private, he sometimes expressed strong disapproval of changes in college life. Not long before his retirement he invited me to dine and stay the night at the lodgings. When I arrived, he was flustered.

'I've made a stupid mistake,' he said. 'I've asked you to dine on one of our ladies' nights.' These had been recently introduced.

'I don't mind,' I said. I thought it a civilized reform.

'I know you don't mind, but I do.' He went grumbling on until it was time to change for dinner.

Of course, when he chose John was capable of showing great self-restraint and great courtesy, and though the ladies who surrounded him at dinner were not particularly sparkling, he was charming to them.

I remember another small incident from that visit which highlighted John's better side. He had gone on for some time about the ladies' night, and when he glanced at the clock he said apologetically:

'I'm so sorry. You will want a wash but we must go down at seven. I have only left you five minutes, but please don't be late.'

I went to my room, where I found Paine, John's butler, tidying up my clothes. He was a pleasant man, and inevitably we fell into conversation. Suddenly, I glanced at my watch and saw that it was three minutes past seven. I made my apologies to Paine and rushed back to John's room.

'I'm terribly sorry. I'm late.'

'You're not late,' said John with a smile of understanding and forgiveness.

'But it's well after seven.'

'You are not late. You were talking to Paine. I heard every word. I only wish all my guests would talk to Paine like that.' It was clear that in John's book cordiality overrode punctuality. And no great harm was done. We arrived at the ladies' night in plenty of time.

*   *   *

Despite the concerns of the All Souls crisis John published some important books and some sixty articles between 1962 and 1968. In 1965 he faced the Franks Commission in February, was in love again, and in the autumn gave the Clark Lectures at Cambridge, 'Mark Pattison and the Idea of a University', to be published in 1967 by the Cambridge University Press. It is a short book of only 148 pages, but though I know there are some who will disagree with me, I must say that I think it is his best. John had been interested in Pattison* at least since the thirties; he mentioned his admiration in a letter to his mother of 1936. Many people knew of this interest, and some hoped that it would result in a *magnum opus* about this great nineteenth-century Oxford figure. John himself occasionally spoke of producing such a work, but unfortunately, it never came to anything. However, the loss of the hypothetical *magnum opus* should not blind one to the merits of the slim volume he did produce.

John's Clark Lectures, given in 1965, were topical in that they gave his own view of the purpose of a university education, and indirectly answered both the Franks Commission and those members of All Souls who had urged the college to accept thirty graduate students. Years before, when John was considering a life at All Souls as Estates Bursar, he had written to Warden Sumner outlining his personal philosophy of the purpose of a scholarly life at All Souls. Whether or not Sumner recognized it, John was in fact quoting Pattison's words: 'Learning is a peculiar compound of memory, imagination, scientific habit, accurate observation, all concentrated, through a prolonged period, on the analysis of the remains of literature. The result of this sustained mental endeavour is not a book, but a man.' It must be added that while Pattison's intellectual scope encompassed European learning, John, with the command of only English and Latin, was limited to the study of English seventeenth- and eighteenth-century literature, and was not equipped to identify himself with his

---

* Mark Pattison, (1813–84). Educated Oriel College. Fellow of Lincoln 1839; For some time associated with Newman and the High-Church party, but withdrew. Failed to be elected Rector of Lincoln 1851. Gave up his fellowship due to disagreements with the new Rector 1855, and devoted himself to study, partly in Germany. Elected Rector of Lincoln 1861. Wrote extremely introspective *Memoirs*. JS was fascinated by Pattison from an early age, seeing reflections of his own character and academic ambitions. He often spoke and wrote of writing a life of Pattison, but though he collected much material, the book was never even started.

hero. But Pattison did offer considerable psychological appeal to John as a sympathetic example of noble failure. His was a tragic and contradictory character: his courage was rooted in total intellectual honesty, and his loneliness sprang from an inability to articulate his emotional needs. In every aspect of his character John found traits with which he could identify, and an expression of an intellectual life which he sought to emulate. That ideal was the very antithesis of the reforming Franks Commission and the invasion of a growing body of graduate students.

All his life, John had a desire to be creative; at school a creative artist, and later a creative writer and, best of all, a poet. There was in John a creative spark: the creative writer reveals himself in *Mark Pattison*; the poet in his self-published *Grave Epigrams*. His account of Pattison's life – his early failure to be elected Rector of Lincoln College, his tortuous marriage to Emilia Strong, and his relentless introspection – is given with the skill of a gifted novelist; a strong narrative is matched by excellent characterization. There was talk some years later of reprinting the book, but it came to nothing – a pity, since it might have found a wider audience in the paperback market. I think it was John's favourite among his own books. His admiration for Mark Pattison was deep-seated, and the idea that he had conveyed something of the man's character to someone previously unfamiliar with him, afforded John particular pleasure.

Mark Pattison cropped up again around 1980, when Colin Haycraft intended to publish a new edition of Pattison's *Memoirs*, originally published in 1885, which he invited John to edit. Something went badly wrong, but there is little surviving correspondence; what does exist is unusually acerbic. Basically, two strongly opinionated men were at odds, and they appeared to quarrel increasingly about the minutiae of Pattison's life. In December 1980 Haycraft wrote a heated letter about a suggestion of John's that Pattison arrived in Oxford in a vehicle drawn by post-horses, when the original text said 'four horses'. John's editorial note was dismissed as 'absolute rubbish'. No doubt John's reply, if it exists, is equally explosive, and although the book reached an advanced proof stage, with a publication date and a British Library number, it never appeared. The proof copy remains on the file, with an introduction by John along with editorial footnotes. I did attempt to get the introduction published in a learned journal, but it came to nothing: I was not qualified to rule on the unresolved disputes between him and Hay-craft. It awaits the attention of a Pattison scholar, qualified to decide who was right and who was wrong, 'post-horses' and all.

Over the years John had collected a number of Mark Pattison's books, letters and papers. These he gave to Lincoln College, Oxford; his Samuel Parr material he gave to St John's College, Cambridge. These two collections form a memorial to two of his lifelong interests, and a reminder of the two *magna opera*, long discussed but never written.

What John did write, he wrote extremely well, but he never possessed the temperament or stamina to produce a good, long book. In athletic terms, he was essentially a sprinter, not a marathon runner. In fact he wrote no complete book after *Sense and Poetry* in 1934. All his books after that date are collections of essays, lectures and broadcast talks, or books which he edited. One cannot deny, however much one enjoys what he did write, that a man blessed with his cleverness and fine prose style could have produced at least one or two books of greater importance.

His essays, some controversial, illustrate his clear style and his sharply analytical mind. His familiarity with Latin gave his English prose strength and clarity. He was a perfectionist – to his own cost – and would agonize over a single word. He was not musical in the normal sense, but he did have an acute ear for the rhythms of prose and poetry. His writing is easy to read aloud; and it was that quality that was later to make him such a good broadcaster.

John may not have enjoyed the effort of writing, but he loved the glory of being published, either commercially or in the many charming little 'vanity publishing' items he put out himself. In old age he was defensive about his failure to publish more significant work. At that time he became untidy: a book removed from the shelf tended to end up on the floor. My first duty on arriving for my autumn stay at Beechwood House was to clear the floor and, more important, to line up the complete works of John Sparrow on a shelf by his chair. It was a long shelf and John would smile with a certain self-satisfaction.

'Are you sure you have found everything?'

'Yes, I have looked everywhere,' I assured him.

'Quite respectable, don't you think?'

I agreed.

To the end of his life, his literary inertia wrestled with this persistent hunger for publication. When I started going through his papers, he asked me to look out for anything, prose or poetry, which might be suitable for publication. The only prose work I found was the proof of Pattison's *Memoirs*. With poetry, John had been there before me and done a most thorough job. Once or twice I thought I had found an unpublished poem, only to discover that he had already included it in *Grave Epigrams*. Despite all this I do not think that John died with any unfulfilled literary ambitions. He would have given his soul to have written just one great poem, but he was realistic enough to know that he never would. For the most part he was satisfied to write essays of literary criticism, with occasional forays into literary controversy.

The fifteen essays in *Independent Essays* illustrate his range. There are straightforward critical essays – mostly book reviews – but also one lecture on 'great poetry', an essay on medieval Latin poetry, and his introduction to the poetry of John Betjeman. They are all written with a marvellous clarity. His respect for fine scholarship, as opposed to what he considered mere academic work, is evident in his praise for R. W. Chapman's* edition of *The Letters of Samuel Johnson*.

One cannot help noticing that six of the essays in the book skirt or confront head on the subject of homosexuality – essays about Oscar Wilde and A. E. Housman and Roger Casement. More direct is the review of Peter Wildeblood's *Against the Law* and a more sociological study of homosexuality, *They Stand Apart*, edited by J. Tudor Rees and H. V. Usill. John nicely called his review 'A Difficult Topic'; a great deal more 'difficult' when he discussed the two books in *The Times Literary Supplement* in 1956. In his final essay in the book he reviewed a book on the Lady Chatterley case, and Lord Radcliffe's Rede Lecture on 'Censorship'. In a note at the end of the book he says that he has decided to omit his two controversial essays about the Lady Chatterley trial published in *Encounter* in 1962, as 'their tone and treatment would have rendered them, I think, out of key with the rest of its contents'. But these two essays were included in *Controversial Essays*, along with pieces on the Warren Report, Adolf Eichmann, long-haired undergraduates, and poetic plagiarism in seventeenth-century Poland.

* Robert Chapman, CBE, (1881–1960). Educated at Dundee High School, St Andrews and Oriel College, Oxford. Worked at the Clarendon Press, a distinguished literary editor and authority on Dr Johnson.

In his controversial writing I think John most enjoyed exercising his analytical, Chancery lawyer's mind; it often made him a frightening adversary. He also enjoyed puncturing what he saw as extreme, 'phoney' liberal attitudes. That was his main purpose in attacking the verdict in the Lady Chatterley case, and the stream of eminent literary figures who attested to the book's purity and literary merits. There was another element: I once asked John if it had amused him to write so publicly about the anal intercourse between Mellors and Lady Chatterley – a practice more often associated with homosexuality. He admitted that it had, but added that he thought 'buggery' a most disgusting practice.

I do not believe that his public writings on homosexuality expressed his personal views on the subject. He might put forward a case for more liberal attitudes, rationally argued. But like many old-fashioned homosexuals, he experienced in his own life an added thrill in being on the wrong side of the law. I found amongst his papers a pamphlet issued by the Homosexual Liberation Movement. John had scrawled across the front of it, 'What an obscene document.' That probably expressed his true feelings on the 'difficult topic' more than any book review in the TLS.

John was outstanding on paper, but not always in life. In 1967 Penn, John's youngest and favourite sister, was suffering from a period of deep depression. John was obviously kind but abnormalities of the mind, even temporary ones, were beyond him; something he could not understand or cope with. I think he had a slight depressive streak in his own nature, but it was under control, and he liked well-ordered lives in others. He was to find his own Achilles' heel in the loneliness of retirement.

Lord Radcliffe had become Chancellor of Warwick University, and at his inauguration in 1967 John was given an Honorary Degree. It is clear from the Orator's opening address that John had already established a reputation which in time made him a media figure. 'Mr Chancellor, Those who believe in the conspiracy theory of society credit MR JOHN SPARROW with being an arch-organiser of that sinister, if fictitious, organisation, the Establishment. It is almost beyond belief that one who has shown so much respect for the clear vision of sheer objective fact should be a subject of so many myths.'

In 1968 Harold Nicolson died, and his sons invited John to give the memorial address. John agreed, but did not wish to make it, as they asked, a combined address for Nicolson and Vita Sackville-West, who had already died in 1962. A compromise was agreed, and John, who had become a master of such occasions, gave a brilliant address which delighted everyone. He loved deserved flattery, and as on many similar occasions, letters of congratulation poured in, all carefully preserved. Several were from people who had only the slightest acquaintance with John; it seemed that everybody wanted to know him. In his own way he had become a public figure, and public figures must accept that they belong to everyone.

That year brought another incident which showed John in a less favourable light. On 6 November Oxford's *Cherwell* magazine published an article by an undergraduate at Wadham – a deliberately vulgar attack on All Souls, with sub-headlines such as 'BUGGER, FILTHY, SLUM, and naming a number of fellows, including the Warden. It was intemperate; it was scurrilous and disgraceful, a misjudged undergraduate prank.

John had a favourite joke, which he wheeled out occasionally: 'Of course, I'm much cleverer than you.'

I would bow my head in agreement to such an obvious proposition.

'When it comes to intelligence' – John liked to separate cleverness and intelligence – 'I'm not so sure.'

I remained silent.

'But,' he said with a regretful smile, 'when it comes to common sense, you are streets ahead.'

There was some truth in this. And had John been blessed with rather more common sense, he would have totally ignored the grotesque *Cherwell* prank. The author hoped to draw blood; silence would have disappointed him.

The trouble was that John could not resist controversy, but he should have realized in this case that the 'lure' was not worth the spilling of a drop of All Souls ink. Letters flew thick and fast: he wrote a formal protest to Maurice Bowra, the Warden of Wadham. Worst of all, he entered into a correspondence with the author of the article; his second letter rejected the author's apology. All this involved a lot of hair-splitting about who was offended and to whom the apologies should be directed.

The only result of this correspondence was to prolong the affair with a sensational front page of the *Cherwell* the following week:

[217]

the headlines ran AB SILENCED IN CENSORSHIP CLAMP-DOWN, and BOWRA AIDS CO-ED BID.

Bowra had the last word. He wrote to John advising him to let the incident die a natural death, not least because the author of the article was likely to do well in his finals and had an extremely bright future. Bowra proved right in both the long and the short term. It is ironic that shortly after this fracas, John should have written in a letter to K Clark that an Oxford friend had asked, 'And how was Maurice at Christmas?' To which someone replied, 'He has given up smoking and listening.' One cannot resist adding that on occasion John could be remarkably hard of hearing. There is another story which suggests that Bowra was more *au fait* with contemporary Oxford than John. The two of them were walking late at night through the town centre, returning from some university dinner. Near the Sheldonian they passed a group of obviously gilded undergraduates, who took no notice of them.

'How sad,' observed John. 'Twenty years ago we should probably have known all of them.'

'No,' replied Maurice Bowra. 'What is sad is that twenty years ago they would have recognized us.'

Bowra had the great advantage of being in charge of an undergraduate college. In All Souls John was isolated from many of the realities of Oxford life.

Of course, the insulting letter in the *Cherwell* was only a small symptom of the attack on authority which swept through universities around the world during the sixties, though it never took a serious hold in Oxford. The walls of the Warden's lodgings were once chalked with radical and offensive graffiti – CHAIRMAN MAO ON SPARROW – MAKE HIM INTO BIRD'S NEST SOUP – and John, ever brave if unwise, harangued a student audience from his front steps. As Atticus wrote in the *Sunday Times*, 'John Sparrow is a made to measure villain for the militants.' John wrote an article in the *Listener* entitled 'Revolting Students', a pun hardly more conducive to serious debate about Oxford's problems than his remark that he loathed the long hair of modern undergraduates, since one could no longer see their necks. It was at about this time that John's right-wing stance on every subject started to become a parody of itself, helped by his transformation by the media into a pillar of the establishment. It used to remind me of Nanny in the nursery saying,

'John, if you continue to pull that face, you will get stuck with it.'
Not that John minded. He enjoyed the disguise, though he ran the
risk that people would start to laugh at him, rather than with him.

At this time John was also travelling a certain amount. In February
1968 he was in the United States, perhaps pursuing his investigation
of the Kennedy assassination and the Warren Report, about which
he wrote a number of articles. In March he stayed at the Villa I
Tatti, Florence, and in August he was in Genoa. Many of these short
journeys abroad are recorded only by the bills for air tickets from
his Oxford travel agent; no existing correspondence explains their
purpose. For example, in the autumn of 1969 he flew to Jersey, but
I have found no explanation for this visit.

Other interests of John's remain largely undocumented. When I
started going through his papers, I expected to find a vast collection
of bills for the books in his large and important library. I found very
few bills or letters from booksellers, some of whom were friends.
John never made even the simplest checklist of his library, and no
doubt his excellent memory served that purpose. However, I found
a number of bills for pictures bought by John during his wardenship
– mainly drawings and watercolours, including a large collection of
watercolours by the Scottish artist James Giles, and some by such
well-known English watercolourists as Thomas Tudor, W. Callow,
G. P. Campion, George Richmond and David Cox. He bequeathed
many of these pictures to museums.

John's life contains occasional surprises, which reveal aspects of
his character known only to his closest friends. He had a wild streak
in his nature, and a curiosity about people; these led him into some
unlikely situations which showed him at his most vulnerable and
likeable.

In the autumn of 1971 John took sabbatical leave for a term, and
in September, after staying for a few days with the Berlins at Santa
Margherita initially, went on to a villa he had rented near Lucca. It
so happened that the daughter of the owner of this property was
staying in her own villa near by. No doubt intrigued that her father's
tenant was the Warden of All Souls, she drove over the day after his
arrival to see if he had settled in. At first John was distant, determined
to assert his independence.

'Can I do anything for you?'

'No thank you.'

'How are you going to manage with shopping?'

'I shall walk to the shops.'

'It's much too far to walk. Would you like me to give you a lift twice a week?'

'No thank you. I'll rent a car.'

'Where?'

'I don't know. I'll find somewhere.'

'Forgive my asking, but do you speak Italian?'

'Well, er, no, not very much.'

'Wouldn't you at least let me help you find a car, and then you'll be independent?'

John, of necessity, thawed and accepted her offer. By the end of a week, strange as it may seem, a kind of love affair had started between them, which was to continue for some years.

John was sixty-five and already portly. She describes herself at their moment of meeting as 'young, pretty, unintellectual, female, covered in babies and happily married'. Without question, she fell in love with John. Reading their letters, I would certainly say that John loved her, which is not quite the same thing as being 'in love' with her. This might, in fact, have strengthened rather than diminished their relationship.

In describing herself, she omitted a vital element in their relationship. She had a marvellous sense of humour, which appealed to John, and must have drawn him to her. They laughed endlessly – when she was not crying on his shoulder – and played tricks on each other. Shortly before John published his collection of poems, *Grave Epigrams*, she dropped a hint that he might dedicate the book to her. When she received her copy she saw the dedication page: 'DEDICATED TO A.N. AT HER REQUEST'. When she looked more closely, she saw that John had had a special label printed to paste over the real dedication to her. They enjoyed both elaborate and simple jokes.

Their love led John into unexpected places; part of him enjoyed such surprises, particularly in the company of those he loved. I used to take him to places that were very 'un-John' – the Lions of Longleat, night clubs, *The Sound of Music* ... He hated them but couldn't refuse me.

There were also long, emotional evenings in the lodgings when she poured out her heart to John. And there were times when he was equally dependent on her, especially when she met his plane after a lonely stay somewhere. One paragraph from a letter he wrote her in November 1972 touches two sides of their close relationship: 'Thank you for the two letters – I won't say more about them than that one, the consoling one (and it was consoling), was one of the nicest, and the other (Peter Pan), was the funniest, you have ever written to me –' They consoled each other and they made each other laugh. Their love for one another continued into John's retirement but was eventually shipwrecked on the rocks of his drinking and his loss of memory.

Nineteen seventy-two was an unfortunate year for John. On 12 February he flew to New York to open the Grolier Club's anniversary exhibition of John Donne, at which he gave the address. He was to have gone on to Boston to speak to the 'Odd Volumes', another distinguished club for book-collectors, but as he was leaving the Grolier exhibition, he slipped on the staircase and wrenched his knee severely. An American specialist advised him to fly home immediately, and when he returned to Oxford he went into hospital for treatment. There was bitter disappointment among the book-collectors of Boston.

The year ended badly. Just before Christmas 'I was struck down by a horrid attack of pneumonia which kept me in bed or out of action for a month.' K and Jane Clark insisted that he came and convalesced with them in Marrakesh. Somewhat reluctantly, he went for ten days. He would probably have welcomed the holiday if K had been alone.

The remaining five years of John's wardenship offer no particular excitements, and are a kaleidoscope of fragments, some brightly coloured, others dull, but none falling into any very obvious pattern. He published some thirty articles and letters to newspapers, his *Lapidaria* series reached *Septima* in 1975, and he published *Grave Epigrams* privately in 1974. There was a continuing flow of correspondence to old and new friends: John Betjeman, K Clark, John Sutro, Cyril Radcliffe, William Plomer and Philip Larkin; letters of 1975 show that he was buying wine from Colin. In the same year he preached that well-received university sermon in St Mary's on 'The Sin of Pride', the kind of short piece he was so good at.

For many years he had been a member of the governing body of Winchester College; one of the Fellows, led by a Warden. They met several times each year to debate the policy of the college, and John, as one might expect, tried to obstruct every suggested change. As he grew older he tended to snooze and snore his way through much of the meetings. It is said that on one such occasion, when he had been snoring fortissimo, he suddenly woke, sat up straight, and said, 'Gentlemen, I do hope that I have not kept any of you awake.' And when the time came for him to retire, he applied his lawyer's mind to the college statutes, employing a clever piece of casuistry to suggest to the Bursar that he was entitled to stand for re-election. The Bursar, Ruthven Hall, was not daunted by ageing Chancery lawyers, and turned down his request.

The Fellows had a fine library, and for several years John was the Fellows' librarian, the day-to-day work done by a professional librarian. The existing correspondence between John and the librarian under him show the most unpleasant side of John's character that I have ever come across. It is obvious that the librarian – something of an empire-builder – was not John's kind of person, but John was unforgivably cold, pedantic, crushing and, most unlike him, blatantly snobbish. The younger man so obviously needed tactful guidance and support, but all he got from John was a sledgehammer. John's letters make gruesome reading, but John at his worst was intolerable.

In 1974 a new horizon opened for John. In September he received a letter from Edward H. Devi, President of the University of Chicago, inviting him to give the Sara Schaffner Lectures in social studies in the autumn of 1975. John replied that he must consult his colleagues about being absent for more than a month, and eventually his visit was arranged for March and April 1976, incorporating a few days in Princeton on the way out. Having sought the advice of Edward Shils, a leading American intellectual at Chicago University and a Fellow of Peterhouse, Cambridge, who spent part of each year in Cambridge, John devised a series of three lectures on liberty, equality and fraternity, published by Chicago in 1977 under the title, *Too Much of a Good Thing*. The lectures were clever and amusing, a blend that John could manage so well, and they were a great success. So was his entire visit. He was fêted by the university, and by Chicago's intelligentsia. There were seminars and one or two minor lectures on the side, interspersed with large lunch and dinner parties, concerts and a visit to the Art Institute. John's programme was arranged by Don Bruckner, Vice-President for Public Affairs, who had met John when he was at Oxford. John enjoyed himself, charmed everyone he met, and returned home a little disorientated by the American social round. He had hardly left before the authorities in Chicago began to consider a second visit.

In the later years of his wardenship John formed a close friendship with Harold Macmillan, who was at that time Chancellor of Oxford University. This involved frequent visits to Oxford, where he could, if he had wished, have spent the night in his own official residence. However, he preferred John's company, and more and more frequently came brief notes, asking to stay the night: '[15 March 1977] My dear Warden, Once more, I have to thank you for a marvellous day. How I enjoyed our evening! Yours ever, HM'. John wrote across the bottom of this letter, 'We stayed up talking till 3.0 am'. How one would like to have overheard some of their conversations.

John retired as Warden of All Souls in 1977, after twenty-five years in that office. Had he been a good Warden? The simple answer is 'No', an opinion I would be nervous of expressing were it not supported by some of the most distinguished Fellows of his time, who were also close friends. Of course, both the question and my answer are too simplistic. John never set out to make life simple, either for his friends or for his enemies.

There can be little argument that John failed in assuming the academic responsibilities one would expect from the Warden of All Souls. He was not an academic and had little sympathy for the academic life. He made no secret of this, and he failed to show any interest in the work of his colleagues – particularly the younger colleagues. In the college's moment of 'crisis' he not only failed to seize the opportunity to put through reforms; he did everything in his power to obstruct change. One might plead that he sincerely believed that he was preserving the college from dangerous intrusions, but it would be truer to say that he was striving to ensure that it remained the way he personally wanted it.

I have already mentioned my conversation with several Fellows of All Souls, of different generations, who deplored John's failure to further the academic reputation of the college, but who at the end of the day found him a most excellent companion at dinner. All Souls is a particularly tightly knit community, and in their social life, for most if not all the Fellows, John was a stimulating Warden, who could make an evening memorable by his cleverness, his wit and his charm.

I, along with countless other friends of John, enjoyed the special pleasure of dining occasionally in All Souls as his guest. I can remember sitting for hours after dinner with an interesting group of people, the conversation – gently orchestrated by John – ranging from poetry to the morality of bullfighting. Throughout his wardenship John received 'bread and butter' letters from such guests as K Clark, William Plomer and, of course, Harold Macmillan, all emphasizing the special pleasure of staying in All Souls.

IX

RETIREMENT

1977–92

Mr John Sparrow has moved from All Souls
to *exile in* Beechwood House.
*A change of address card sent to John Sutro
in November 1977*

JOHN SPARROW retired from the wardenship of All Souls at the
end of the Trinity term 1977, having reached the age of seventy
the previous November. He was succeeded by Sir Patrick Neill,
QC, who had been elected to the wardenship earlier in the year.
John, although a comparatively wealthy man, with ample means to
buy a house or flat for his retirement had – deliberately, one feels –
made absolutely no provision for his new life. I have no evidence to
support my belief that, right up to the last minute, he was hoping
that All Souls would allow him to continue living in the college in a
suitable set of rooms. He must have looked to the precedent set by
Maurice Bowra, whom Wadham allowed to go on living in college
when his own wardenship ended. It is said that this arrangement was
not a success; nor was it more likely to be in John's case, if indeed
All Souls ever considered such an arrangement. I find it unlikely that
they ever did do for a moment.

All Souls did offer John the ground floor of Beechwood House,
on the edge of Iffley village – an attractive eighteenth-century house
he had bought during the development of the Visiting Fellows scheme.
John accepted the offer, not least because he had nowhere else to go.
It was, in fact, a large and agreeable flat, looking out onto a lovely
garden, and in later years, when the concept of '*exile*' had faded, he
often remarked, looking down the long lawn and listening to the
birds, 'It's really very pleasant here.'

John's negative, gloomy view of his retirement was sadly a self-

fulfilling prophecy. His dismay at leaving All Souls – despite the fact
that he could still dine there, and often did – blinded him to the fact
that his retirement was not an end, but an opening to many new
opportunities; most important of all, it meant continued contact with
old friends and the chance to make new ones. At the time of his
retirement he was still much in demand: the BBC were keen to
continue broadcasting his talks, partly polemic, partly humorous. He
could have lectured anywhere – at solemn academic occasions or at
more light-hearted gatherings at undergraduate societies and schools.
And publishers remained eager to print the scraps from his table.
He had enjoyed great success at Chicago University in 1976 and
had been invited to return in 1978. Edward Shils told me that,
had the second visit gone well, it was likely that he would have
been asked to return each year for two or three months as a visiting
professor. It was an opportunity that most men in retirement would
would have jumped at. These years should have been happy and
rewarding for John, keeping him in contact with a wide variety of
people.

Only a few letters to John survive from friends wishing him well
in retirement. Harold Macmillan wrote thanking him for all his kindness and hospitality, and saying that he would seek him out in 'the
environs of Oxford'. Sadly, he never fulfilled his intention. John
received a sympathetic letter from Goronwy Rees, and another from
K Clark saying that John's silence suggested that he preferred to
make the difficult adjustment alone. It was a misjudgement made by
many of John's friends.

In the company of close friends John was still his old self. In
November, with typical thoughtfulness, Colin, with three of John's
other friends, including myself, arranged a dinner at the Travellers'
Club to mark John's retirement. We asked John to invite an
additional guest of his own choosing and, to our delight, he asked
John Betjeman. Colin ensured that the dinner was memorable, but
what really made the evening was the hilarious charade acted out by
the two Johns, a performance they had been perfecting since their
undergraduate days. We had joined together to buy John a present
– a Waterford decanter. The mysterious, wrapped parcel was laid at
his place. Betjeman looked at it with childlike curiosity. He had
hardly sat down before he said to John, 'Do let's open the parcel.'

'No,' said John, with a headmasterly tone. 'After the port.'

'Why not now?' said the wheedling Betjeman.

'After the port,' countered the headmaster.

In this familiar game, the roles of schoolboy and pedagogue might suddenly be swopped. The hilarity and pleasure of the evening was best summed up in John Betjeman's letter of thanks to Colin. 'The banquet for Spanzbury [one of the versions of Hanbury by which he always addressed John] could not have been more enjoyable. I think Spanzbury himself was pleased and touched. He was looking every inch the Ironmaster's boy he is with those sturdy footballer's legs and a suit from the school tailor.' For John it was probably one of the few bright interludes in the last months of 1977.

There is no doubt that John's retirement started a serious disintegration in his character, which led in the eighties to a notorious period of drinking. It is always difficult to chart the course and analyse the causes of such a 'break-up', particularly in John's case, since until the later stages he was not under any kind of medical supervision. His decline was not monitored by anyone qualified to diagnose his condition.

There is some evidence in his letters that he was already worried about his loss of memory before his retirement, but since he had long enjoyed an exceptionally good memory, he may simply have been impatient with the slight memory loss which many begin to experience around the age of seventy. According to his brother and sister, there was a history of abnormal loss of memory in the family, but that might be explained by the fact that so many members of the Sparrow family lived to a great age. It is impossible to say whether John's condition was hereditary, or simply a normal deterioration in old age, made worse by years of drinking, but by the time he reached his late seventies his memory was obviously in shreds.

The first clear sign that something was seriously wrong occurred during his second visit to Chicago University in the spring of 1978. He got off to a bad start. Foolishly, probably because he was not in the mood to put together another original series of lectures, he compromised by agreeing to speak on Renaissance Latin poetry, a subject on which he was a world authority, but which was not going to attract a large audience, or the kind of enthusiasm his first lectures had generated. It should have been obvious to anyone that such lectures would be 'caviare to the general', and how easy it would have been for him to attract a larger audience by speaking on seventeenth-

or nineteenth-century British poetry. Perhaps it was part of his growing mental inertia that he did not foresee the lack of attraction of Renaissance Latin verse.

This second visit to Chicago was not a success either for John or for the university. He was lonely and worried about his memory; he missed the adulation he had received in 1976, and was depressed by the low attendance at his lectures. All his letters home are full of homesickness.

There were brief moments when the best of John reasserted itself. In May he was invited by Professor William Calder to visit the University of Colorado at Boulder to give an informal talk on Mark Pattison. I wrote to Professor Calder, who had, I discovered, moved to the University of Illinois, asking him if he remembered John's visit and talk in 1978, some fourteen years earlier. He responded with a long letter describing John's visit as if it had happened yesterday, leaving me in no doubt that both John and his talk were engraved for ever on the minds of everyone who had attended. They had all been fascinated by his talk and enchanted by John. When in sympathetic company, John was so good at creating what one might call 'weekend' relationships. It is sad to think that if he had had the energy to conjure up a more interesting series of lectures for his second visit to Chicago, he might have repeated the success of 1976.

But that is probably a simplification, and what Edward Shils later told me suggests that while John was capable of capturing an audience over a weekend, his performance at Chicago was blighted by more fundamental problems. The authorities there were not much concerned with large audiences, and were quite happy for small classes to benefit from John's erudition, but they did expect his classes, whatever the attendance, to be properly presented. Shils, a man of great kindness who had taken to John, realized that all was not well. He went to see John shortly before his final lecture and found him confused, unprepared and miserable. He did what he could to organize John and his last lecture, and John fumbled his way through it, but he was not asked to Chicago again.

I think that John gave his first broadcast for the BBC in 1968, since 'Revolting Students' was published in the *Listener* on 4 July that year; he also published in *A Listener Anthology* in 1970. Over the next few years he gave occasional talks – three in 1969, two in 1974, and a talk on Forrest Reid, and a contribution to a film about

John Betjeman in 1976. In the year of his retirement he gave six talks on 'Words', which established him as a popular broadcaster, with consistently high ratings and a certain amount of fan mail. John had always been fond of reading aloud, and was very good at it. He had no difficulty in transferring that skill to broadcasting.

In 1979 he moved on to a series of more general subjects, starting with light-hearted talks on 'Equal Rights', 'Growing Old', and 'Beards', among others. He contributed four more talks in the 'Words' series in 1980: 'Headlines', 'Beautiful Words', 'Anagrams' and 'Semicolons'. In 1982 there followed 'Post Offices', 'Lonely Hearts' and, a favourite hatred, 'Dogs'. A collection of his talks, *Words on the Air*, was published by Collins in 1981.

It is clear from John's correspondence with the BBC that they were anxious for him to continue with these talks. But much as he enjoyed giving them, he found writing more and more of an effort and was constantly late in delivering his scripts. His producer grew desperate; a frantic letter from her begins 'Dear Mr Sparrow, We thought of using blood instead of ink . . .' But neither threats nor persuasion had any effect on John's growing unreliability and he was dropped.

No doubt John's excessive drinking overtook him slowly, and was part of his general disintegration. I was living abroad throughout the seventies, but I remember my first visit to Beechwood House, when I had heard nothing about John's drinking. He was sitting at his table, staring out over the garden, and seemed subdued. As we began to gossip about this and that, his old vitality returned. The only sign of drink was a bottle of Cinzano on the dining-table. He pressed me to help myself, but I refused and he declined a glass. There seemed nothing wrong with him, but I realized that he was desperately lonely. It was at about this time that he wrote a charming poem called 'A Day with Myself'. I did not read it until some years later, but it summed up perfectly his mood then. Quite simply, he *was* in exile, and I think it was partly his loneliness which drove him to drink.

By the 1980s John's excessive drinking, particularly on his nightly visits to dine in All Souls, was becoming a cause for scandal. He was caught by the police driving dangerously under the influence of drink. Forced to return to Beechwood House at night by taxi, he became notorious among the taxi drivers of Oxford. More serious, there was a disgraceful scene in University College, where he was dining – and drinking – when, as some kind of pathetic, drunken protest, he lowered his trousers in the face of a lady fellow. In 1987 he was banned from dining in All Souls.

These events were deplorable, and tragic because John had established a reputation for himself which further isolated himself from his friends in Oxford and elsewhere; he never managed to shake it off, even after his recovery. At the height of the crisis his brother Tim did his best to intervene, but it was his old friend Sally Owen who really saved him. She was the widow of the classical philosopher Gwil Owen, and had known John when her husband was a professor at Oxford. Learning of John's plight, and immediately suspecting that much of his problem was rooted in loneliness, she took steps to organize his life: she made sure that he was properly looked after, took him out, and invited him to stay. Her care and kindness – and, no doubt, patience – very quickly worked a cure.

I became aware of all this only when I made my annual visit to John in, I think, 1987. I was about to ring the bell of Beechwood House when I noticed a piece of paper taped to the door and headed in capital letters and an unfamiliar hand 'MR LOWE'. It was a message from the male nurse now looking after John. We had never met, but he begged me not to bring any drink into the house, and if I took John out to lunch at the local pub, not to allow him more than one glass of wine or half a pint of beer. He himself had had to go out, but would be back in the afternoon, when he would explain everything.

John seemed his normal self, although his memory had deteriorated further, and I did take him out to lunch to an Iffley pub just up the road. We had sandwiches in the bar, and John accepted a glass of wine without comment, and never asked for a second. He did, however, bring his umbrella, with which he proceeded to poke the landlord's enormous Alsatian dog. It was no doubt a latter-day and ill-timed gesture in support of his anti-dog campaign. I begged him to stop, fearing the anger of both the landlord and the dog. Eventually, nothing worse happened than our removal, with the remains of our lunch, to the dining room. The landlord was tolerant and familiar with John's erratic behaviour. I should add that John's needling of the wretched dog was nothing to do with drink. It was the kind of stupid 'joke' he might have been guilty of at any time.

That afternoon I met the male nurse. I told him how easy it had been to limit John to one glass of wine, and he confirmed that John was almost cured of serious drinking, providing it was not put in his way. He apologized for the severe tone of his note, but said that his work had been made difficult by some friends of John who sneaked bottles of gin into Beechwood House, with disastrous results.

From then on, I saw a lot of John until his death, but he never showed any craving for alcohol, and though he would have a drink on occasions of celebration, he would go without for months. Some people in Oxford – those who had never liked him – described him as 'a confirmed alcoholic'. If that was the case, he made a remarkably quick and easy recovery, given an organized life and regular company.

At that time I met Sally Owen, who had done so much to rescue John. There was a moment of crisis when the male nurse suddenly left, and unavoidably John had to be put in a nursing home for a short stay. He hated it, and the memory of it made him more appreciative of his home at Beechwood House. Most important, and by great good fortune, a nurse-companion was found to look after him. Inge Gerstl quickly took to John, and was kind and masterly when he was difficult. Since he soon became very fond of her, he was usually very co-operative.

Inge, like Sally, saw that it was essential to do everything possible to relieve John's loneliness, so she not only looked after and spoilt him, but offered endless hospitality to his friends and spoilt them too. I think I was the main recipient of her kindness.

In 1987 I had agreed to write the 'portrait', and for the three years before his death I stayed for several weeks each autumn at Beechwood House. The first year I slept on the floor in the sitting room. This was not a total success. John was now eighty-one, and often woke in the middle of the night. At about 3 a.m. I would hear the door of my room open, the light would go on and, standing in the doorway, very much awake, John would say with a smile, 'I hope that I am not disturbing you.' Then he would settle himself comfortably on a sofa, assuring me that he was only staying 'a few minutes'. He was often still there at five.

I cannot remember what we talked about through the night – or through the day, for that matter. John's memory loss was erratic. He always knew who I was, even when I arrived after several months' absence. Other old friends, who came just for an occasional day, eluded his memory, though he was good at hiding the fact. Of course, he still liked to tease. Occasionally he would say to me, 'I know who you are, but could you remind me of your name.'

Former friends of his would sometimes say to me, 'I can't think why you go to see John Sparrow. He's gone over the top.' That view was sadly borne out by those who dropped in for an hour, giving John insufficient time to get them in focus, or those who were not really close enough to him to penetrate the mists that shrouded his memory. At that moment in his life he needed old friends with time and patience. I can only say that I enjoyed my visits enormously, and part of what I had always enjoyed, particularly his humour, was still intact.

I think it is safe to say that he enjoyed the last few years of his life: Beechwood House had become a real home to him; he was wonderfully looked after by Inge Gerstl, and a few loyal friends and colleagues visited him. Sometimes he just sat and thought, sometimes he watched videos of famous soccer matches, and sometimes he dozed. And between whiles he talked, if there was someone to talk to, or turned the pages of a favourite book, seldom reading it, but enjoying the old pleasure of having it in his hands.

In the last year of his life, at the age of eighty-five, his legs ceased to work, and it became difficult to move him about. He hated being 'manhandled' up and down: his best moment of the day was when he was finally settled back in bed, relaxed and ready for some evening company before he went to sleep. Those evenings are my last memory of John, as I had to return home about three months before he died on 24 January 1992, fortunately in the company of one of his closest friends.

His humour survived longest. His bed was surrounded by favourite authors, from his collection of Christina Rossetti to his books by Forrest Reid. But for the last hour of those days he always chose the verse of Edward Lear and Lewis Carroll and, needless to say, his own *Grave Epigrams*. By then, he seldom read aloud, but required me to do so. I was always nervous of reading his verse, as several poems had lines with a slightly emphasized syllable; if you failed to get it right, the rhythm of the line was destroyed. I always missed it, and was always corrected. Lear and Carroll were easier, and after certain poems or bits of nonsense verse John would say, 'I like that very much. Read another.' I would start to read another but, looking up, I saw that John had drifted off to sleep. It was the end of another day, moving rapidly towards the end of his long life.

X

THE MAN

―――

Here, with his talents in a napkin hid,
Lies one who much designed, and nothing did;
Postponing and deferring, day by day,
He quite procrastinated life away,
And, when at length the summons came to die,
With his last breath put off – mortality.

An epitaph for himself, written by John Sparrow

OHN SPARROW, to a greater degree than most, presented different sides of his character to his friends, his acquaintances, his
colleagues, and to those he disliked. All these variations were
part of the same man, but their diversity makes it difficult to
bring them together into an authentic portrait, recognizable to all
who knew him. I have worked on his biography with the advantage
and disadvantage of a close friendship which lasted over forty years.
It helped me that I had known one face of my subject very well. That
at least gave me a context into which to put the events of his life.
But I suffered from having fixed in my memory a picture of John
Sparrow which I was often to find did not fit with the memories of
others. It has been further confusing because, in their own way, all
the memories are valid.

Since I began to work on this book in 1988, I have talked to, or
corresponded with, dozens of people who knew John in various ways.
There were occasions when I began to wonder if we were talking
about the same man, so different were their impressions from my
own. John had many friends: quite a small number were very close,
and many were friendships based on some common interest. After
he became Warden of All Souls and something of a public figure,
many were anxious to be considered his friend; even a close friend.

I remember talking to a book-collector who had certainly known
John well, but was anxious to show that he had known John much

better than me. I was impressed but somehow I did not see him as a close friend. Just before I left I could not resist putting his 'close friendship' to the test. 'I wonder,' I asked, 'what John used to say to you about his homosexuality?'

'Good gracious!' the man said, throwing his arms wide in a gesture of openness. 'We never discussed anything like that.'

I have yet to meet a *close friend* with whom John did not discuss the subject so central to his character. I do not mean that all his close friends were homosexuals. Several were, but the others accepted John as he was, and were always prepared to discuss the subject with sympathy and humour.

I have already written a good deal about John's homosexual activities and attitudes in the course of this book. I hope that I have made it clear that this side of his nature coloured every fibre of his being, every action and every thought. In most respects his attitude to his sexuality was old-fashioned: on the whole one loved one's friends and bought one's sex. John did not flaunt his homosexuality, but nor did he make great efforts to hide it.

John had a reputation for being predatory with undergraduates, which I think was exaggerated. I got to know John early in 1951, shortly after I had come up to New College, and because we had book-collecting and a sense of humour in common, we became friends almost immediately. I knew that John was a homosexual, but I was not alarmed when he invited me to stay with him in Venice in August 1951. One or two of my contemporaries advised me not to go, but I ignored them.

I am glad I did. Not only did John behave perfectly, without causing me one moment of embarrassment, but he gave me one of the most enjoyable and stimulating holidays of my life; the holiday opened up a friendship that lasted until his death. There was a postscript to our Venetian holiday. The following term Raymond (later Sir Raymond) Carr, then a Fellow of All Souls, who had taught me at school and became a good friend, wrote to John accusing him of perverting his former pupil. John, who was quite innocent, and did not like Raymond, was torn between righteous indignation and the pleasure of simply being righteous. And for the rest of his life he remained proud of how well he had behaved in Venice, jokingly boasting about it. I remember arriving at Beechwood House in the last year of his life. A bright but rather scatty young nurse opened the front door, and before I could say a word she said, 'You're John Lowe, the one he never slept with.'

'That's quite true,' I replied, 'but how did you know?'

'Oh, he told me this morning while I was helping him with his bath.'

I do not think John exerted any bad influence over me. He never tried to overawe people with his cleverness, but he was quite severe in his demands for intelligence, good manners and maximum effort. I found among the letters congratulating him on the election to the wardenship one from John Buxton, my English literature tutor at New College. Buxton ended his letter telling John that he had much improved my work. John had indeed opened my sensibility to new depths in literature.

If homosexuality was one pillar of John's character, a deep selfishness was the other. I do not mean the petty kind of selfishness common to most people, but a deep-rooted self-concern which prevented him from using his considerable talents for the benefit of others, particularly within the framework of the institutions he served. It was apparent at Winchester and was noted in his school reports. It was evident at Oxford, and after that at the Chancery Bar. If he had remained at the Bar, he might have attained high office, but according to some of those who knew him there, his reluctance to sit on administrative committees – essential steps for promotion – might have jeopardized his chances of being more than a successful silk with a specialized and lucrative practice. It has been said that he could have become Master of the Rolls, but those who knew him best at the Chancery Bar doubted his ability to show the selfless application to the more boring parts of legal life necessary to achieve that.

It must already be obvious that it was selfishness that flawed his wardenship of All Souls; he was determined to keep the college as he liked it, without really considering its role for the future, or its contribution to the life of the university or, indeed, the wishes of his colleagues. One can only surmise that John would not be elected Warden today, and I still find it surprising that the college elected him in 1952.

From where did John's selfishness spring? Was he born selfish, or did his early years encourage this deep egotism? It was probably a combination of genes and youthful experience. It is clear that John's mother nurtured him as her most gifted child and to some extent their family life centred around him. The Antiquarian Society was obviously John's scheme, and its funds were immediately appropriated by him to support his own book collection. It is hard to believe that his brother and sisters had the slightest interest in rare editions of Elzevirs. And he must have been supported in this by his mother. Tim and Daphne both claim that all the children were enthralled by the Antiquarian Society. Perhaps then, as later, John charmed those around him in order to get what he wanted.

John was not always loyal to his close friends, including friends to whom he owed a great deal. There is no doubt that he tired of Maurice Bowra as they both grew older, disparaging him and laughing at him behind his back. Perhaps stranger – although clear in John's letters to his mother – his affection for Cyril Radcliffe had waned, perhaps since the latter had married – a deplorable course of action in any friend of his. But Radcliffe's affection for John never wavered. There was a sad occasion when the Radcliffes invited him to spend Christmas with them at their Warwickshire home. John accepted, but at the last moment cried off with a lame excuse. It was clear that he did not wish to go. Shortly afterwards Cyril Radcliffe wrote him a perceptive note, saying that he was saddened not so much because John could not come, but because he obviously did not mind not coming.

All deeply selfish men like to have their own way, and John was no exception. Not often, but occasionally, when he felt he was being thwarted, he would respond with a flaring temper. In the course of my own long friendship with John I experienced only two attacks, both momentarily alarming. The first was wholly deserved. John was trying to encourage me to write a bibliography of Forrest Reid. It did not interest me, but as an undergraduate I was too nervous to speak out, and no doubt appeared to be procrastinating in the face of his generous help. We were standing in my rooms in New College and, without any warning, John suddenly shouted at me, 'For God's sake stop talking about it and get on with it.' Though his tone was harsh, it was excellent advice which I have followed ever since. But it was strange advice coming from that dilatory friend.

The second and more alarming explosion occurred over supper at Beechwood House, when John must have been about eighty-three. I was sitting with John and Inge Gerstl, chatting peaceably about his dislike of bearded students. I remarked that it was a strange irony that while John had spent so much time attacking the bearded young, I had spent much of my life administering a trust which handed out scholarships to bearded young artists. My remark touched a deep nerve. John went white and rigid and, turning to me, said with extraordinary force, 'How dare you speak to me like that at my table.' Inge calmed him down in a second, and immediately he was full of apologies, begging my forgiveness. It might have been a matter of old age, but it wasn't. Fierce temper was innate to John, and was perhaps a symptom of his selfishness.

In 1975, not long before John's retirement, I was dining in All Souls as his guest, and staying the night at the lodgings. After an excellent dinner we retired to the common room and I talked to a recent Prize Fellow who had been at New College with my son. Then I returned to John, who was obviously engaged in a rather acerbic conversation with another recently appointed Prize Fellow who, I learned later, had been given his fellowship against John's wishes. I could see at once that both men, while in no way drunk, had had one glass of claret too many. John was needling the younger man and, unwisely, he thought he would needle John. Suddenly, John's temper flared, and it was as if he had turned a flame-thrower on his junior. It was a horrible spectacle and the scene remains engraved on my mind. The young fellow had been impertinent, but a Warden of nearly twenty-five years' experience should have taken that in his stride. I was horrified and, on our way back to the lodgings, did not disguise the fact. John, typically, was immediately mortified, and asked what I thought he should do. I suggested that he sit down immediately and write the kind of 'olive branch' note he was so good at. He followed my advice. I did not read the note, but I am certain it was masterly. John, when he wished, was equally good at breaking and making the peace.

There is no pleasure in writing about John's failings, but they belong to the portrait of the man. He had an exceptionally fine analytical brain, ideally suited for the drafting work he was required to undertake at the Chancery Bar, but beyond that, it made him a formidable adversary in any kind of controversy, a fine critic of prose and poetry and, when he wished, a Machiavellian manipulator of daily affairs. He had no interest in speculation, such as philosophy or religion. He was a pragmatist, who preferred to deal in facts and strict critical analysis. In literature he could recognize less precise qualities – the sentiment of Christina Rossetti, one of his favourite poets, and the Celtic magic of W. B. Yeats. His library was well stocked with nineteenth-century poets in those charming, elaborately bound editions illustrated by Birket Forster and other artists of the sixties. John had little interest in fiction: in his correspondence with William Plomer, both poet and novelist, he frequently discussed his poetry, but never mentioned his novels, and probably never read them.

I once asked John if he would rather have been a famous poet or a famous novelist. 'Oh, without doubt, a famous poet,' he replied. 'I mean, after a good dinner, with a glass of claret on one's desk, a great poem might be written in an hour. But a novel; goodness, it might drag on for years.'

John's interests were more concerned with the world around him than the world at large. He was a distinguished Latinist and, following his youthful study of John Donne, he developed a deep knowledge of seventeenth-century English literature, matched by a wide understanding of eighteenth- and nineteenth-century writing. These interests were evident in his superb collection of books, which reflected every aspect of his expertise.

Books remained one of the greatest pleasures of John's life, and he built up one of the finest private libraries assembled in Britain in this century, a collection discriminating yet wide-ranging. He was essentially a bibliophile, a collector whose library reflected his personal interests rather than particular themes. But where his interest was engaged, he was tireless in making his collection of a favourite author complete. I remember that we had both collected a particular illustrated edition of *Enoch Arden*, its covers decorated with an attractive blind-stamped rope pattern. John had two copies of this book, the cover in different colours. He then discovered that I had an edition in a third colour. The race was on. I cannot now recall the outcome, but I am sure that John acquired more different editions than me.

Of course, the *Enoch Arden* was at the more frivolous end of his library. His collection of some 2,000 books of Renaissance Latin verse, bequeathed to All Souls, was as fine as any in the world. His knowledge of seventeenth-century literature, supported by an almost uncanny serendipity, brought real treasures to his library. There are stories told by those who accompanied John to bookshops of how his hand was always first to the dusty little volume, invariably a neglected rarity. John was also an active collector of papers and letters of literary characters who interested him, like Samuel Parr, Mark Pattison, Walter Pater and A. E. Housman.

After John's death his generous bequests to several institutions of books, papers and pictures revealed the richness of his library, and even after these books had been removed, the remainder still furnished a major sale at Christie's on 21 October 1992, in addition to a smaller sale at the South Kensington auction room on 18 December. Unfortunately, John never kept any kind of record of his library, and no comprehensive catalogue was made after his death – in many cases the Christie's catalogue lotted up books together, without giving complete details.

Many of John's bequests went to libraries which had been important to him – accompanied by money for the purchase of further books. The Bodleian received fifty volumes, the Codrington, New College and Winchester College twenty-five volumes each, the librarians of each institution to make their own choices. His Walter Pater material was given to Brasenose College, his collection of books by William Cowper to the Cowper and Newton Museum, Olney, and his Nathan Drakes to the library of York Minster.

John's pictures went to various museums: the James Giles watercolours to the Aberdeen Museum and Art Gallery, work by William Etty to York City Art Gallery, drawings by J. P. Neale to the Oxfordshire County Museum, and a landscape by Derwent Lees to the Birmingham Museum and Art Gallery. There was a more important bequest to the Ashmolean, with work by Boudin, Prince Hoare, Arthur Hughes and J. E. Millais. There were also bequests of books and pictures to friends.

John had enjoyed acquiring his library, but he was not acquisitive in the sense that he wished it to become his memorial. At heart he was a book-collector, and apart from his special bequests he wished his library to be sold and returned to the booksellers' shelves, so that other collectors might have the opportunity to share his pleasure.

From 1952 John had encouraged the newly formed Oxford Bibliographical Society, a group of serious undergraduate book-collectors. At the end of each term the members were invited to 'the Warden's meeting', to see and discuss John's books. John would explain the importance of each recent acquisition, and his particular passion for association copies, illustrating the many forms which an 'association' might take. These meetings typified his generosity to other collectors, young and old.

For all his intellectual cleverness, there was a certain provincialism about John; shades of a Wolverhampton childhood and youth. This was not a social classification, but a certain narrowness in his outlook and his way of life. The Betjeman family used to joke about his heavy, 'hairy' suits. He did have the air of somebody comfortably old-fashioned, outwardly conventional and impatient with anything faddish. And when he read poetry in his precise, carefully enunciated manner, there was something faintly old-maidish about his performance. Although he had travelled the world from Germany to Burma during the war, these experiences seem to have left no mark on his imagination, and once the war was over he usually contented himself with repeated visits to Italy – particularly to his beloved Venice.

John's short-lived desire to enter parliament was, I think, only an alternative to making up his mind to do anything else. He took a superficial interest in politics, but he would have been bored to distraction by life in the House, and might well have taken to the bottle rather earlier in life. He was a vain man, with a theatrical streak, and the idea of dramatic appearances in court, in parliament, or in some other arena, appealed to that side of his nature. He was basically fearless, and a gifted speaker, but he occasionally suffered from nerves. I have a tape of the address he gave at Cyril Radcliffe's memorial service: faced with such a distinguished congregation, his voice betrays his nervousness.

I first remember John in his early middle age, just over forty. He was of medium height, stocky in build, and with that lock of dark hair hanging over his brow. He was striking rather than good looking, with a certain saturnine air. His great charm lay in his smile – a smile of both lips and eyes, which immediately erased his sterner gaze. Again, he was vain about his appearance, always wishing that he was more obviously handsome, though he admired his hands sufficiently to have them sculpted. Of course, he made a joke of all this, but vanity was part of him none the less. Towards the end of his life he regretted that his Oxford career had not earned him a knighthood. He would have enjoyed being Sir John Sparrow or, as he hastened to add, making a joke of his ambition, Lord Sparrow. I do not think that his failure to gain a title implied a final sense of failure at All Souls. I suspect that he saw his career as Warden as a long fight to preserve what he believed to be in the interest of the college in the face of inevitable but destructive 'change'.

He did, in a certain sense, admit to a failure in himself: throughout his life he was unable to reconcile the promptings of his head with those of his heart. During his last years he often spoke of his deep admiration for Isaiah Berlin, who was obviously so successful in achieving a harmony between his intellect and his great generosity of spirit. When I was helping John to tidy up his affairs, if a serious problem arose, he would immediately say, 'We must ask Isaiah.'

John could be maddening to deal with. Many of the letters I have quoted show his 'gift' for procrastination, circumlocution, contradiction, self-deprecation, and every other twist and turn – often all in one letter. He would take three pages to argue himself out of one position into another, and the next three returning to where he had started. He did this equally well, if at greater length, in conversation. The golden rule, in nearly every case, was to avoid reaching a decision.

I do not know why John has not received more credit for his writing. I suppose that if you do not produce what is expected of your intellect and your academic position, people are disappointed and do not give your work proper consideration. John was extremely versatile, but the academic world regards versatility as hardly better than dilettantism. He wrote prose perfect enough to be a model for anyone, but his critics have been concerned not so much with the quality of his style as the quantity of his output. Even his correspondence demonstrates his talent. He often denied his ability to write a good letter, but would invariably go on to produce some kind of convoluted masterpiece. His letters had that admirable quality of being absolutely John.

This is not the place to attempt a full literary criticism of all John's published work. In reviewing his life certain books have already received some attention. There were scholarly collections of Renaissance Latin poetry, notably the seven volumes of *Lapidaria* (1943–75), his anthology of *Renaissance Latin Verse*, edited with A. Perosa (1979), and, most original, his four Sandars Lectures in bibliography, given at Cambridge in 1964, a study of inscriptions in Renaissance art. The lectures were published by the Cambridge University Press in 1969 under the title *Visible Words*. It is not a long book, but it shows the depth of John's learning in this field, and was a publication worthy of a warden of All Souls.

No doubt it was the lawyer in John that gave him his more general taste for controversy. There is no doubt that he was on the look out for subjects that lent themselves to his style of attack and, often, demolition. Among his papers were one or two files in which, with the help of contributions from friends, he was collecting material for fresh onslaughts. In one he was preparing an attack on the extremes of contemporary modern art. On a less serious level, William Plomer and other friends sent him newspaper cuttings in support of his running campaign against dogs.

John's bibliography is enriched with a number of slim, privately published works, some the 'vanity' publications of the author, others produced by universities and booksellers. None is more typical of these rare editions, or of its author, than *Some Reflections of a Bibliophile*, published by the Minnesota Center for Book Arts in 1986. It is in every way a charming publication, but fragile and issued in a limited edition of 200 copies. Few readers are ever likely to enjoy it. The text is a delightful blending of John's biblio-philic knowledge, experience and humour. 'We should get on very well in Bodley, if it wasn't for the readers,' remarked a member of the staff to John – no doubt a philosophy that much appealed to John himself. And he offered four 'golden' rules to aspiring book-collectors:

1. Never lend anyone a book.
2. Never sell a book.
3. Never give anyone a book.
4. Never read a book.

He does confess that he has not always obeyed these rules.

Ambitions die hard. As a small boy, John had voiced his determi-nation to be a great poet. In his eighties, of all his books, the one he took most delight in was his collected poems, *Grave Epigrams and Other Verses*, printed by Simon Rendall, Bembridge, in 1974. The slightly strange title came from his study of Dr Parr, as he explained in an introductory note: 'I remember once having made this observa-tion to Edmund Burke, that it would be no bad definition of one sort of epitaphs, to call them grave epigrams. He repeated the words "*grave*

epigrams", and gave me the credit of a pun, which I never intended'
(Sir Joshua Reynolds, writing to Dr Samuel Parr, 31 May 1791).

The collection of poems is not limited to epitaphs, though in different forms there are several of those. When John decided to publish this collection of verse, he searched high and low for any suitable scrap, so keen was he to leave behind him a poetic legacy. Going through his papers after his death, I never found any poems not already included in *Grave Epigrams*, with the one exception of the poem I have quoted on p. 114. Shamefully, I must confess – though I never told John – that I mislaid one long and excellent poem that he sent me in about 1952. For years I had kept it in the back of a commonplace book. When I started this biography, I searched for it, but it had vanished along with any memory of it. Other poems, sent to friends over the years, may well have been lost.

John's poetry is undoubtedly clever, but several poems, even the lightest, touch deeper chords of emotion which are easily missed in the brilliant light of his word play. His celebrated epitaph to Maurice Bowra illustrates this perfectly.

C. M. B.

Which of the two, when God and Maurice meet,
Will occupy – you ask – the judgement seat?
Sure, our old friend – each one of us replies –
Will justly dominate the Grand Assize:
He'll seize the sceptre and ascend the throne,
Claim the Almighty's thunder for his own,
Trump the Last Trump, and the Last Post postpone.
Then, if his strong prerogative extends
To passing sentence on his sinful friends,
Thus shall we supplicate at Heaven's high bar:
'Be merciful! you made us what we are;
Our jokes, our joys, our hopes, our hatreds too,
The outrageous things we do, or want to do –
How much of all of them we owe to you!
Send us to Hell or Heaven or where you will,
Promise us only, you'll be with us still:
Heaven, without you, would be too dull to bear,
And Hell will not be Hell if you are there.'

It is a brilliant epitaph – not only to Bowra, but to his circle. It is clever and amusing, but it is more. Behind the word play there is the affectionate farewell to an old friend, not always valued, but appreciated at the end.

The collection contains poems that are simply good jokes:

> He raised the glittering goblet to his lips
> And drank the ambrosial liquid to the dregs;
> He kissed the face that launched a thousand ships –
> And killed the goose that laid the golden eggs.

That was a particular favourite of John's, but then, to tell the truth, so were most of the poems in the book, which I read to him over and over again in the last years of his life. By the time he reached old age Pattison and Parr had faded away, as had Coventry Patmore – although he was still remembered in John's version:

> To an Angel in the House
>
> A pat on the head
> Sends me happy to bed,
> I wish – how I wish – you'd do that more!
> Cold words and neglect
> Leave me wretched and wrecked:
> Don't send me to Coventry-pat more!

Such light verse reminds one of John's most important quality: his profound sense of fun. Each criticism of John's character is to a greater or lesser extent redeemed by that smile – sometimes puckish, sometimes deprecating, sometimes softening severity – that was constantly transforming his face. Few things are harder to define – or to record – than someone's humour, especially when it is so wide-ranging. John's wit was powered by his quick intelligence, but in addition to the now famous *bons mots* he delighted in 'situation comedy' and a variety of pranks and boyish fun. If selfishness and homosexuality were central to his character, so was the sense of humour that made him such a wonderful companion.

John will long be remembered for certain witty sayings, funny enough to survive the context of the moment, although the attribution is not always certain. Many remember him for 'One Sparrow does not make a Sumner', but his own letter to Isaiah Berlin, quoted in the election chapter, gives the authorship to his friend. But it was Isaiah Berlin who confirmed to me that John had indeed described All Souls at the time of the Suez crisis as 'A hotbed of cold feet'. There was another All Souls occasion which produced a joke wrongly attributed to others. A. L. Rowse complained that John had read none of his books. 'Do you know *Tudor Cornwall*, John?'

'No,' replied John, and gestured to the figure on his right. 'Do you know Stuart Hampshire?'

Such ripostes were quick-witted, but most were born of the moment, within seconds unmemorable.

John enjoyed practical jokes. He once hid me behind a tree in the Warden's garden and, when his unsuspecting guests arrived for tea, encouraged them to give their opinion of the absent guest. An even more elaborate situation is well described by Jeremy Lewis in 'Tea with Warden Sparrow', published in the *London Magazine* in 1993. Arriving at the lodgings, never having met the Warden before, he was instantly enrolled as a 'Housman expert' to help fight off a group of incomprehensible Japanese Housman experts who had also come to tea. John was a marvellous off-the-cuff stage-manager on such occasions, and nobody enjoyed his impromptu productions more than himself.

But John's humour went far deeper than clever witticisms or more rough-and-tumble practical jokes. Humour was in the very fibre of the man, so often redeeming his failings, and adding that special charm to his company. It frequently softened the hard edges, the expression on his face pointing up his jokes, and lent him a great warmth. John was *sui generis*, and it was his humour that contributed so much to his uniqueness.

This sense of fun also formed part of John's gift for friendship, a gift too often shared only with acquaintances and his small group of close friends, though he could make complete strangers warm to him. His friends happily put up with his teasing: so often he would turn this biting wit on himself.

John's close friends may find some of my comments on his character too severe. To them, he was kind, often unselfish, a sympathetic listener to troubles which were of little interest to him, and marvellously supportive. Of course, he chose his close friends; his colleagues seldom saw these qualities. I met several of John's closest friends during his lifetime, and I think all of them – the Betjemans, the

Nicolsons, the Stones and others – would have used the same word to describe him: lovable. For anyone who knew John really well, no other word would do. He conjured up laughter, and he demanded affection. If there was a tragedy in his life, it was his inability to share these gifts more widely and more equably.

APPENDIX
BOOKS BY JOHN SPARROW

Half-lines and Repetitions in Virgil. Clarendon Press, Oxford, 1931.

Sense and Poetry: Essays on the Place of Meaning in Contemporary Verse. Constable & Co; Yale University Press, 1934.

Poems in Latin, together with a few Inscriptions. Compiled by John Sparrow, Oxford University Press, 1941.

Poems in Latin, second series. Oxford University Press, 1942. Limited edition, 100 copies.

Lapidaria. Cambridge University Press, 1943. Limited edition, 100 copies.

Selected Poems of John Betjeman, chosen, with a preface by John Sparrow. John Murray, 1948.

The Coldstream Guards, 1920–1946, by Michael Howard and John Sparrow. Oxford University Press, 1951.

Lapidaria Altera. Cambridge University Press, 1951. Limited edition, 200 copies.

A.E. Housman, an annotated Hand-list, by John Carter and John Sparrow. (Soho Bibliographies, no. 2). Rupert Hart-Davis, 1952.

Lapidaria Tertia. Cambridge University Press, 1954. Limited edition, 125 copies.

Robert Bridges: Poetry & Prose; with appreciations by G.M. Hopkins (and others) ... with an introduction and notes by John Sparrow. Clarendon Press, Oxford, 1955.

Lapidaria Quarta. Cambridge University Press, 1958. Limited edition, 160 copies.

Independent Essays. Faber & Faber, 1963.

Lapidaria Quinta. Cambridge University Press, 1965. Limited edition, 200 copies.

Controversial Essays. Faber & Faber; Chilmark Press, New York, 1966.

Mark Pattison and the Idea of a University. (The Clark Lectures given at Cambridge, 1965) Cambridge University Press, 1967.

Line upon Line; an Epigraphical Anthology. Cambridge University Press, 1967. Limited edition, 500 copies.

After the Assassination: A Positive Appraisal of the Warren Report. Chilmark Press, New York, 1968.

Visible Words: a Study of Inscriptions in and as Books and Works of Art. (The

Sandars Lectures in Bibliography given at Cambridge, 1964) Cambridge University Press, 1969.

Grave Epigrams (poems by John Sparrow). Simon Rendall, Bembridge. 1974. Limited edition, 200 copies.

Lapidaria Sexta. Cambridge University Press, 1969. Limited edition, 200 copies.

Lapidaria Septima. Rampant Lions Press, Cambridge. 1975. Limited edition, 200 copies.

Too Much of a Good Thing. (Three lectures given at the University of Chicago in 1976.) University of Chicago, 1977.

Words on the Air. (A selection of John Sparrow's talks for the BBC.) William Collins, 1981.

Leaves from a Victorian Diary. Introduction by John Sparrow. Alison Press, London, 1985.

Some Reflections of a Bibliophile. Minnesota Center for Book Arts, 1986.

INDEX

This index includes references to John Sparrow's publications mentioned in the text. A complete list of his books is given in the Appendix at the end of the book, pp. 249–50